Muhlenberg's Ministerium, B.
and the Churches of the Twenty-First Century

Muhlenberg's Ministerium, Ben Franklin's Deism, and the Churches of the Twenty-First Century

Reflections on the 250th Anniversary of the
Oldest Lutheran Church Body in North America

Edited by

John Reumann

WILLIAM B. EERDMANS PUBLISHING COMPANY
GRAND RAPIDS, MICHIGAN / CAMBRIDGE, U.K.

© 2011 Wm. B. Eerdmans Publishing Co.
All rights reserved

Published 2011 by
Wm. B. Eerdmans Publishing Co.
2140 Oak Industrial Drive N.E., Grand Rapids, Michigan 49505 /
P.O. Box 163, Cambridge CB3 9PU U.K.
www.eerdmans.com

Printed in the United States of America

17 16 15 14 13 12 11   7 6 5 4 3 2 1

Library of Congress Cataloging-in-Publication Data

Muhlenberg's ministerium, Ben Franklin's deism, and the churches of the
    twenty-first century: reflections on the 250th anniversary of the oldest
    Lutheran church body in North America / edited by John Reumann.
        p.   cm.
    Includes bibliographical references.
    ISBN 978-0-8028-6246-4 (pbk.: alk. paper)
    1. Evangelical Lutheran Ministerium of Pennsylvania and the Adjacent
    States — History — Congresses.   2. Muhlenberg, Henry Melchior,
    1711-1787 — Congresses.   3. Lutheran Church — East (U.S.) —
    History — Congresses.   I. Reumann, John Henry Paul.

    BX8061.P4M85   2011
    284.1'3 — dc22

                                                            2011016001

Contents

INTRODUCTION: Occasion and Events 1997-2006, the 250th Anniversary of the Ministerium of Pennsylvania, and the 300th Anniversary of the Birth of Benjamin Franklin

In August 1748 six Lutheran pastors, plus lay people from ten congregations, gathered in Philadelphia under the leadership of Henry Melchior Muhlenberg (1711-1787). He had been sent from the mission center in Halle, Germany, to minister to these people. A new church building was dedicated. The Ministerium of Pennsylvania was formed (for all of North America!), and a candidate for the gospel ministry was ordained. What were to become characteristic emphases in much of East Coast Lutheranism (and beyond) appeared, including stress on the Reformation Confessions and a common form of liturgy for worship.

So began Lutheran ecclesiology in the New World. Synods descended from the Ministerium continue to this day in the Evangelical Lutheran Church in America; influences have stretched far beyond, among other Lutherans and ecumenically. So began organized Lutheranism in the English-speaking world. So too began an experiment with how Reformation Christianity would take shape apart from the state churches of Europe, in an increasingly pluralistic culture, in a more multireligious (and irreligious and Deist) setting. So began a broader encounter for German and Scandinavian Lutherans with Christians from other lands, languages, and confessions (or lack of them). What we call "ecumenism" was raised as an issue, even though the term did not yet exist.

As the third millennium begins, churches — Lutheran and indeed all churches of tomorrow — wrestle with how heritage should and can be maintained and how new needs are to be met. That is common agenda for Christians generally. Exploration of the Muhlenberg Ministerium and East-Coast Lutheran heritage can have much to offer for tomorrow, and not just in Lutheran circles.

1

Anniversaries like this 250th of Muhlenberg's Ministerium always present dangers as well as opportunities. The past may be held up too easily as a model to be repristinated for the future (though the mood in America generally and U.S. Lutheranism in particular as the Evangelical Lutheran Church in America began in 1988 was often somewhere between benign neglect and active repression of past history and roots). The past may also be looked at as all-glorious, in a triumphalistic way (Lutheran loathing of "theologies of glory" does not always prevent that). One task of historians is to keep us from such temptations.

To reexplore, critically and discerningly, Muhlenberg and the Ministerium in light of subsequent events and the multifaced situation today, was the aim of a planning group[1] set up to mark this 250th anniversary in a series of events.

There was an initial gathering of historians, pastors, bishops, church leaders, and members of local congregations and church institutions at Christ Lutheran Church, in Baltimore's Inner Harbor district, January 31–February 1, 1997. Convocations at the three seminaries of the ELCA's Eastern Cluster took up aspects of the Muhlenberg heritage during 1997-1998, in Philadelphia, in Columbia, South Carolina, and in Gettysburg, Pennsylvania. On the national scene this history provided a focal point for the ELCA's Churchwide Assembly in Philadelphia in the summer of 1997. Countless congregational observations and local history displays were held.

The climax was a symposium on "Roots for New Plantings" in "The Church That Was Planted and Grew: Carrying on the Muhlenberg Tradition and Ministry," August 7-9, in Allentown, Pennsylvania. Appropriately this took place at the ELCA college named for the Patriarch of the Lutheran Church in America, though his three sons have also received attention at Muhlenberg College: John Peter Gabriel (1746-1807), pastor in Virginia and American major general in the Revolutionary War; Frederick Augustus (1750-1801), pastor and political leader, first Speaker in the U.S. House of Representatives; and Gotthilf Henry Ernst (1753-1815), pastor in Lancaster, botanist, and president of what is now Franklin and Marshall

---

1. The Planning Group for the entire project was convened by Dr. Kenneth C. Senft, of the Mission Resource Institute, Gettysburg, which provided staff and financial support. Committee members included George Handley, Darrell Jodock, John Jorgensen, Donald K. Maehl, Robert Marshall, Mark Oldenberg, John E. Peterson, John Reumann, Louise Shoemaker, Richard N. Stewart, Nelvin Vos, and Harold Weiss.

College. A statue of the turtle named for him stands before the science complex on the Allentown campus. On this significant family, Paul Wallace's book, *The Muhlenbergs of Pennsylvania,* remains a standard introduction. Not to be overlooked is Henry's wife, the mother of their six sons and five daughters, Anna Maria Weiser (daughter of a famous Indian interpreter), whom you will meet in a new way in one segment below.

The pages that follow are selected from presentations at these events connected with the 250th anniversary celebrations. They are not mainly about Muhlenberg's family, interesting as that topic is, but about Henry Melchior's work in mission and church organization, in local congregations and especially beyond the separate isolated hamlets and city parishes; his emphasis as a pietist on experience of God in Christ, while remaining a Confessional Lutheran, even an orthodoxist, yet aware of the growing impact of reason and the Enlightenment; and his work with other Christians, in ecumenism, involving both Christian identity and cooperation (or lack thereof) with other churches. These were the themes identified by the planning committee that were explored in a variety of ways.

The essays in this volume are organized around an encyclopedic yet quite readable overview of Muhlenberg's beginnings, subsequent developments over two and a half centuries, and the current scene, in the four keynote areas. Dr. Robert Marshall, President of the Lutheran Church in America 1968-78 and Senior Scholar at the Lutheran School of Theology, Chicago, made this presentation at the Baltimore gathering in 1997.

The Plenary Address at the Muhlenberg College Symposium in 1998 was given by John Reumann, Philadelphia Seminary, whose entire life has been spent on the territory of the old Ministerium of Pennsylvania. He (re)read Muhlenberg's *Journals* and much else for a fresh look at the anniversary events. Responses to both these papers are included, some of them taking exception to keynote emphases. Closely related is the opening keynote address at the Symposium by H. George Anderson, Presiding Bishop of the ELCA and a church historian of Colonial America, especially in the South.

The creative arts were not neglected during the anniversary. A hymn is included, commissioned for the occasion, with words by the late Herman G. Stuempfle, President emeritus of Gettysburg Seminary, and music by Stephen G. Williams, Allentown. Also a play about Muhlenberg and one of his opponents, by John Trump, a pastor in South Carolina; and Louise Shoemaker's reading of the letters of Mrs. Muhlenberg. For those who approach Muhlenberg and the Ministerium with little knowledge of past history (an increasingly common situation), the address by Philip Krey to a synod assembly may be the best starting point in this volume. As an indication of how things have changed since Muhlenberg's day, it is fitting to include the Symposium sermon by an African American woman, then pastor at historic Trinity Lutheran Church on Germantown Avenue in Philadelphia, Barbara Berry-Bailey. The August 9, 1998, dedicatory address by Gettysburg College professor Charles Glatfelter, given after the archeological investigation and restoration of the Muhlenbergs' house in Trappe, Pennsylvania, is also included.

It was hoped to have these essays in print by the year 2000. There was delay on the part of some authors, however, in getting a text to the editor. Some meanwhile published their pieces elsewhere. What was to go into the volume became a matter of fresh selection. Details had to be worked out with a publisher. The editor went through two bouts with cancer, and then had to honor a commitment to put all else aside and complete his commentary on Philippians for the Anchor Bible. In the spring of 2006 it was possible to return to the task of putting the volume together.

By 2006, the successor synods of the Ministerium of Pennsylvania had advanced further into a new millennium. What seemed burning issues in 1997-1998 had often changed shape and importance. By now it was the tercentenary of the birth of Benjamin Franklin, with major emphasis on the Founding Fathers of our country, especially in Philadelphia. As the essays were reedited, a striking fact became apparent: almost no one in 1997-1999 had bothered with the Deists of Muhlenberg's day, yet they were a formative factor in the shaping of America, with its new emphasis on secularity. The closing part of this volume therefore looks at Muhlenberg's Ministerium and Benjamin Franklin's Deism, especially Nature's God and the Virtues, as pointers from the past for the present age.

IN MEMORY

John H. P. Reumann (1927-2008), Editor and Contributor, and Robert J. Marshall (1918-2008), Planner and Contributor, both died after these events were held and the essays written, but before this book could be published. The Planning Group responsible for the Muhlenberg Tradition Series dedicates this book to the vision of John Reumann and Robert Marshall and to their memory.

I. The Church That Was Planted and Grew

An overview on Muhlenberg's Ministerium of Pennsylvania (and North America), the church that was planted and grew over the next two and a half centuries, was provided by Dr. Robert J. Marshall, retired President of the Lutheran Church in America, in a four-part address at the initial anniversary event in Baltimore, January 31, 1997. This overview paid attention to the beginnings in Muhlenberg's colonial and Revolutionary days, to subsequent Lutheran history, and to the current situation in the American and world context. The "keynote themes" were those worked out by the Planning Committee: Mission, Organization, (Personal) Experience or Piety, and Ecumenism or the varied relationships with other Christians in the pluralistic American religious scene. Much of this has been lived history and experience for Dr. Marshall. The paper is not documented with the endless footnotes that might have been added, on point after point. Its strengths include the clarity of the storyline for the heritage and history of Muhlenberg's Ministerium and Eastern Lutheranism (the only kind that then existed in what was becoming the United States) in the "new worlds" of the last quarter of the second millennium. A much-abbreviated version appeared under the title "The Church Still Being Planted," in *Currents* 25 (1998): 85-101. It was a deliberate decision by Dr. Marshall not to try to cover other Lutheran traditions in America outside the history linked to the Muhlenberg beginnings. They deserve full treatment, in their own right, elsewhere.

The Church Still Being Planted:
A Survey History of Muhlenberg's Ministerium

Robert J. Marshall

The title is one adopted for observance of the 250th anniversary of the Lutheran Ministerium, the oldest continuous Lutheran organization in America, other than a few congregations. Recalling the first meeting of the Lutheran Ministerium in August 1748, this description of the church, coined by the convener of that early meeting, provided a fitting theme. Henry Melchior Muhlenberg (1711-1787), the pioneer Lutheran pastor, experienced and articulated in this phrase the contrast between the firmly established church in Europe and the church in the "New World," with its instability and open future.

The situation of the church in America today is not entirely different from what it was in colonial times. The dynamics of American culture, mobility of the population, continuing immigration, changing neighborhoods, and the ever-pressing mission challenges of the New Testament place the church in a situation where it might gain helpful insights from the Muhlenberg tradition as it developed through the years. Four subtopics are presented here: (1) mission, (2) church organization, (3) personal Christian experience, and (4) ecumenism. These are each pursued from (a) Muhlenberg beginnings, through (b) two centuries and more of history, to (c) lessons for confronting current situations.

Mission

Beginnings

Henry Melchior Muhlenberg has deservedly been called a "Missioner Extraordinary."[1] Yet he was a missionary made and not born. His life as a missionary began in his early twenties when he was a student at the new University of Göttingen in the German state of Hannover (1735-1737). Associates, including Prof. J. Oporin, helped him experience a renewal of faith that led him to volunteer as a teacher of poor children who could not afford to go to school. The next step was at Halle, which, under A. J. Francke, was already a mission center. He began as a teacher, then was ordained in 1739 to serve as a pastor. He had wanted to go to India. Pennsylvania came as a second choice.

As a missionary from Halle, he was assigned to provide pastoral care to German emigrants. He was accountable to the directors at Halle and he continued to send them reports until the end of his life.

Muhlenberg soon learned that hardships could characterize a missionary ministry. The fourteen-week voyage across the Atlantic brought severe bouts with seasickness, bad food and water, threats from pirates and enemy ships, and a rowdy crew. In addition to scolding the crew, he conducted worship for them when they requested it. He found greater pleasure in personal ministry to a Lutheran Salzburger family on board, refugees who settled in Georgia.

Once located in eastern Pennsylvania at the three congregations that had sought a pastor, Muhlenberg began in 1741 his regular travels on horseback to serve all three. He covered tiring distances at night as well as day, through snow and rain and flooded rivers as well as in the scorching heat of summer. His pay was so little that he borrowed money to buy clothes and a better horse, then later, land and a parsonage.

Gradually the scope of his mission became clear to Muhlenberg. He had agreed to a three-year term. As the end of the time came near, he realized the continuing, indeed growing, need for pastoral ministry in America and he decided to stay, to build a house, and to marry. It was then, in 1745, that he began to describe the church situation where he was working as "Ecclesia Plantanda" — the church still has to be planted.[2] His mission continued for the rest of his life.

1. Helmut T. Lehmann, "Missioner Extraordinary" (1992); see General Bibl.
2. Theodore G. Tappert, in E. C. Nelson, ed., *The Lutherans in North America* (Philadelphia: Fortress, 1975), p. 56.

During that time an ever-expanding territory was demanding his attention. Muhlenberg was called upon to come to this place or that, either because a group of people had not had pastoral services for a long while, or because there was a quarrel they hoped he could settle. When a second missionary (Peter Brunnholtz) arrived, from Halle, Muhlenberg arranged for him to serve the Philadelphia congregation, while he himself took the congregations farther out in the country, whence it would be easier to reach new places still more distant. He traveled west to Lancaster and York; south to Frederick, Maryland; east to Raritan, New Jersey, and New York City; and then still farther in every direction.

The motivation for it all came from his sense of personal benefit from having received the gospel, and the conviction that all people needed it as much as he. Muhlenberg was ready to hold worship in homes or barns, in public buildings or open fields. He was willing to preach in German or English to make certain the message would be understood. When he was in Charleston, South Carolina, he had decried, like a true missionary, the neglect of the slaves' religion. He regretted the difficulty and failure of missions to the Indians. Yet he confined his own missionary work to German immigrants, as he had been assigned, and he had more to do than one missionary could manage.

He sympathized with the people he served. Many had come as indentured servants, and even when liberated they often struggled desperately with poverty. The church provided schools that taught not only Luther's Small Catechism and the Bible, but reading, writing, and arithmetic to assist in earning a living. As was customary at Halle, Muhlenberg was also equipped with herbs and medicines to assist the ill.

Yet the focus of mission in the Muhlenberg tradition was clearly being established as reaching people with the gospel by every possible means.

Subsequent History

In the years after Muhlenberg, as the population moved ever westward, the Ministerium that he had led began in 1805 to recruit pastors for summer service as itinerants among new settlements. The New York Ministerium, which first met in 1786, and then regularly from 1792 onward, and the North Carolina Synod, which was formed in 1803 — bringing the number of synods to three — did likewise. Later, full-time missionaries were sent.

There were outposts in Indiana, Michigan, Illinois, Minnesota, Canada, Kentucky, and Tennessee.

In Ohio the Lutheran church owed its beginnings to a frontiersman, John Stough, chosen by the people to be their preacher. He traveled east to be licensed by the Pennsylvania Ministerium in 1794; then, ten years later, to be ordained. The Pittsburgh Synod was organized with the Great Commission of Matthew 28 in the preamble of its constitution. Into the twentieth century, the growing population and expanding territory made "home mission" a daunting task.

New forms of mission began to develop. In the 1840s William Passavant from Pittsburgh began to promote "inner mission" to reclaim people spiritually and rehabilitate them physically. Health, education, and welfare, as well as better worship forms, were all included. To aid in such work the first deaconesses came to the New World from Germany.

"Foreign missions" were advocated, using Muhlenberg as the model of a missionary who had left his homeland to serve overseas. In 1842, exactly one century after Muhlenberg's arrival in America, John C. F. Heyer arrived in India as a missionary from the Pennsylvania Ministerium. Between terms in India, Heyer engaged in ministry in Minnesota.

During the Civil War, the Pennsylvania Ministerium provided chaplains for the Union forces. One of them was Passavant. After the Civil War, with the heirs of the Muhlenberg tradition divided among three organizations, home missions not only continued but took on new forms. Lutherans had missionaries at the ports of entry to the United States to assist immigrants, and they maintained seminaries in Germany to train pastors for service to immigrant congregations in America.

While other church bodies had organized in the Middle West to serve immigrants from various predominantly Lutheran territories in Europe, often absorbing earlier missions begun by eastern synods, those from the Muhlenberg tradition took a new approach and organized English-language congregations from Ohio to the Pacific.

When the spiritual heirs of Muhlenberg combined into the United Lutheran Church in America at the close of World War I, they had missionaries overseas in Asia, Africa, and Latin America. Yet their work in foreign missions did not match proportionally the overseas work of some other Lutheran churches in America.

After World War I put the use of the German language into steep decline, home missions became largely a matter of establishing new English-language congregations. The exceptions came from newer immigrant groups, such as those from Slovakia, Hungary, and Finland.

After World War I, the new United Lutheran Church (formed in 1918) developed a growing emphasis on social concerns. Political advocacy had begun by the eastern synods in the early nineteenth century. Such issues as temperance and Sabbath (Sunday) observance had been at the head of the list. Some synods in the North, notably the Franckean Synod, had declared slavery to be a sin. While those in the South might show concern for the religion of the slaves, once the Confederacy had formed, they tended to declare that slavery was not a sin. Such conflict in viewpoints had encouraged the predominant pattern among Lutherans to consider social action an individual matter. With the United Lutheran Church in the 1920s, however, public issues became a regular part of the church's agenda. Later it published three volumes on "Christian Social Responsibility."[3]

Other new ministries, in which the United Lutheran Church took the earliest initiative, included pastoral service specifically for students at universities, and radio programs such as the National Radio Pulpit aired by the National Broadcasting Company (the "Knubel Hour," with ULCA President F. H. Knubel, and Paul Scherer, professor at Union Theological Seminary, New York).

The war had brought cooperation with other Lutheran church bodies to serve soldiers and sailors and to care for orphaned missions, places that had been cut off from support by Lutheran mission societies in Europe. World War II increased such cooperation and added home missions in war-industry towns, especially through "Lutheran World Action." After the war, campus ministry was among the additions to cooperative work.

Through church mergers — the Lutheran Church in America (1962), the Evangelical Lutheran Church in America (1987) — the Muhlenberg tradition was joined with other Lutheran traditions that agreed on the breadth of concerns and forms of mission needed in order to reach people with the gospel.

Current Situation

At the beginning of the twenty-first century, the church formed from a mixture of Lutheran traditions will be repeatedly assessing where it is

3. Harold C. Letts, ed., *Christian Social Responsibility,* 3 vols. (Philadelphia: Muhlenberg Press, 1957).

headed with home mission, global mission, and social mission. Memories of great endeavors during the quarter century following World War II are dying out with the generation that experienced them, and the trends suggest the question, "What next?"

During the "religion boom" following World War II, new congregations were established by the hundreds for mobile, fairly prosperous, white middle-class families. In the ULCA Muhlenberg's words were turned into a motto, "The Church Must Be Planted." The church widened its mission in those years to assist existing strategically located congregations (often urban) to survive and serve a diversity of peoples. Now a shortage of funds requires the difficult task of establishing priorities and long-range strategies.

Time was when congregations could be mobilized by the thousands to join in uniform evangelism programs to attract new members and reactivate the inactive. Presently many congregations insist upon greater freedom to pursue their own mission initiatives and emphasize the distinctiveness of their circumstances.

Global mission responded to the new independence of former colonial territories and assisted in organizing autonomous churches in those places. Rather than concentrating on a limited number of mission fields that had won a degree of loyalty among members of the supporting churches in America, emphasis has been placed upon projects that will allow greater flexibility as change may require. New loyalties have been engendered by developing relationships between specific churches overseas, or sections of them, and individual synods or congregations in the ELCA ("partner synods" or parishes). Reductions in income and consequently in long-term missionaries have been matched by encouraging many short-term volunteers. Although conversions are far from out of date, the greater respect for peoples of other cultures has called for putting demeaning attitudes aside, and for engaging in interfaith dialogue. Such dialogue has become appropriate at the home base in America, too, as religious diversity has increased.

World War II overseas relief aid generated donations of goods (food, heifers, clothing) by the trainload and by the tens of millions of dollars. World Hunger appeals have continued to elicit generosity for overseas emergencies, at the same time that disaster emergencies at home have been gaining more support. Efforts overseas have moved toward promoting self-help community development. Government support for such work by churches has diminished from earlier times, when it provided the major proportion, to the present more modest amounts.

At home the "War on Poverty" increased the reliance by governmental units upon the church's social service agencies. Lutheran agencies received additions largely from government to their existing funding and have reached a total from all sources approaching two and a half billion dollars annually, the largest service program of any Christian communion. But as the ideal of a humanitarian government wanes, both in overseas and domestic services, church agencies face major priority and strategy decisions.

The enthusiasm among segments of the church's membership for the civil rights and anti-war movements in the 1960s was later replaced by environmental concerns. In each instance, corporate response by the church has been expected by some, in the form both of official statements and of action for the common good of humanity.

In a society with strong forces for "earn-your-own-way" individualism, and a widespread belief that everyone has a chance to "make it" in a free society, the church may join in the debate over definitions of freedom, justice, and peace, and about the causes of poverty, delinquency, and violence. It can espouse self-help and ecological responsibility as causes deserving nurture. It will want to minister to those who are already church members, comforting them as needed, challenging them when possible. The mission has grown to be as diverse and complex as modern life, but it still exists only because the church has received the gospel given by God for new life in Christ.

Responses

After each segment of Dr. Marshall's presentation, there were responses from several persons knowledgeable about the topic and its history or who might see it from a particular vantage point, as parish pastor, layperson, woman, or person of color. They had great freedom on what to say. The aim was to lead into discussion of the topic today. **Raymond Bost** *and* **Charles Glatfelter** *(see pp. 208-13, below), as historians, went into fuller detail about the United States emerging two centuries ago when, as it was once put, "Everything, so to speak, has been started anew." The expansion and trauma of mission in such a time were noted. Dr. Bost particularly picked up on developments in the South; see his 1998 article, "The Muhlenberg Tradition Moves South," and "Continuing the Muhlenberg Tradition in the South" (pp. 35-49, below).*

Organization

Beginnings

There were Lutheran organizations in America before Muhlenberg's arrival. As early as the 1620s and 1630s there were Lutherans in the Dutch colony along the Hudson River, but they had trouble receiving governmental approval for a pastor until the British gained control in 1664. Along the Delaware River, again in the 1630s, Lutherans were dominant in the Swedish colony. In the Virgin Islands, Danish Lutherans built Frederick Church in 1666. In the 1730s along the Savannah River, the Salzburgers settled after fleeing persecution in Austria. In addition, by the time of Muhlenberg's arrival in America, there were Lutheran settlers in Nova Scotia and in Maine, as well as in his assigned destination of Pennsylvania.

Although congregations survived in these places, larger Lutheran organizations did not. In New York and northern New Jersey, in 1725, William Christopher Berckenmeyer organized fourteen congregations into parishes, structures that had disintegrated by 1751. In New Sweden the congregations were a district of the Skara diocese in the homeland and later came under the Archbishop of Uppsala. Under authority of the Church of Sweden, the first Lutheran pastors were ordained in America (notably the German Justus Falckner, in 1703). Their church buildings might also have been the first built. The first Indian missions were conducted by a Swedish Lutheran pastor, John Campanius. When Sweden gave up its colony to the British, however, the congregations aligned with the Anglican Church. In Ebenezer, Georgia, the Salzburgers not only built church buildings but also an orphanage, the first Lutheran social ministry institution in America. Yet with the American Revolution, these efforts withered and the colonists began to scatter. No Lutheran organization survived from any of these beginnings, except a few congregations.

It was three congregations in Pennsylvania that helped determine the course of Muhlenberg's life. New Hanover, Providence (or Trappe), and Philadelphia, all established by 1730, organized as the "United Congregations" in 1733 and appealed for a pastor from Europe. The initiative of responsible laymen was matched by their faithfulness, as they waited for nine years. Their organization already included deacons and elders, who met Muhlenberg and agreed on how he should proceed to get acquainted and establish his leadership in congregations.

Muhlenberg was accustomed to a much more secure and ordered organization of the church than he found in America. In his hometown of Einbeck, where he had been baptized, catechized, and confirmed, there were church buildings centuries old, pastors and other church personnel who were trained, assigned, and supervised by an ecclesiastical organization for the town and its territory, with the government providing legal and financial support. None of this existed in Pennsylvania. At Halle he had known the complex of institutions built by A. H. Francke with support from wealthy landholders. By cooperation with the ecclesiastical authorities of Saxony, he had been ordained in Leipzig. The Halle mission network included ties in London with the court chaplain Ziegenhagen, who was the point of contact for the Pennsylvania congregations. The young Muhlenberg benefited from some time with Ziegenhagen before setting off for a minimally structured and almost totally undisciplined church environment.

Fortunately Muhlenberg proved to be a master organizer, and several features of his developments survive to this day. He relied on authoritative documents, such as his ordination certificate, to displace self-appointed ministers who had no such authorization. Since he wanted a proper call from each congregation, he asked the leaders to sign a document that he had drawn up to specify the division of responsibilities.

A few years later, in 1748, Muhlenberg invited to a meeting the four pastors who had followed him from Halle, the Swedish provost, and John Christopher Hartwick who had come from Hamburg, Germany, to serve a parish in New York and had visited Muhlenberg two years earlier. The date was August 15 on the calendar in use at the time. It would be August 26 on our current calendar. The occasion was the dedication of a sizeable new church building by the Philadelphia congregation. The stated purpose was "closer union of the preachers," plus "mutual consultation and agreement in matters concerning all the congregations."[4] Laymen from some ten congregations were in attendance to report on their congregations and to provide advice when requested. Only the pastors would vote.

Muhlenberg wanted approval for an order of worship, which he and a couple of other pastors had developed. The liturgy that was adopted was the best that Lutherans would have, according to traditional standards, for another century.

Uppermost of items on the agenda was ordination. There were never

---

4. *Documentary History* (from *Hallesche Nachrichten*, Muhlenberg's reports to Halle), pp. 3-42.

enough pastors. Schoolteachers had to be tutored in private to prepare for ordination and be licensed to preach. Muhlenberg held to the policy in Germany that the church should provide for the examination and ordination of candidates. He did not want to practice private ordination as some had done (like J. C. Stoever, Jr.). Muhlenberg made it clear that he did not believe that ordination conferred any "inherent power" or effected any "personal change," but that ordination provided the authority to hold the office of pastor and to perform the functions of the office.[5]

The new organization assumed significant responsibilities for strengthening good order in the church, but it did not have much structure of its own at the beginning — no officers for the first two years, no regular annual meetings until 1767 — and was considered an experiment by Muhlenberg. After all, the mission of the church over an expanding territory and growing population was too demanding to allow much time for seeing to its organized embodiment beyond congregations. Then too Muhlenberg could be counted on to serve as Senior, not only because of his length of tenure and the expectation of the Halle fathers, but even more because of his forceful leadership. The organization did not feel the need for a constitution until 1781, when it finally settled upon a name, Evangelical Lutheran Ministerium of North America. As other synods formed, the name was changed to Evangelical Lutheran Ministerium of Pennsylvania and Adjacent States. Districts or conferences were allowed, where pastors located near each other could meet.

In the meantime, in 1762, Muhlenberg had developed a constitution for St. Michael's congregation in Philadelphia. The form he used had origins in sixteenth-century Amsterdam, where Lutherans were a minority free church, much like Lutherans in America. The form had been adapted in London, in New York, and among the Salzburgers in Georgia. It provided for the congregation to elect its pastor and its lay leaders.

In all of the texts that Muhlenberg developed for organizational purposes, a confessional basis was included. In the call for a pastor, the constitution for a congregation, and constitution for the Ministerium, there was reference to the Augsburg Confession and often to the other Lutheran symbolical documents. In the order of worship there was the Creed.

He had adopted a polity that would survive through these 250 years and many changes in church structure. The laity were members of congregations, where they had defined powers and responsibilities. The pastors

5. Tappert, in E. C. Nelson, ed., *Lutherans,* p. 47.

were members of a ministerium, which would decide about discipline of its members and about who qualified for ordination. The structures indicated that the church was both local congregations and a more universal reality, a fundamental aspect of the Muhlenberg tradition.

Subsequent History

For over half a century after Muhlenberg's death in 1787, responsiveness to the American environment seemed to influence Lutheran organizations more than loyalty to Lutheran identity.

In a new constitution adopted in 1792, the Pennsylvania Ministerium did not include any reference to the Lutheran Confessions. Neither was acceptance of the Confessions required for ordination. In accord with government by the people, which was developing in the new nation, lay delegates were now allowed to vote at Ministerium meetings.

Since the conferences were forming separate synods, the Ministerium proposed a General Synod to maintain unity. Quite the opposite resulted. Synods began to divide between those that favored, and those that opposed, a General Synod, which was finally founded in 1820. The Ministerium itself remained a member for only a couple of years. Fear of centralization and disagreement about confessionalism were among the reasons for withdrawing. Some Ministerium congregations were more interested in relations with the Reformed Church than with Lutheran unity.

S. S. Schmucker became president of Gettysburg Seminary, organized in 1826, the first Lutheran institution to endure until the present (Hartwick Seminary survived from 1797 to 1940). Schmucker strove to make the General Synod a viable organization, and by the 1850s most eastern synods had joined again, including the Pennsylvania Ministerium. In the interest of Americanization, however, he proposed slight emendations to the Augsburg Confession, a move that engendered new debates and divisions.

In another fifteen years the General Synod had broken into three parts, dividing the heirs to the Muhlenberg tradition. The Civil War had caused the southern synods to organize on their own United Synod, South. Renewed concern for confessional identity brought a withdrawal of half of the northern synods that remained, to form the General Council in 1867, under the leadership of the Pennsylvania Ministerium. Each part had its own seminary, a new one in Philadelphia, and one in the South since 1830.

By 1888, however, the kinship felt by the three groups had led to cooperation in producing a worship order, the Common Service Book. In 1918 they came together in the United Lutheran Church in America on the basis of the Lutheran Confessions.

By that time, Muhlenberg would have been gratified at the number of Lutheran institutions. His plans to build institutions in Philadelphia had gone unfulfilled. In the 1840s William Passavant had begun starting orphanages, hospitals, a college (Thiel), and a seminary in Chicago. No Lutheran can claim credit for more institutions than he. Others were at work beginning in the 1840s, which was a boom decade for founding institutions. One college, in Allentown, Pennsylvania, was named for Muhlenberg.

Muhlenberg would have been surprised by the complexity of later church structure. Besides synods, there were boards and committees within the synods and within the churchwide organization of the ULCA. In addition, cooperation brought participation in the Lutheran World Convention and in councils of an interdenominational makeup.

Disagreements about the inspiration of Scripture, lodge membership, and interchurch relations divided Lutherans and were issues on which the ULCA held distinctive positions. For Lutheran unity the ULCA considered subscription to the Lutheran Confessions sufficient. In 1962 it merged with Lutherans of three other traditions to form the Lutheran Church in America (LCA). Then in 1987, Lutherans of a still greater mix of traditions formed the Evangelical Lutheran Church in America (ELCA).

The international organization had become the Lutheran World Federation at the close of World War II. In America, the organizations that were bringing the greatest variety of Lutherans together were Lutheran World Relief and Lutheran Immigration and Refugee Service. Confessional identity was a unifying force when it came to service, although theologically it could be divisive.

Current Situation

As the ELCA faces the future, some prognosticators are predicting that megachurches (self-sufficient, all-inclusive congregations) will dominate among church structures. Others predict a disintegration into house churches small enough to assure a congenial group committed to service according to a New Testament model.

If complex denominational structures persist, congregations will still continue to experience pressures to expand their involvement in local mis-

sion, even as they are challenged by the church body to worldwide cooperation and a universal vision. Where Lutheran institutions, such as colleges
and social service agencies, no longer serve predominantly church constituencies, constant attention to defining their church relationship will be
needed. Synods and churchwide structures will be called upon to serve a diversity of people and still maintain unity with a clear identity and integrity.

In a society that has developed a proliferation of voluntary organizations, the church has reason to assess which of its programs deserve priority on the basis of clearly combining Christian faith with effectiveness in
Christian service.

The ELCA has an excellent description of the "nature of the church"
in its constitution (Chapter 2.02):

> The church exists both as an inclusive fellowship and as local congre-
> gations gathered for worship and Christian service. Congregations
> find their fulfillment in the universal community of the Church, and
> the universal Church exists in and through congregations. This
> church, therefore, derives its character and powers both from the sanc-
> tion and representation of its congregations and from its inherent na-
> ture as an expression of the broader fellowship of the faithful. In
> length, it acknowledges itself to be in the historic continuity of the
> communion of saints; in breadth, it expresses the fellowship of believ-
> ers and congregations in our day.

The ELCA statement copies substantially a similar statement that was in
the LCA constitution. The dual nature of the church echoes the structures
that Muhlenberg defined over two centuries earlier.

As a corporate entity in a free society, where people are to decide the
direction of the nation, the church faces the question whether it has a responsibility to serve as a conscience for society, as moral guide or goad. As
an organized group of people, what is the church's responsibility to its own
members? What claim to their time, talent, and treasure is proper, compared to their divine calling to other institutions, such as families and
those structures providing for daily work and for civic order? How does
the church teach stewardship in a society that can exaggerate the need for
material goods while it is raising the standard of living for some and increasing the difficulty of survival for others?

Organization for the church is more than a framework. It is people in
dependable and purposeful relationships. Along with all the human needs

that the organized church may serve, it will want to be a seedbed for mission, for planting the gospel in people's lives, for growth as a confessing church in whatever its social setting.

RESPONSES

*Responses in connection with "Organization" by **Mark Oldenberg** and **Kay Dowhower** lifted up the openness to new needs in society that Muhlenberg's descendants faced and the variety of ministries in the nineteenth century. The comments of **A. Gregg Roeber** (pp. 50-52, below) exhibit a historian's necessary caution about lines too easily drawn from past to present; he suggested a Muhlenberg (and opponents) more "confessionalist" than often assumed.*

Personal Experience

Beginnings

Henry Melchior Muhlenberg understood the course of his life to have been determined by his experience shortly after he began his studies at the University of Göttingen. He believed God had rescued him from "boozing" and "brawling" with the wrong associates (*Journals* 1:3). God's agents had been three students from the University of Halle and Professor Oporin. He credited the theological courses with awakening his deeply personal awareness of sin and justification by Christ, and with strengthening his faith for the power of a new life.

Such experience needed continuing renewal. Muhlenberg spoke of daily repentance. He believed in reflecting on the spiritual significance of a day's events and keeping a record in a journal.

Muhlenberg replayed his own experience in his ministry to other individuals and families. When someone was ill or dying or wanted counsel, Muhlenberg would read to them from Scripture, discuss the pertinence of the text, encourage the persons to respond by describing their feelings — if with tears, so much the better. He would lead them in a confession of sin and of faith, pray with them, and assure them of God's grace. His basic premise was that "theoretical knowledge, without practice and experience, leaves a person in the lurch when trouble comes" (*Journals* 1:489).

In advising a man who wanted to work for the Lutheran church, Muhlenberg recommended the study of the Bible, the Lutheran symbolical books, and such authors as Luther, Arndt, and Spener in order to acquire "the fundamental biblical and theological truths and experience them" (*Journals* 1:182). He believed a pastor should have experienced the truth of the doctrines that he was expected to teach and preach. It was not enough to stick to the "unaltered Augsburg Confession with an unaltered heart" (*Journals* 2:387; 3:427).

Yet experience was not self-sufficient. Only the Word of God, the promise of the gospel, provided the source of trust and assurance of salvation. Muhlenberg disagreed with George Whitefield, the Methodist evangelist, who was often in America, and taught that every adult needed a conversion experience. Muhlenberg defended infant baptism, took care to provide for catechization, and held the sacrament of the Lord's Supper to be an integral part of the life of faith. As a result Muhlenberg has been dubbed an "orthodox pietist."[6]

For worship experience, he wanted the traditional liturgy. Although he knew that his Germans considered the sung liturgy of the Swedes to be too "papistical," and that the immigrants had come from different locations and liturgical traditions, he solved the problem by using as a basis the liturgy in use among the Lutherans in London and introducing some variants from several Reformation liturgies in Germany.

Muhlenberg thought of experience with particular reference to feelings, convictions, and the motivating power of the will in relation to Jesus Christ. Today's analysis might consider his cultural background as a part of his experience and thus explain (1) his adherence to a certain brand of Christian tradition, (2) his desire to perpetuate a scholarly professional ministry, and (3) a historical liturgy. These indeed belong to the Muhlenberg tradition.

Subsequent History

After Muhlenberg's time, his combination of pietism and tradition began to lose out. The pressure from rationalism and Deism in small measure, and from revivalism in large measure, made the Confessions seem less important.

---

6. Lehmann, "Missioner Extraordinary," pp. 9-10. Cf., further, Robert F. Scholz, "Was Muhlenberg a Pietist?" *Concordia Historical Institute Quarterly* 52, no. 2 (Summer 1979): esp. 50-58.

During Muhlenberg's last years, the Enlightenment in Germany had caused Americans to question the wisdom of seeking pastors from there. Any attempt to make rationalism fit with supernatural revelation was too confusing for most people, even when it was attempted by the Halle graduate who had become president of the New York Ministerium, Frederick Quitman (reason overcomes superstition).

The Pennsylvania Ministerium made "experimental religion" a constitutional requirement for the clergy. By that was meant "an individual experience of the struggle against sin and its eventual conquest through the power of Christ," aided by "mutual edification" and "consideration of Bible truths" among pastors.[7] Sermons were to aim for edification and were to be judged by their practical value. Emotional intensity, greater than had characterized pietism, became prevalent in revivalism during the first half of the nineteenth century.

S. S. Schmucker, in his inaugural address at Gettysburg Seminary, highlighted "fervent piety" as a prerequisite for theological education. Like Muhlenberg, his experience included scholarly learning, but not with quite the same commitment to the Lutheran Confessions. Rather, at Princeton where he studied, the battle of biblical revelation against rationalism probably contributed to Schmucker's later effort to adjust Lutheran confessionalism to his experience of religious pluralism in America. But it should be remembered that he showed a concern for the Confessions at a time when some Lutherans were ignoring them altogether.

The worship experience among Lutherans also reflected current trends. The traditional form was revised and replaced. Historic elements, even the Creed, were dropped. With responsive liturgy gone, the congregation participated in little more than hymn singing. Prominence was given to the sermon and to "prayers from the heart."

In the 1850s a shift began. Germany was experiencing renewed interest in historical origins, and changes were introduced in Pennsylvania by immigrant pastors who became leaders in the Ministerium. Some historic liturgy was introduced in 1855. The English translation became the English Church Book of the General Council, then of the General Synod and of the United Synod, South. The Muhlenberg tradition in worship was getting back on track.

In the latter part of the nineteenth century, intrusions by scientific

---

7. H. George Anderson, in E. C. Nelson, ed., *Lutherans*, p. 90, citing *Documentary History*, pp. 250, 252, 257.

learning were becoming a part of experience to be considered by religious leaders. The influence was felt in "natural theology" and in biblical studies. Before the Civil War natural science was largely a matter of collecting flora and fauna and organizing them according to species. Some Lutheran pastors like G. H. Ernst Muhlenberg gained recognition for their notable contributions. Theologically the emphasis was placed upon the harmony between science and the Bible.

A change occurred when Louis Agassiz and Charles Darwin presented their challenging theories. Although rejection of the new science prevailed among Lutherans, Milton Valentine at Gettysburg Seminary, as early as 1884, and later Henry Eyster Jacobs at Philadelphia Seminary and John A. W. Haas (Muhlenberg College) asserted that the new scientific theories, if proven, posed no threat to Christian faith.

Literary and historical criticism of Scripture struck closer to home. Again there were strong opponents. Early in the twentieth century, however, Jacobs and Haas were claiming that verbal inspiration of Scripture was neither necessary nor Lutheran. F. H. Knubel, who would become first president of the ULCA, agreed.

In 1938 the ULCA adopted the Baltimore Declaration, which held that the Bible received its authority from its message. Charles M. Jacobs had developed the case for considering the Word of God in a threefold sense: gospel message, Jesus Christ, and Scripture in which Christ is central. This ULCA formula survived to be largely adopted in the ELCA Constitution (Chapter 2.02, "Confession of Faith").

After two hundred years of the Muhlenberg tradition, there was a characteristic readiness to adjust to the cultural environment, as well as an expectation that experience should correlate with a confessional understanding of Scripture.

Current Situation

Today the role of experience in Christian life is commonly termed "spirituality." Can Muhlenberg's combination of pietistic experience and confessional commitment shed light upon a Lutheran type of spirituality? If so, both studied understanding and emotional feeling would be included, along with certain specific activities.

These activities would involve Bible study and prayer in private and in groups. In public worship, hearing the Word and receiving the sacraments would receive priority in a setting of prayer and praise. Christian fellowship would emphasize giving and receiving comfort and counsel with other Christians. The desired result: experiencing the presence and the power of God, together with motivation and commitment for Christian living. In church and out, generosity and ethical conduct would be a constant concern.

For worship today, there are contrasting trends. On one hand, an increase in liturgy and symbolism in worship has pushed the historical horizon back to pre-Lutheran traditions. On the other hand, there are freer forms of worship preferred by some congregations. Or a congregation may offer a choice at different services. Will conformity or diversity prevail in the foreseeable future? How can Christian community be experienced, in spite of diversity and fragmentation in society?

Two aspects of present-day experience deserve special attention — one of more recent development, the other of longer duration.

Forms of experience as part of a new social consciousness have received explicit expression in recent decades. The "Black experience" and the "feminine experience" are examples of special insights and concerns of a particular group that deserve the attention of the church for the benefit of the whole society. Since the movements include nonreligious people, the church needs to encourage its members to share their perceptions of the Christian grounds for participation and for a positive contribution by the church. A Lutheran church body may adopt an official policy statement for social goals and social action, but then it must foster specific study and action programs.

A more longstanding aspect of modern culture — science — is concerned with provable natural causation and process, and it should not be expected to prove or disprove the existence of God. Although the church can acknowledge the degree to which everyone is indebted to scientific discovery and the resulting technological development, it also needs to recognize that science is continually theorizing, and debating probabilities, in order to correct or augment its findings, rather than to promote absolute determinism.

In a free society where many divergent interpretations of life experiences are available, Christians still have reason to wonder at the hiddenness as well as at the grace of God. Amid the imperfections of human attainments and understandings, Christians may seek a wholistic involvement of faith with social and intellectual challenges of our time, while spiritual strength remains greatly dependent upon traditional resources.

RESPONSES

Muhlenberg and "Experience" introduced an area of authority often stressed nowadays by Liberation and Feminist theologians. Responses by **Sherman Hicks***, an African American pastor and former bishop (***Mary Havens***, Lutheran Theological Southern Seminary faculty, dissertation on Zinzendorf, was unable to be present), Paul Baglyos, Luther Routte, and others led to discussion of ministry to Negroes/Blacks and whether, by standards of "correctness" today, Muhlenberg was a racist (see Jeff G. Johnson and Michael Cobbler 1998). The response by* **Robert Scholz** *(pp. 53-59, below) placed spiritual experience for Muhlenberg clearly within scriptural and doctrinal norms, while also arguing that in the postmodern "paradigm shift" the Muhlenberg tradition suggests a "continuing role" for "the subject's experience in the face of authenticating norms."*

Ecumenism

Beginnings

Encountering new dimensions of religious pluralism in America, Henry Melchior Muhlenberg made himself at home by being friendly toward other churches, but selectively so. He was ready to cooperate with Presbyterians and Anglicans, and even with a revivalist preacher such as George Whitefield, but especially with the German Reformed. He might preach in their churches and they in his. Interestingly, when he had preached in a congregation with both Reformed and Lutherans present, he recorded that he had preached in a manner that would offend neither group. Although he could cooperate to this degree, he cautioned against allowing union churches to produce laxity in teaching.

He had the most trouble with Moravians. When Muhlenberg left Germany, Count von Zinzendorf was under the ban in Saxony and forbidden to enter Hannover. He was being criticized by pietists and orthodoxists alike. Upon disembarking at Charleston, Muhlenberg heard about a conflict between pro-Moravian and anti-Moravian Lutherans and Reformed in the very place where he was headed. The part of the congregation in Philadelphia that had accepted the preacher sent by the Moravians had taken over the church building and locked out the others. Eventually the court returned the property to those who had rejected the Moravian preacher.

Muhlenberg met with Zinzendorf, who questioned his legitimacy. Muhlenberg found fault with the Moravians' de-emphasis of the Law, repentance, faith, and sanctification in their effort to focus on the love of Jesus. In addition they appeared to hope to dominate in a union of German Christians. Although Moravians eventually gave up any such aggressiveness and Zinzendorf regained good standing in Europe, they continued to be among those less acceptable to Muhlenberg.

Muhlenberg did not consider Quakers and Anabaptists to be "church people," because of their attitude toward sacraments. He took exception to various "specious sects," because they relied only on proof texts, or accepted sudden conversions, or opposed churches and their sacraments.

Even where Muhlenberg was friendly, he remained doctrinally discriminating. After an Anglican had praised the divine institution of episcopal succession, Muhlenberg responded, "the terms 'episcopi' and 'presbyter' are synonymous in the apostolic writings; and succession was dragged through deep mud during the dark ages" (*Journals* 1:323). He set a pattern of selective openness with other churches, which became characteristic of the Muhlenberg tradition.

Subsequent History

After Muhlenberg, friendliness moved toward formal arrangements. For several years the New York Ministerium agreed that the Episcopal Church should serve English-language Lutherans. Later the influence of the Oxford Movement brought "high church" tendencies not appreciated by Lutherans, and the agreement was terminated.

In South Carolina, again for a few years, some Lutheran and Reformed ministers formed a united organization, the *Unio Ecclesiastica*. There was much talk of a similar union in Pennsylvania, where there was already cooperation in church buildings, a hymnal, and the founding of Franklin College (today Franklin and Marshall).

Friendliness now extended to Moravians. The North Carolina Synod even elected a Moravian to serve as secretary, then as president. Methodists were out of favor, however, because the "enthusiasm" in their worship was attracting Lutherans away from their home congregations.

In the mid-nineteenth century S. S. Schmucker sought Protestant unity on the basis of fundamental scriptural teachings; but he did not include Unitarians, Campbellites (Disciples of Christ), Baptists, and certainly not Roman Catholics or those espousing Deism. He was a leader in organizing the International Evangelical Alliance in 1846.

In contrast, Charles Porterfield Krauth, interested in Lutheran unity, led the General Council in developing the Akron-Galesburg Rule of 1872-75, to oppose sharing pulpits and altars with non-Lutherans.

The General Synod allowed freedom in such matters. Then in 1908 it became a charter member of the Federal Council of Churches, but left in 1917 to join in forming the United Lutheran Church in America.

The ULCA worked out its ecumenical policy in the Washington Declaration of 1920. It advocated cooperation in interchurch endeavors. Prepared by F. H. Knubel and Charles M. Jacobs, the content had been presented earlier in an inter-Lutheran meeting, in a paper, "Essentials of a Catholic Spirit," but it was not well received there by some Lutherans.[8]

The ULCA was developing two criteria for ecumenical cooperation: (1) the "evangelical principle" for alliance only with churches that confessed Jesus Christ as divine Lord and Savior, and (2) the "representative principle," which required that only official representatives of churches, and not co-opted individuals, would have power to vote. Since the Federal Council did not honor either principle fully, the ULCA held only a consultative relation to that organization.

The ULCA and its antecedents had participated in interchurch world mission conferences and the International Missionary Council, and in most meetings of the international Conference on Faith and Order and the Conference on Life and Work.

In planning for the World Council of Churches, the ULCA took the lead in mobilizing Lutheran support, both at home and abroad, for representation according to confessional families rather than by national constituencies. Abdel Ross Wentz won the case in committees and at the First Assembly in 1948. Franklin Clark Fry held high office in the WCC Central Committee.

In 1950 the ULCA took a leading part in applying its ecumenical principles in the formation of the National Council of Churches of Christ in the USA (NCCCUSA). On the same basis, synods and congregations were encouraged to join state and local councils of churches.

In all of these ecumenical developments, the ULCA was consistent with the Muhlenberg tradition of interchurch relations on a selective basis.

---

8. F. W. Meuser, in E. C. Nelson, ed., *Lutherans*, pp. 408-10.

Current Situation

In the 1960s a new ecumenical development involved all churches that would be in the ELCA, namely bilateral dialogues, first with the Reformed-Presbyterian churches, then the Roman Catholic Church, and finally the Episcopal Church. Later dialogues have included Methodists, Baptists, Conservative Evangelicals, Orthodox, and Moravians. International dialogues have been held under the sponsorship of the Lutheran World Federation.

This development led to a major shift taking place in ecumenism. For about twenty-five years after World War II, the conciliar movement dominated the ecumenical scene. Now interconfessional dialogues are front and center.

Councils of churches have been a comprehensive type of organization. They incorporate most major Protestant denominations and Orthodox churches, and their programs cover most areas of church activity. Since the disruptions of the 1960s, however, they have suffered from declining support and retrenchment in program. In the NCCCUSA a salient feature has been the prominent place of "Black" churches. In addition to the growth of membership in the WCC from churches in developing nations, Lutherans have had great interest in the study of *Baptism, Eucharist and Ministry,* a multilateral process for matters usually reserved for bilateral dialogues. A key figure at a crucial point in the process was William Lazareth, who, as a graduate and faculty member of the LCA seminary in Philadelphia, could be called a representative of the Muhlenberg tradition and Eastern Lutheranism.

In contrast to the broad representation and programming of the conciliar movement, dialogues have usually involved a small group of specialists limited to study and discussion of the theology and polity of two confessional families. Bilateral dialogues are thus narrow in scope, usually on issues that have in the past been divisive, but go deeply into the topics discussed, as the essence of the church.

From this very focused activity have come proposals for "full communion," thus suggesting broad and profound implications from the dialogues. According to the "Declaration of Ecumenical Commitment" adopted by the 1991 Churchwide Assembly of the ELCA, full communion with another church involves not only intercommunion, sharing pulpits, and transfer of members, which have already been practiced quite generally, but interchangeability of ordained ministers, common commitments of evangelism, witness and service, and common decision-making.[9] In the past, decisions about this variety of matters would have been made separately over a considerable period of time and with due attention to particular conditions that pertain in each case. It remains to be seen what difference full communion will make as a commitment to work with other churches on a whole panoply of involvements.

By adopting the "Formula of Agreement,"[10] which had already been approved by the Presbyterian Church (USA), the Reformed Church in America, and the United Church of Christ, the way has been opened to actual experience with full communion. A joint committee is to "coordinate implementation." Based as it is on *A Common Calling: The Report of the Lutheran-Reformed Committee for Theological Conversations, 1988-1992*,[11] the Formula breaks new ground. It specifically notes, with refreshing and uncompromising honesty, not only "agreement on the essential matters of the gospel," but also "important theological differences." In the past such differences would have been sufficient to prevent altar and pulpit fellowship. Instead, "the varying emphases" are declared to "provide complementary expressions of the church's faith in the Triune God," not "disagreements that need to be overcome," not church-dividing, but "diverse witnesses to the one gospel that is confessed in common." "Complementarity" is the new key word. Confessional complementarity is matched by another new emphasis: "mutual affirmation and admonition." The churches affirm each other because their diversity is needed for adequate witness, and they admonish each other because none of them claims to be perfect. Theological dialogue is to continue, even as the churches develop new dimensions of cooperation.

Full communion between the ELCA and the Episcopal Church in the USA followed a somewhat different pattern. In addition to a quite complete "Agreement in the Doctrine of the Faith" from a summary of the international Anglican-Lutheran doctrinal consensus,[12] the agreement re-

---

9. *1991 Churchwide Assembly, Evangelical Lutheran Church in America, Reports and Records*, vol. 2 (Orlando, 1991), pp. 353-58; the policy statement is reprinted as *Ecumenism: The Vision of the Evangelical Lutheran Church in America* (Chicago: ELCA, 1991).

10. *Ecumenical Proposals: Documents for Action by the 1997 Churchwide Assembly* (Office of the Bishop, Evangelical Lutheran Church in America, Chicago, 1996), pp. 18-22, esp. p. 19 for quotations.

11. Edited by Keith F. Nickle and Timothy F. Lull (Minneapolis: Augsburg Fortress, 1993).

12. *Called to Common Mission (A Lutheran Proposal for a Revision of the Concordat of Agreement)*, November 1998, paragraph #5. Cited hereafter, above, by paragraph #.

quires the ELCA to change its installation of bishops to conform with Episcopal polity (#12). The change involves "the historic episcopate."

The Episcopal Church has had "bishops in this historic succession" and the ELCA has not (#11). To effect the change, the ELCA has agreed that future installations of bishops will include the laying-on-of-hands by at least three bishops who are in the episcopal succession (#19). Further, the ELCA agrees that "bishops shall preside and participate in the laying-on-of-hands at the ordination of clergy" (#20), a practice that has in the past usually involved a bishop, but not necessarily, since any ordained minister could perform the rite if authorized by a bishop. The ELCA has agreed to make constitutional and liturgical changes to provide for the new practices. In the meantime, the Episcopal Church will recognize as authentic the ministry of those in the ELCA who were ordained, and the bishops (who were installed without the historic succession) as "priests/priests exercising a ministry of oversight *(episkopē)* within its synods" (#15). To do this, the Episcopal Church has had to enact a temporary suspension of a seventeenth-century restriction in the "Preface to the Ordination Rites" of *The Book of Common Prayer* (#16). It has also accepted the fact that the ELCA will continue to differ in (1) its view that the historic episcopate is not necessary for full communion (##13, 18); (2) continuation of full communion with churches that do not have the historic episcopate (#25); (3) practice that does not think of the rite for placing in office bishops, deacons, deaconesses, or diaconal ministries as ordination (##9, 14), and (4) understanding and practices that bishops are not bishops for life (#18). Hence there was more detailed spelling out of differences between the two churches and which of them could be tolerated in contrast to those that required change. Two assemblies of the ELCA were required (1997 and 1999), and lengthy debate at both, before the ELCA approved full communion with the Episcopal Church by a required two-thirds majority. Still, a minority in the ELCA has continued active opposition to the action taken.

In contrast, full communion with the Moravian Church was adopted by the ELCA with little debate.

In this new ecumenical era, how many further patterns for full communion will be adopted? How will inconsistencies be avoided, in order to minimize the possibility of conflict eventuating with one church or another over the course of time? As always in ecumenical relations, more than sentiment and personal preferences will be needed in order to take all three of the emphases of John 17:17-23 seriously: the truth of God's Word, the mission of being sent into the world, and unity through Christ.

At the same time, the ELCA has become concerned about relations to Judaism and to some extent (but increasingly) with Islam and other religions. Such inclusiveness has influenced the composition of some local councils or conferences of churches, which only in the last couple of decades have begun to include Roman Catholics.

In the past 250 years Lutherans have moved ever outward in interchurch relations, from informal friendliness and sharing to formal organizations and agreements, but with selectivity concerned for confessional commitments to the gospel. With people of other faiths, the emphasis had fallen on dialogue, mutual understanding, and cooperation for community wellbeing. The diversity of peoples and the complexity of structures are greater, but the need for planting the church in a changing society remains the same.

RESPONSES

*The responses reflected how lively an area ecumenism was in 1997, when attention was being given throughout the ELCA to proposals for "full communion" with three Reformed/Presbyterian churches and a Concordat with the Episcopal Church. The Joint Declaration on the Doctrine of Justification between churches of the Lutheran World Federation and the Roman Catholic Church, to be signed in Augsburg, Germany, on October 31, 1999, was taking shape in this period. The response by **Walter Wagner** reflected the ELCA-Moravian document for "full communion," taken up and approved in the ELCA Assembly in 1999. His presentation was published as "A Key Episode in American Lutheranism: Muhlenberg and Zinzendorf's Encounter" (1998), later expanded into a book (Wagner 2002). Among the principles that Wagner set forth at Baltimore were "Do your historical homework about the other side"; "[R]eexamine the confluence of politics and personalities in ecumenical discussions"; "Order and Vision, the Muhlenberg and Zinzendorf principles, are fundamental to ecumenical ventures and self-understanding." These remarks raised questions about how a church's ecumenical representatives are to be committed to its principles and at the same time open to other views. At Baltimore, time permitted little opportunity to hear, let alone discuss, the response of **Frederick K. Wentz**, which is reproduced below (pp. 60-67).*

RESPONSES TO ROBERT MARSHALL'S
SURVEY HISTORY

Mission: Continuing the
Muhlenberg Tradition in the South

Raymond M. Bost

Much that was significant in the life and work of Henry Melchior Muhlenberg was not unique to his life and ministry. He was a thoroughly committed Christian; German Lutheranism of the eighteenth century molded his life, and he drank deeply at the springs of that Christian movement known as pietism. But as Muhlenberg filtered the strains of biblical Christianity, German Lutheranism, and pietism through his own personal experience as a pastor in colonial America, he produced a blending of those elements that would significantly shape the future development of Lutheranism in what became the United States of America. This essay seeks to demonstrate how selected concerns in the Muhlenberg tradition were manifested in Lutheranism in the South, through the Henkel and Stirewalt families.

Organizational and Confessional Concerns

German settlements in Muhlenberg's Pennsylvania were a significant cultural influence on the budding state of Pennsylvania. Germans also settled in the Southeast before the American Revolution, but, for several reasons, they did not have the cultural impact of German settlers in Pennsylvania. In explaining the failure of the Germans as a group to assume "cultural importance" for the South, Randall M. Miller has observed,

> German immigration to the South encompassed too broad a time span, was too irregular, and drew from too many diverse sources within "Germany" to impose a single cultural order anywhere. Still,

large numbers of Germans settled in the southern region from the colonial period through the 19th century, and within their areas of concentration they built and maintained German subcultures that thrived into the modern era in several instances, at least in attenuated forms.[1]

William Penn's famed colony provided the geographic locale for most of Muhlenberg's ministry, but his influence was not confined to Pennsylvania and places beyond its borders to which Muhlenberg was briefly called to deal with "troubles in Zion." Through Muhlenberg's Ministerium and its impact on a young ministerial candidate named Paul Henkel, many of the concerns dear to Muhlenberg's heart were passed along to Lutherans in the South.[2] Since many of those concerns were not just reflections of Muhlenberg's personal thinking but were generated by scriptural themes embraced by Lutheranism, those concerns continued to manifest themselves long after their espousal by persons like Muhlenberg and Henkel. Prominent among those concerns were two whose development in the South will be the focus of this study: (1) fostering ecclesial structures to provide for the spiritual development of Lutheran Christians through worship centered in the preaching of the Word and administration of the Sacraments, and (2) the concern for mission outreach to the unchurched.

An acute shortage of clergy was a prominent characteristic of Lutheran church life in the days of Muhlenberg. Concern to provide an expanded and more dependable supply of clergy fed the concern to create supra-congregational organizations and schools of theology. Synods and a General Synod were organized, the latter establishing Gettysburg Theological Seminary in 1826. Despite the creation of Lutheran theological schools in New York, Pennsylvania, and South Carolina, Levi C. Groseclose, a North Carolina pastor, wrote to William A. Passavant in 1850 that in his area Lutherans were "a mere handful of ministers and people," with every minister having far more work to do than he could possibly do well:

---

1. "Germans," *Encyclopedia of Southern Culture,* ed. Charles Reagan Wilson and William Ferris (Chapel Hill: University of North Carolina Press, 1989), p. 429.

2. Henkel's long apprenticeship under the Halle pietists who dominated the early Pennsylvania Ministerium was discussed in a presentation at the Baltimore conference, which focused on Muhlenberg and the founding of the Pennsylvania Ministerium. See Raymond M. Bost, "The Muhlenberg Tradition Comes South," *Concordia Historical Institute Quarterly* 71, no. 3 (Fall 1998): 128-34.

Oh! that the Lord would raise up, qualify, and send forth more effi-
cient laborers into his vineyard, that the waste places of Zion might be
built up. Oh, Lord, revive us! Make us strong in faith and self-denial,
and abundant in every good work! Pardon me, dear brother, for in-
dulging in the foregoing reflections. "From the abundance of the
heart, the mouth speakest." A sad picture this, of one of the oldest
Synods in the United States! Where we ought to have at least one hundred ministers, we have twelve![3]

Most Lutheran synods in the South elected to unite with the General
Synod created in 1820, but the Tennessee Synod declined to do so out of respect for the vehement opposition to the creation of that body by their early
leader, David Henkel, and their continuing doubts about the General
Synod's commitment to confessional Lutheranism. The Civil War ruptured
the bond of unity created for Lutheran synods in the General Synod. Statements by former colleagues that seemed designed to place all the blame for
the tragic conflict squarely on the shoulders of the South made it difficult
for many Lutherans in the South to think of returning to the General Synod
immediately after Appomattox. But with the Confederate States of America
forcibly persuaded to return to their former role as parts of the United
States, the decision to continue a separate general ecclesiastical body for Lutherans in the South seemed to require some sort of public explanation. A
reason advanced for sustaining a Southern version of the General Synod in
the South had to do with Lutheran unity and confessional identity.[4] The

3. *The Missionary* 3, no. 9 (September 1850): 67 and 70.

4. In August 1866, a committee of three pastors appointed to formulate a rationale
for the action recently taken to maintain a separate organization for Lutherans in the
South gave four reasons for preferring to continue a separate existence. One of those reasons was that the Lutherans in the South wanted to affirm their confessional identity, a
move that was not expected to win applause in the old General Synod where some en-
dorsed S. S. Schmucker's "Definite Synodical Platform." "Pastoral Letter," *The Lutheran
Visitor* 1, no. 8 (August 1866): 185.

In adopting the constitution for the new body before the end of the year, the Virginia Synod explicitly affirmed the fact that it was but renewing a confessional position
adopted earlier. "In this action the Synod has simply reaffirmed the doctrinal basis which
it adopted in 1861, at Mt. Tabor, Va., when it instructed its delegates to the proposed convention for the formation of the General Synod, to favor the Augsburg Confession un-
qualifiedly as the bond of union between our Southern Synods." *The Lutheran Visitor* 1,
no. 12 (December 1866): 281.

fact that the Lutheran tradition was cast in a clearly minority role in the South, and the fact that *Southern* Lutheranism itself was divided into two camps, led even before the Civil War to concern to heal the breach between the Tennessee and other Lutheran synods in the South. Beginning in 1820 as a split between the North Carolina and the newly created Tennessee Synods, the schism divided families and congregations as the Tennessee Synod moved throughout the Carolinas and Virginia, in particular, encouraging Lutherans to embrace a distinctly confessional understanding of their Reformation heritage.

By the spring of 1867, serious thought was being given to the future of the Evangelical Lutheran General Synod of the Confederate States in America. The editor of *The Lutheran Visitor* encouraged his readers to consider the issues to be confronted by the forthcoming convention of the South's general body for Lutherans. He noted that some, no doubt, would long for a "higher type of Lutheranism than that displayed by our synods, in the past, or even at the present. . . ." Partisanship, however, must, he believed, be avoided. "**Festina lente** [make haste slowly] is the motto by which we should be governed in any contemplated change of **government, worship,** or **doctrine.**" Clearly fearful that those wanting to see the general body move to a stronger confessional position would divide rather than unite Lutheranism in the South, Editor Miller urged a concern "to study and practice those things which make for peace."[5]

On Thursday morning, May 23, 1867, delegates to the convention that would act on the future shape of the Lutheran church in the South met at Staunton, Virginia. Georgia had two delegates present, South Carolina seven, North Carolina five, the Southwest Virginia Synod five, and the Virginia Synod eight. The Tennessee Synod, which had not been a member of the previous body, was invited to participate in the assembly and sent a commissioner. Editor Miller was convinced that the attendance of a representative from the Tennessee Synod provided "strong grounds to expect" a union of that body with the reorganized general body for Lutherans in the South, a development "which will doubtless be followed by the addition to the Gen. Synod of the Holstein [sic] Synod.

---

5. "General Synod," *The Lutheran Visitor* 2, no. 4 (April 1867): 117. Since it was no longer appropriate to have the words "Confederate States of America" appear in the official title of the Southern general synod, the designation "Evangelical Lutheran General Synod in North America" was adopted. Despite shifting titles, it was generally known as the General Synod South until it became the United Synod, South.

We fervently pray that we all may soon be one, even as **Christ and the Father are one.**"[6]

From its reorganization as the Evangelical Lutheran General Synod of North America, the general body for Lutherans in the South longed to be a broadly inclusive body. When the North Carolina Synod declared that it favored "every proper measure which has as its object, the union of all the Synods **in these United States,** upon the great doctrines of the Lutheran Church, as set forth in the Augsburg Confession," it quite probably reflected sentiments that could be echoed in other Lutheran synods in the South.[7] However, the hope of immediately enjoying close fellowship with the Tennessee Synod was not realized. Tennessee was not satisfied with the confessional stance of the body, and by 1870 a second divisive issue had manifested itself. Synods supporting Southern Seminary were concerned about its future location, and the North Carolina Synod hoped to provide the new home for the school. Several sites in their state seemed to the North Carolinians suitable for a Lutheran school of theology. Initially it appeared that North Carolina's bid for the school had carried the day, but objections to the initial decision were voiced, the matter reconsidered, and the decision made to locate the school of the prophets in South Carolina. Not only was the school to be located in the Palmetto State, but the first two professors to be named were chosen from the pastoral ranks of the South Carolina Synod. Convinced that their neighbors to the north and south were intent on acting together against the best interests of the southern church in gen-

6. *The Lutheran Visitor* 2, no. 7 (July 1867): 202. The Holston Synod was an offshoot of the Tennessee Synod, created out of the desire to have a synod more compact than the Tennessee Synod, which prior to the creation of the Holston Synod had significant clusters of congregations in both Carolinas as well as Virginia and Tennessee. Those in Tennessee became the Holston Synod.

The Holston Synod moved promptly to apply for admission to the general body for Lutherans in the South and was unanimously received. *The Lutheran Visitor* 3, no. 6 (June 1868): 185.

7. *Minutes of the Sixty-eighth Session of the Ev. Lutheran Synod of North Carolina held in Pilgrim Ev. Lutheran Church, Davidson Co., N.C., August 23d-28th, 1871* (Salisbury, NC: J. J. Bruner, Book and General Job Printer, 1871), p. 6. Emphasis added. The Committee on the President's Report responded to the resolution he presented with two resolutions of its own, the first of which deprecated "the causes that have produced divisions in our beloved Zion" and prayed "that all such divisions, may speedily be healed." The second declared that "we stand prepared to be governed by the indications of the great Head of the Church, in reference to any general organization sound in faith, that is likely to bind the church in the unity of the spirit and the bond of Peace" (p. 12).

eral and its North Carolina Synod in particular, the North Carolina Synod in 1871 withdrew from its General Synod affiliation.[8] At the same time, North Carolina elected to again test the water with regard to a closer working relationship with the Tennessee Synod. North Carolina's conversations with Tennessee produced no immediate reunion, but may well have helped to pave the way for the union fifteen years later of the Tennessee Synod and other southern synods as they created the United Synod, South.[9]

Ecclesia Plantanda

It has often been assumed that Muhlenberg derived much of his inspiration for missionary endeavor from what was understood to be his motto, *ecclesia plantanda*, a phrase that has been translated as "the church must be planted." Scholars, however, assure us that Muhlenberg did not utilize the phrase to proclaim a missionary imperative. Rather, in using the phrase *ecclesia plantanda*, Muhlenberg was distinguishing the church as it was coming into being on North American soil in his own day from the church he and so many of his contemporaries had known in "the Old Country."[10] But this concern for the emerging church, *ecclesia plantanda*, was certainly a prominent part of the outlook of Henry Melchior Muhlenberg, Paul Henkel, and those in the South who later shared their understanding of the Church, its message, and its mission.

8. North Carolina's representative proposed Charlotte, Concord, and Lincolnton as prospective sites for the school. The General Synod elected to consider yet another North Carolina site, Mount Pleasant, the home of North Carolina College.

9. William Edward Eisenberg, *The Lutheran Church in Virginia, 1717-1962* (Roanoke: Virginia Synod, LCA, 1967), pp. 223-24. While Tennessee's confessional identity remained strong and delayed her being united with other Southern synods, Tennessee actually went through "a more basic change of character" than any of the Lutheran synods in the South, the change coming in its attempt to sustain the use of the German language and in its church polity. Hugh George Anderson, *Lutheranism in the Southeastern States, 1860-1886: A Social History* (The Hague: Mouton, 1969), p. 47.

10. The distinguished historian of early German Lutheran and Reformed developments in Pennsylvania, Charles H. Glatfelter, seconds the view of the late Theodore G. Tappert in insisting that to read *ecclesia plantanda* as though Muhlenberg were declaring a mission imperative is, in fact, to miss his meaning. Muhlenberg often contrasted *ecclesia plantanda*, the church now emerging, with *ecclesia plantata*, the planted church, reinforcing this understanding. Charles A. Glatfelder, "Muhlenberg West of the Susquehanna," *Lutheran Theological Seminary Bulletin* 72, no. 4 (Fall 1992): 5.

As the "New South" began to emerge following the demise of Reconstruction, Lutherans in the South could at last begin to look beyond the persistent evidences of the trauma that had overwhelmed the nation in the 1860s. The concern for missionary activity that had manifested itself in ante-bellum days in the creation of missionary societies soon revived, and as Lutherans found themselves working more closely together in the United Synod, South, it was to be expected that a concern for mission would soon become apparent. Interest in overseas or "foreign" missions had been stimulated when missionary W. P. Schwartz visited the State of South Carolina before the Civil War, and interest in his work in India continued as Southern Lutherans cooperated with the earlier version of a general synod in supporting his missionary endeavors in India. Now with a slowly reviving economy and the growth of towns, Lutherans began to sense the need to follow their members as they moved into what would become the South's urban areas. As the Evangelical Lutheran General Synod South held its last convention prior to becoming a part of the new United Synod, South, its president reflected on mission opportunities close at hand:

> In addition to Richmond, Atlanta, and the State of Mississippi, which have been so often and so earnestly presented to your consideration, we may also mention Augusta, and the Southside of Savannah, in Georgia, Orlando, and other points in Florida, and a number of hopeful points in Alabama, where judicious missionary labor would yield early and abundant results.[11]

When the United Synod met the following November at Ascension Church, Savannah, Georgia, the body learned that it no longer had the services of Schwartz in India, but disappointment relating to that missionary endeavor did not dampen the interest of the United Synod, South in supporting mission work overseas. In 1887 the Board of Missions of the United Synod, South had already begun gathering information relative to establishing an American Lutheran mission in Japan, and by 1891 it could an-

11. The Report of President W. S. Bowman, *Minutes of the Last Convention of the Evangelical Lutheran General Synod South, of the Second Convention of the Evangelical Lutheran Diet, and of the First Convention of the United Synod of the E. L. Church in the South, held in St. Mark's Church, Roanoke, Virginia, June 23-28, 1886* (New Market, VA: Henkel & Co., Printers, n.d.), p. 5.

nounce the appointment of its first missionary to Japan, James A. B. Scherer, a third-generation Lutheran pastor's son who was a native of Rowan County, North Carolina.[12] By 1893, J. N. Lenker could report,

> The American Lutheran mission is located in Saga, where Rev. Scherer is also at present employed in a government school. A native helper has been employed and the missionaries have begun to hold services. They feel that their work has now fairly opened, and they are well satisfied with the beginning which has been made. A recent letter reports that they have baptized their first convert. The United Synod proposes to expend $4,500 a year on its foreign mission station.[13]

The very gifted but in some respect atypical missionary Scherer would have to cut short his formal career as a part of the Lutheran mission in Japan because of illness. He would go on, however, to serve as a professor at Lutheran Theological Southern Seminary, as president of Newberry College, and as president of the technical school that emerged as the California Institute of Technology. But in the era that ushered in World War II, he was most widely recognized as a spokesperson for understanding the importance of developments in Japan.[14]

As noted above, Scherer was a native of Rowan County, North Carolina, and that same county figures prominently in the story of another Lutheran family that was to play a notable part in the overseas mission work of Lutherans. Captain John Stirewalt, a Pennsylvania native, moved to Rowan County, North Carolina, where he is said to have constructed for his congregation the first pipe organ to be built in the state. A devout member of Zion (later known as "Organ") Lutheran Church near Salisbury, he

12. Scherer was soon joined in Japan by his Roanoke College classmate and roommate, the Rev. R. B. Peery, the two being 1890 graduates of the school.

13. J. N. Lenker, *Lutherans in All Lands: The Wonderful Works of God*, 3rd ed. (Milwaukee: Lutherans in All Lands Company, 1893), pp. 645-46. Grace Lutheran Church, Winchester, Va., under the leadership of Pastor I. G. M. Miller, committed itself to provide Missionary R. B. Peery's annual salary of $750. William Edward Eisenberg, *This Heritage* (Winchester, VA: Trustees of Grace Evangelical Lutheran Church, 1954), pp. 153-54.

14. James A. Scherer, "A Pioneer Lutheran Missionary in Japan: James A. B. Scherer," *Currents in Theology and Mission* 19, no. 5 (October 1992): 326. Shortly after accepting the presidency of Newberry College, Scherer published three books reflecting his understanding of Japanese "history, culture and morality," two of the three being substantial publications issued in both Great Britain and the United States.

would live to see his congregation sharply divided in terms of loyalty to the North Carolina and Tennessee Synods. As New Market, Virginia, the home of the Henkel Press, gained increasing prominence as a center of thought and influence for the Tennessee Synod, Captain John's sons, Pastor John N. and Jacob, elected to move to New Market. Death would claim the young pastor before he could make the move, but his wife, a daughter of Paul Henkel, returned to Virginia with her brother-in-law. Jacob, who married Henrietta Henkel in 1833 and was ordained by the Tennessee Synod in 1838, would labor for more than thirty years as a Lutheran pastor.

The Jacob Stirewalts continued the participation of the Henkel and Stirewalt clans in the life and work of the Tennessee Synod by providing the Synod with Pastors Jerome Paul and John Nathaniel Stirewalt. The latter was the father of the notable Lutheran missionary, Arthur Julius or "A. J." Stirewalt (1881-1968). A. J. attended the Tennessee Synod's young college, which would become Lenoir-Rhyne, and then moved on to the Chicago Lutheran Seminary in Maywood, Illinois. Accepting the call of the Tennessee Synod to serve as a missionary in Japan, he was ordained in 1905 and served in Japan for the next sixty years, sixteen of those years after his official "retirement" in 1952.[15] Stirewalt's work in developing social service agencies for the welfare of the Japanese people was so outstanding that, despite the fact that his "retirement" came less than a decade after the bombings at Hiroshima and Nagasaki with their more than 200,000 casualties, Emperor Hirohito presented him with the Fourth Order of the Sacred Treasure and granted him an extended private audience on the occasion of his "retirement." Among the institutions to which A. J. Stirewalt contributed were *Kyushu Gakuin*, a school for boys in Kumamota that he founded and directed, as well as homes for widows, orphans, and the aged, which he also founded and operated.

As noted above, Pastor Jacob and Henrietta Henkel Stirewalt not only begat a pastor son named John Nathaniel but one named Jerome Paul as well. A native of New Market, Virginia, Martin Luther Stirewalt, Sr. (1882-1960) was a son of Pastor and Mrs. Jerome Paul Stirewalt. Educated

15. *Life Sketches of Lutheran Clergy, North Carolina Synod of the Evangelical Lutheran Church in America and Antecedents, 1773-1999* (Salisbury: Historical Works Committee, North Carolina Synod, 2001), p. 470. His work, begun under the auspices of the Tennessee Synod and the United Synod South, continued under the United Lutheran Church in America. After retiring to Kobe in 1952, he joined the faculty of the Lutheran Bible Institute sponsored by a Norwegian Lutheran mission, serving there until he returned to Virginia shortly before his death.

at Lenoir-Rhyne College, Chicago Lutheran Seminary, the University of Chicago, the University of Virginia, and Northwestern University, he would occupy one of the most prominent Lutheran pulpits in the Southeast for nearly a decade. But having taught even before he was ordained, he would spend much of his professional career in teaching ministries, serving at the Chicago Lutheran Seminary, Lutheran Theological Southern Seminary, and Lenoir-Rhyne College.[16] His daughter, Catharine, would carry on the Muhlenberg-Henkel-Stirewalt concern for fostering the development of the church, *ecclesia plantanda*.

In September 1939, Catharine Amelia Stirewalt (1908-2001) was the focus of attention at a church formerly served by her father, Saint John's Lutheran, Salisbury, North Carolina.[17] There a special service was held for the setting apart of a missionary. This event was the culmination of Catharine's decision to offer herself to the Board of Foreign Missions of the United Lutheran Church in America for mission work overseas. Before the end of the month, she was on a ship bound from San Francisco to China. The crossing "was smooth and the weather most pleasant." A brief stop in Japan provided an opportunity to see something of the Lutheran mission work there.

> From Light Brigade days I have heard of the kindergarten work in Japan. One day I suddenly realized that I was sitting in a kindergarten in Japan, seeing the children and teachers doing their work.[18]

On October 19 she arrived at Tsingtao (Qingdao), Shandong Province, where Lutherans had a congregation, a hospital, and a school of nurs-

---

16. A son, Martin Luther, Jr., also found a career in the church's educational ministries, teaching at Lenoir-Rhyne and Hamma Divinity School, serving as Dean of Hamma as it carried out one of American Lutheranism's boldest experiments in theological education. His scholarly publications on letter forms in antiquity and the New Testament include *Studies in Ancient Greek Epistolography*, Society of Biblical Literature Resources for Biblical Study 27 (Atlanta: Scholars Press, 1993) and *Paul, the Letter Writer* (Grand Rapids: Eerdmans, 2003).

17. Ms. Stirewalt graduated from Carthage College in 1929 and had just completed a Master's degree in the joint program offered by the Biblical Seminary in New York and New York University when she was set apart for mission work in China.

18. Ms. Stirewalt's Christmas letter to friends in the United States, 1939 (Mission collection, James. R. Crumley Jr. Archives, Lutheran Theological Southern Seminary, Columbia, SC; hereafter cited as Crumley Archives).

ing. This was projected as the base of operations for her missionary endeavors, but her initial assignment was to study the Chinese language, and to that end she was sent north to Beijing (Peking) where she enrolled in the College of Chinese Studies.

> The first ten weeks were very busy studying Chinese. We had four teachers from the language school and a class of ten. We got up at five-thirty, had breakfast, and at six-forty-five sat around our dining-table in class. We had classes until noon, then ate, rested, studied, went swimming and occasionally hiking. We went to bed soon after dark because we do not have electric lights and it is hard on one's eyes studying Chinese by a kerosene lamp; and because we had to get up so early in the morning.[19]

While studying in Beijing she made several trips back to Tsingtao, and was able to spend some of the summers of 1940 and 1941 in Peitaiho Beach, a "very lovely summer resort," working with teachers of Chinese there.

With initial language studies completed, Catharine, along with a missionary couple she had been in school with, was assigned to the mission in Tsimo, thirty miles from Tsingtao. The Lutheran enterprise at Tsimo included an established congregation, a school, the mission compound itself, and a small hospital. Catharine's assignment was to prepare to replace the teacher, Clara Sullivan, who was scheduled for a furlough. "We were getting the Fall programs underway and the new missionaries were finding their places and learning to use the Chinese language when things came to an end with the attack on Pearl Harbor."[20] The longstanding struggle of China as confronted with Japan's expansionist interests had seen the Chinese Nationalists increasingly release their claims to the rich and fertile coastal lands of northern China, including Shandong Province. Lutheran mission activities had continued after the Japanese became the dominant military power in the province, but with the attack on Pearl

19. Letter of Catharine Stirewalt to "Margaret," possibly Margaret Poole of Salisbury, N.C., September 1, 1940. Crumley Archives.

20. Ms. Stirewalt recorded in notebooks some of the highlights of her mission experiences 1939-1941 and 1947-1949. These notebooks were typed by the Rev. Dr. M. L. Stirewalt, Jr., and a copy of the typescript placed in the mission collection at the Crumley Archives. The author has drawn most of his information about Catharine's experience in China from the document cited as Catharine's ms. and from Catharine's correspondence.

Harbor and America's response of declaring war on Japan, the situation of American missionaries in Shandong became quite different. Catharine and her colleagues were now "enemies" of the government. Japanese soldiers came into the mission compound at Tsimo the same day their planes attacked Pearl Harbor. The missionaries were relieved of their duties and confined, first at the Tsimo mission compound, then moved into a house, then moved again.[21] Next came a move from Tsimo to the mission compound in Tsingtao, where the hostage missionaries were confined to buildings associated with the hospital, which was permitted to continue its operation since it was staffed by a Chinese doctor. Here the internees were reasonably comfortable as they had a Chinese cook who could leave the compound and do their shopping. It also helped that their captors permitted them to leave the compound and walk the city streets for three hours each day.[22]

The following summer, the governments of the United States and Japan began negotiating an exchange of prisoners. Thinking the war would surely be over soon, Catharine and other single missionaries decided against participating in a prisoner exchange. In the fall, the internees noted a change in the attitude of their captors after it became public knowledge that the United States had shipped 120,000 of its own citizens off to internment camps simply because they were of Japanese extraction. Instead of continuing to enjoy the relative comfort of the familiar mission compound in Tsingtao, Catharine and some of her companions were moved to an old hotel in the city where the single women were housed on cots in what had once been the hotel's ballroom, while the missionary families, irrespective of size, were reduced to no more than one room per family. Here the internees would observe the passing of Thanksgiving and Christmas.

In March 1943, moving time came again, this time to Weihsien, a city

21. The uncertainty, hardship, and frustration associated with these early days of 1942 in which the missionaries moved three times in two weeks is described by Catharine's friend, Mrs. M. D. Shutters, in a letter Catharine asked her to write to her parents, Pastor and Mrs. M. L. Stirewalt, Sr. The letter, dated August 17, 1942, is owned by Mr. Luther Sowers of Salisbury, N.C., who kindly shared a copy with the author who then placed the copy in the Crumley Archives.

22. This luxury could only be enjoyed in the hours immediately after noon when the streets were virtually deserted. When Chinese persons were encountered, they usually sought to avoid the missionaries lest they be seen as fraternizing with "the enemy." The internees were required to wear identifying armbands when outside the mission compound. Catharine's ms.

west of Tsingtao, where American missionaries were being detained in a Presbyterian missionary compound.[23] Catharine was one of fifteen single women assigned to sleep on cots in what had been a large classroom there in earlier days.

Rumors began circulating among the internees in August that a second exchange of Japanese and American prisoners of war was being negotiated. No longer living in the expectation that the war would be a short one, there was no hesitation this time about participating in an exchange. So at the end of August 1943, Catharine found herself along with several other single women on the hard wooden seats of a third-class passenger train car en route to Nanking. Seventy-two hours later, having had no respite from the punishment meted out by the wooden train seat nor any opportunity for sleep, Catharine and her companions reached Nanking where they boarded a train for Shanghai. Reaching that metropolis, the exhausted travelers enjoyed the refreshing experience of a good night's sleep at Saint John's University before undertaking the next leg of their journey.

That came on the *Teia Maru,* a ship that had been adapted for troop transport and was now en route from Shanghai to the Portuguese colony of Goa. On the ship the meals were arranged by sittings, since not all the passengers could be fed at one time. Catharine recalled that on one occasion a group of Roman Catholics passed by them just after the first sitting for breakfast, and the Catholics were overheard to remark that they had just had "another Lutheran breakfast." An inquiry as to their meaning evoked the response, "The Diet of Worms!" When Catharine and her associates went to their sitting for breakfast, they were able to confirm the fact that both the bread and the porridge were thoroughly infested with weevils.

On October 19, four years to the day after her arrival in Tsingtao, Catharine and her colleagues were exchanged for Japanese prisoners of war and boarded the *Gripsholm,* "and what a glorious sight that large, gleaming white ship, flying the Swedish flag and the Red Cross flag. . . ." After the rigors of internment, life aboard the *Gripsholm* evoked an enthusiastic response.

The cabins the unattached women were assigned to were quite deep in the ship, but were clean and had only two passengers in most of them. Also, the run of the ship was ours and on the decks, chairs and chaise

23. For a description of life in this compound in 1943, see Langdon Gilkey, *Shantung Compound* (New York: Harper & Row, 1966).

lounges were available. There were magazines so we could catch up on the news; stores where we had Red Cross credit and could purchase long-needed items; and most important of all, letters from home folks from whom we hadn't heard for a full two years.

And there was food. Fresh fruit tasted extra good.[24]

On December 1, 1944, missionary Stirewalt was reunited with family and friends at a reception at the Prince George Hotel in Manhattan. Then it was off to a well-deserved period of rest and renewal.

The spring of 1945 found Catharine Stirewalt enrolled at Union Theological Seminary, New York City. In the fall she began a year of service to the Deaconess Community of the United Lutheran Church in America, serving on the staff of the Deaconess School in Baltimore.

With World War II ended, plans soon evolved for Catharine to return to her field of service, China. In midsummer of 1947, she sailed from San Francisco for Shanghai, flying from there to Tsingtao where she would join the staff of the Bible School operated by the Lutheran mission. But the China to which she returned in 1947 was not the one she had left in 1943. In April 1944, the Japanese launched a military offensive, Operation Ichigo, with the objectives of destroying the main fighting forces under Chiang Kai-shek and gaining control of airports that might be used to launch airstrikes against Japan. Since this operation targeted Chiang's elite military units and registered significant victories for the Japanese, Chiang was left with limited military strength to oppose the spreading Communist influence when Japan surrendered to the United States in August 1945. Civil war followed in China, and while initially it appeared Chiang's more numerous forces would be able to carry the day, in January 1949, approximately 300,000 Nationalist troops surrendered to the Communist forces and resistance to the Communists ceased north of the Yangtze River.[25] The last hope of carrying on Lutheran mission work in Shandong Province evaporated, and Catharine Stirewalt and her American colleagues returned to the United States, thus concluding her formal career as a missionary serving overseas.[26]

24. Catharine's ms.

25. For an overview of the dramatic increase in Communist military forces and influence in the years following 1936, see J. A. G. Roberts, *Modern China: An Illustrated History* (Phoenix Mill, Gloucestershire: Sutton Publishing Limited, 1998), pp. 201ff.

26. In October 1949, a Proclamation announced the creation of the People's Republic of China.

Concerns for church organization and for reaching unchurched persons who were like sheep without a shepherd were conspicuous themes in the ministry of Henry Melchior Muhlenberg. In the post-bellum South, Lutherans again struggled to foster the organization of congregations and synods and a supra-congregational Lutheran entity that would shepherd synods in a distinctly Lutheran fellowship. In doing so, Lutherans in the Southeast were clearly reflecting identification with a strand of the Muhlenberg tradition. And in recognizing the claims of the *ecclesia plantanda* as well as those of the *ecclesia plantata*, Lutherans in the South again reflected their kinship with Muhlenberg, who, in accepting the role of missionary in the New World, did so much from his field of service in Pennsylvania to shape Lutheranism in the United States as we know it today.

Organization: Muhlenberg, Ecclesiology, and Confessional Witness

A. Gregg Roeber

At the 1993 Muhlenberg Conference in Philadelphia I summarized my assessment of Muhlenberg's unresolved tensions between an objective, confessional Lutheran understanding of the church as those gathered around the correct preaching of the Word and similarly correct administration of the Sacraments, and his early emphasis on subjective, experiential religion.[1] Muhlenberg evolved in his confessional ecclesiology from the "Self-Biography" years and the anonymous *Send-Schreiben* published in 1741 to his later insistence on unqualified subscription to the unaltered *Augustana* and his devotion to commentaries on it by 1748, the date of the Ministerium's founding in Pennsylvania. The nine-volume work of Gustav Reinbeck, *Reflections on the Augsburg Confession*,[2] provided not only Muhlenberg but also his successor, J. H. C. Helmuth, with a more rigorous defense of a distinctly Lutheran theology of the church.

Muhlenberg's rather weak sacramental theology never actually questioned the objective efficacy of the sacraments. But he never purged himself, either, of a tendency toward "receptionalism" and synergism in his emphasis on the "truly awakened" and those who had demonstrated a rational understanding of grace's efficiency. In his musings on polity, too, Muhlenberg openly admired the Presbyterians for their efficiency and ability to impose tight discipline, and to organize educational and charita-

---

1. A. G. Roeber, 1998, "Henry Melchior Muhlenberg: Orthodox Pietist," Lehmann Memorial volume, pp. 1-15.

2. *Betrachtungen über die in der Augspurgischen Confession enthaltene . . . göttlichen Wahrheiten,* in nine parts (Berlin: Haude, 1731-47); cf. *Journals* 3:613-15 and passim thereafter (Sept. 15, 1784).

ble foundations. Gradually drawn into deeper considerations of episcopal polity from his conversations with his best friend among the clergy, the Swedish dean, Carl Magnus Wrangel, Muhlenberg nonetheless repeatedly observed that while episcopal ordering was ancient and legitimate, it was not of divine origin.

The actual structure of the Ministerium reflected Muhlenberg's mix of admiration for a presbyterial polity with his growing awareness that subscription to the confessional symbols had to proceed hand in hand with the Lutheran Church's spread. Whether the Senior's death can be related in causal fashion to the 1792 decision of the Ministerium to absolve its pastors from confessional subscription, one can only speculate. It is not accurate, however, to suppose that immediately thereafter the way was paved for Schmucker's later "Americanizing" agenda. Not only Helmuth and Jacob Goering of York, but the Henkels refused to concede confessional witness. Even at his most irenic, Muhlenberg had never countenanced communion with other churches, despite his personal friendship (for example) with the German Reformed pastor Michael Schlatter.

The "Muhlenberg Tradition," then, I would argue, is not serviceable for those who wish to see an unbroken line stretching from ingenious "planting" of the Lutheran Church to pulpit and altar fellowships with Reformed and Anglicans in the late twentieth century. Muhlenberg grew skeptical of the mixing of confessional traditions, even while always somewhat envious of the Reformed groups' numerical and institutional edge in North America. Annoyed with the claims to privilege and the princely trappings of episcopal office, Muhlenberg tilted more toward the congregational offices of "elder" and "presenter" among the laity and similar borrowings in polity from the German Reformed and Presbyterian traditions — even while insisting on closed communion as the norm for Lutheran ecclesial life.

At best, however, eighteenth-century pietism, in whatever guise, is a weak reed upon which to rely in discussing ecclesiology, if one takes seriously theological roots for such a discussion. If one is content to see the pastoral office itself, and all other dimensions of ecclesial life including social witness in the form of orphanages, counseling centers, and the like in purely functionalist terms, or to derive the pastoral office as well as all other forms of witness and priestly office from baptismal priesthood, perhaps the case is different.

It is never wise to succumb to a triumphalist version of a particular tradition's self-image. Perhaps alongside Muhlenberg and his contributions, future discussions would do well to consider studying his opponents as well. The German orthodox confessionalists of Bach's Leipzig, theologians like Valentin Ernst Loescher, and cranky types like New York's redoubtable Pastor Wilhelm Christoph Berckenmeyer provide salutary reminders of the shortcomings of Muhlenberg and his pietist contemporaries that they, and many of their admiring descendants, have been loath to acknowledge.

In its striving for inclusivity and ecumenical openness, it would still pay the ELCA to remember that, whatever the apparent limitations of the more conservative confessional understanding of church and *communio in sacris* represented by the Lutheran Church–Missouri Synod and its foreign sister churches, Muhlenberg himself shared that same perspective, as did and do the Roman and Orthodox churches. An odd kind of unity exists here in mutual agreement to observe those ecclesial bounds, however tragic and scandalous they appear. Those who find such boundaries no longer significant should be intellectually honest enough to admit that Muhlenberg, and the past two hundred-plus years, are thereby rendered even more remote and irrelevant to their claims. A "that was then, this is now" mentality strikes most of us historians as arch and uninformed. The burden of proof, then, lies with those who would demonstrate that the theology of what constitutes the church no longer speaks for the kind of confessional witness Muhlenberg himself represented. I remain unconvinced.

Personal Experience in the Muhlenberg Tradition

Robert F. Scholz

Henry Melchior Muhlenberg was called to colonial Pennsylvania in 1742 to serve three Lutheran congregations in the Philadelphia area and to develop the Lutheran Church in that British-American province. The objective of this paper is to describe the role "experience" played in planting the Lutheran Church in North America and (therefore) in shaping the Muhlenberg tradition, its authority, and influence.

By 1748 the guiding principle of Muhlenberg's ministry — *Ecclesia plantanda* ("the church must be planted") — bore enough fruit to warrant forming the Pennsylvania Ministerium for congregational oversight.[1] Muhlenberg's role as Ministerium Superintendent was to provide pastors and catechists for the many "lost sheep" roaming the unfenced countryside of Pennsylvania and adjacent provinces. Children and adults were either gathered through Holy Baptism and what Muhlenberg described as a "covenant" of good conscience between the individual and God, or reincorporated through conversion, that is, a return of those previously baptized to an active faith in Jesus Christ. This faith was now to be sustained by the Holy Spirit's edifying work, manifesting the meaning of Baptism in the lives of the converted. Though concerned with the conversion of unchurched adults he encountered in America, Muhlenberg steadfastly in-

---

1. Muhlenberg's legacy of *ecclesia plantanda* has been treated at greater length in Robert F. Scholz, "*Ecclesia Plantanda,* the *Uncertain* Muhlenberg Legacy and the New York Experience," in the Lutheran Historical Conference volume, *Missionary to America: The History of Lutheran Outreach to Americans. Essays and Reports, 1992,* pp. 9-41. Cf. William J. Mann, *Life and Times of Henry Melchior Muhlenberg* (Philadelphia: General Council Publication Board, 1911), p. 89.

sisted upon the sacramental efficacy of Baptism for children and adults. For both, the sacrament was the way in which God redeemed all his children — young and old — as a new creation "against which the gates of hell shall not prevail" (*Journals* 1:701, cf. 209; 2:87, 295, 313, 391, 494; 3:340).

With time, Muhlenberg's missionary principle was extended to *Ecclesia plantanda et colligenda*, "the Church must be planted and gathered." The Latin *et colligenda* ("and gathered") was added to more accurately convey the method of planting and the importance of the harvest. The church grew as congregations were formed of members gathered by the gospel's call. One thinks, and rightly, of Luther's understanding of the Spirit's work in his explanation to the Third Article of the Creed:

> I believe that by my own understanding or strength I cannot believe in Jesus Christ my Lord or come to him, but instead the Holy Spirit has called me through the gospel, enlightened me with his gifts, made me holy and kept me in the true faith, just as he calls, gathers, enlightens, and makes holy the whole Christian church on earth and keeps it with Jesus Christ in the one common, true faith. (Kolb-Wengert, *The Book of Concord*, 355-56)

It was this work of the Holy Spirit — calling and gathering into "true faith" and therefore making holy, that is the key to the kind of religious experience that Muhlenberg emphasized — or what he repeatedly referred to as "sanctification." It was the experience of the Spirit's work in calling, gathering, and enlightening persons in the church that Muhlenberg valued and that he passed on to successive generations of Lutherans. It was not experience *per se* that was valued, but experience as sign of the Spirit at work in the lives of congregations and their members. Thus he counseled a prospective pastor seeking to join the Ministerium that he should read the Holy Bible diligently, become "acquainted with all the symbolical books," and study the writings of "such highly enlightened fathers of our church as our blessed Luther, Arndt, Spener, and others, so that he might lay upon his soul the fundamental biblical and theological truths, *and experience them*, and thus be able to transmit them to others" (*Journals* 1:173, 298-303, 323-25).

Spiritual experience shaped in relation to Scripture and doctrine, experience of what doctrine and Scripture taught, a piety appropriately modeled on the confessional norms of the faith — this is the kind of experience the Muhlenberg tradition emphasized. As he often remarked, it was not enough for a Christian to adhere to "the unaltered Augsburg Confession with an unaltered heart." Muhlenberg displayed in his own experience and ministry the normative influence of the Augsburg Confession, the evangelical dynamic of Law and Gospel, and the existential reality of sin and forgiveness. He had an especially close working knowledge of the Small Catechism and its theology, focusing his understanding of Christian piety on Luther's explication of Baptism as a daily dying and renewal. He drew heavily on Luther's "Preface to Romans," which contained key words — grace, faith, flesh, and spirit — and such experiential emphases as "the daily wrangling" that "continues as long as we live." Muhlenberg reminded the Ministerium's teachers and leaders of the key distinction made in Luther's *Commentary on Galatians* "between the righteousness of the law and the righteousness of Christ," adding in his own words that "this distinction is easy to be uttered in words, but in use and experience it is very hard, although it be never so diligently exercised and practised." The experience was necessary for those who would be "instructors and guiders of consciences" so that in times of temptation they might "be able to instruct and comfort both [their] own consciences and others, and to bring them from the law to grace, from active and working righteousness to passive and received righteousness." As he put the matter to another pastoral candidate, "theoretical knowledge, without practice and experience, leaves one in the lurch when a test comes."[2]

For Muhlenberg, as for Luther, the spiritual discipline of study and meditation, traceable to its origins in the monastic discipline of St. Benedict, was essential to daily existence in a state of grace. In simplified form, he urged such a piety on the laity; he practiced a more developed form himself and insisted upon it for his ministerial colleagues. For Muhlenberg the reading of and meditation on the Word of God for its hidden wisdom, which was imparted through the workings of the Holy Spirit, was so important that it came before pastoral visitation and the cure of souls in his list of priorities. Why? For Muhlenberg, as for Luther, the struggle for personal and exegetical insight into the renewing Word of God was part of the daily struggle with *Anfechtung*. Behind Muhlenberg's own experience lay the paradigmatic experience of Luther as described by the reformer in the "Preface" to his Latin works:

2. Martin Luther, "Preface to the Epistle of St. Paul to the Romans," in John Dillenberger, ed., *Martin Luther: Selections from His Writings* (Garden City, NY: Doubleday, 1961), pp. 23-24; "A Commentary on St. Paul's Epistle to the Galatians, 1531," p. 107. *Journals* 1: 155, 325.

I beat importunately upon Paul . . . most ardently desiring to know what St. Paul wanted. At last, by the mercy of God, meditating day and night, I gave heed to the context of the words, namely, "In it the righteousness of God is revealed, as it is written, 'He who through faith is righteous shall live.'"[3]

This piety which Muhlenberg urged on his parishioners focused on the experience of the Pauline dynamics of Law and Gospel, the struggle of revealed sin in search of repentance, the warfare of flesh and Spirit, and the contest between two kinds of righteousness — all aspects of rebirth that comes through water and the Spirit in the new life of Holy Baptism. Where parishioners asked about "exercises of piety," Muhlenberg urged on them daily reading of the Bible, the Small Catechism, and Johann Arndt's *True Christianity*, with prayer to "God in all simplicity" to "bless this to their souls." Aware of the experiential pitfalls common to such spiritual exercises, Muhlenberg warned another parishioner in dealing with her religious experience to "hold fast to Gospel promises" not by "putting trust in feelings" but by daily putting off of the old . . . and putting on the new" (*Journals* 1:298-303, 323-25).

In a word, Henry Melchior Muhlenberg's emphasis on Christian experience was an emphasis on the experience of Reformation faith, as found in and shaped by Scripture and the Confessions. It was the active, experiential appropriation of this faith that drew the scattered sheep of the Lutheran diaspora in colonial North America to reenter the fold of active personal faith and congregational life. The disciplined experience of faith through daily study and prayer focused attention on the Spirit's work in the struggle of putting off the old and putting on the new — that wrestling with sin and grace and the attention to the experience of those who were simultaneously justified and sinners *(simul justus et peccator).*[4]

As a pastor he showed unceasing regard for the struggles with evil and the dictates of sensitized consciences among the justified who faced the realities of life on America's first frontier. Rape, incest, domestic violence, disputes among neighbors, drunkenness and alcoholism, the physi-

3. Dillenberger, *Luther,* p. 11.

4. For a more detailed analysis of Muhlenberg's use of spiritual experience, see Robert F. Scholz, "Henry Melchior Muhlenberg's Relation to the Ongoing Pietist Tradition," The Lutheran Historical Conference, *Lutheranism and Pietism: Essays and Reports, 1990,* pp. 40-66.

cal and economic hardships of rural life, frontier violence, ethnic conflict — these received his constant attention, for they profoundly affected the lives of children, women, and men. Primitive schools permitted only the briefest and most superficial formation of youth in knowledge and godliness, while lax courts all but ignored domestic conflict and the human vices accompanying it. Where the life of the flesh was so much in evidence without the countervailing force of law, culture, or religion, *simul justus et peccator* was a harsh and painful reality in the life of his parishioners (*Journals* 1:267-68, 354, 378-79).

It was to counteract this kind of dreadful experience and the accompanying stress that wore down lives, that Muhlenberg sought to "lay a foundation of true Christianity in the hearts of the people" and then to build and to heal them from the inside out. In echoes of Luther on the freedom of the Christian, Muhlenberg also addressed human freedom and the drive for material security in the raw, new land of license and liberty. He distinguished between two callings — the temporal and the heavenly — so that both might be properly fulfilled. By encouraging auditors to "seek first after the Kingdom of God and His righteousness" through the experience of struggle and renewal, he thought also to provide "for their own proper needs in due order" (*Journals*, 1:354).

For his pastoral dedication Muhlenberg developed a reputation as a pietist, an epithet often applied as a term of derision. I have avoided the term because it tells us too little about Muhlenberg. In the first place, his Halle-nurtured piety was balanced by his adherence to Lutheran orthodoxy (certified at ordination by the orthodox Lutheran consistory), a tradition of systematic theology which he conscientiously taught others and applied himself in his ministry. More to the point, using the term pietist masks a fundamental cultural shift occurring in early modernity — the shift of attention to the conscious, feeling, experiencing, thinking subject and its capacity for reasoning and feeling that was occurring in religious thought and political theory in the late seventeenth and eighteenth centuries. The point can be made by reference to Muhlenberg's near contemporary, the Leipzig cantor, Johann Sebastian Bach, who also displayed a blend and balance of orthodoxy and pietism in his church music. While Bach's Masses reflect the orthodox confessionalism of the Lutheran tradition and its poets, especially in the use of the ecumenical creeds and the Reformation chorales, his Cantatas and Passions were permeated by the spirit of pietism, especially the recitatives and arias for individual voices, with their intense subjectivity, moral earnestness, and

Rococo devotion.[5] What Bach conveyed for emulation in his music, Muhlenberg modeled in his sermons and teaching.

By the end of Muhlenberg's active career, the American Enlighten-ment experience in political and religious liberty had come to diminish the normative, confessional aspects of this Christian experience. The emphasis on experience now stood alone, or in alliance with rationalism. And where it came to be valued for its own sake — as with revivalism and "new mea-sures" practices — the Lutheran Church opened itself to the prevailing emphases on emotions and feelings against which Muhlenberg had once warned. In New York Lutheranism, the area of developing Lutheranism that I have studied most closely, the planted church grew for a time using these means of gathering, but ultimately failed in mission efforts to sustain itself using these modified understandings of experience.[6]

To continue gathering and planting, the Lutheran Church would eventually return to a confessional understanding of Word and Sacrament in nurturing Christian faith. This crucial change in emphasis, which oc-curred with the rise of modern confessionalism — a paradigm shift as im-portant in our time as was the rise of pietism to Muhlenberg's era — saw a reversal of the relationship between experience and dogma, a reversal that remains normative today. Whereas Muhlenberg emphasized experience as the litmus of true Christianity, it is dogma's norming of modern "spiritu-ality" — our contemporary equivalent of religious experience — that was until recently considered the hallmark of an authentic Christian.

Today, in a culture hungry for, and infatuated with, many different forms of "spirituality," Christian religious experience in the Muhlenberg tradition is important to the contemporary work of (re)evangelization for three reasons. First, in its own balancing of experience and doctrine it can restore the current imbalance that overemphasizes reason and belief at the expense of reflection, prayer, meditation, and the experience of the Spirit's work. Just as Muhlenberg insisted on the continuing role of doctrine for in-terpreting experience and shaping authentic Christian faith, so we need to insist on the continuing role of the subject's experience in relation to au-

5. Christoph Wolff, *Johann Sebastian Bach: The Learned Musician* (New York: W. W. Norton, 2000), pp. 113-14, 253-59; and Jaroslav Pelikan, *Bach Among the Theologians* (Philadelphia: Fortress, 1986), chs. 4 and 5. See also Günther Stiller, *Johann Sebastian Bach and Liturgical Life in Leipzig* (St. Louis: Concordia, 1970), p. 200.

6. See Scholz, "Ecclesia Plantanda," pp. 21-41; also, Robert F. Scholz, *Press Toward the Mark: History of the United Lutheran Synod of New York and New England 1830-1930* (Metuchen, NJ/London: Scarecrow Press, 1995), esp. ch. 7, "Parallel Problems."

thenticating norms. Second, Muhlenberg's pastoral theology offers a still accessible, scripturally based systematics of spirituality rooted in the teaching of Luther and the Confessions of the Lutheran Church. It bears careful study by Lutherans in an age searching for viable systems of spirituality.

Finally, the origins of that trajectory of spiritual wisdom in the western church, to which the Muhlenberg tradition stands witness in honoring the thought of Arndt and Luther, also bear careful study. Luther and Arndt themselves reflect a spiritual tradition of Christian faith experience lying behind the Reformation and grounded in the spiritual insights and practices of St. Bernard and St. Benedict.[7] This is especially so regarding the meditative reading of Scripture *(lectio divina)* that so profoundly shaped a mature Christian faith in the first centuries of the church, and that can still be seen in the pastoral theology of Henry Melchior Muhlenberg.[8] It has recently been argued that, without recovery of catholic piety, the spiritual tradition that Arndt, Spener, and Muhlenberg represent is doomed to extinction — indeed, it is already dead.[9] This suggests that the future of mission work in the Muhlenberg tradition is linked to a larger set of ecumenical issues that the Lutheran Church now faces. In any case, as Muhlenberg well knew and we must remember in our own way, *ecclesia plantanda et colligenda* is all about harvesting the ripe fruits of a faith both evangelical and catholic.

7. Cf. "Spirituality and Spiritual Formation: A Position Paper of the Faculty of the Lutheran Theological Southern Seminary," I.7, cf. III.9, in *Currents* 27 (2000): 351, 354.

8. See the important study by Jean Leclercq, *The Love of Learning and the Desire of God: A Study of Monastic Culture* (New York: Fordham University Press, 1982), esp. "personal experience," pp. 211-12.

9. See Robert L. Wilcken, "Lutheran Pietism and Catholic Piety," in *The Catholicity of the Reformation,* ed. Carl E. Braaten and Robert W. Jenson (Grand Rapids: Eerdmans, 1996), pp. 79-92.

Muhlenberg Ecumenism into Century Twenty-One

Frederick K. Wentz

The Muhlenberg tradition (from Lutherans in the eighteenth century, including later H. E. Jacobs and A. R. Wentz) and ecumenism was outlined in five periods, as to (a) context, (b) Christian response to that context, and (c) the Henry Melchior Muhlenberg tradition:

I. 1750-1800
 (a) Rising pluralism, free environment, religious wilderness, threat and opportunity
 (b) Denominations emerge ("those Christians denominated . . .")
 (c) Henry Melchior Muhlenberg and the Ministerium
II. 1800-1850
 (a) One nation, good feeling, fluid/unformed society. Often loss of identity in sloppy ecumenism: "We're together because we're German. . . ."
 (b) Growing consensus, Evangelicalism, revivals and voluntary societies, denominational competition
 (c) General Synod, denominational rebuilding; S. S. Schmucker: the idea of and need for councils
III. 1850-1900
 (a) Conflict, immigration, urbanization, and industrialization
 (b) Breakup of Evangelicalism into liberals and fundamentalists; a minority high church or "catholic" movement
 (c) Henry Melchior Muhlenberg tradition split; dialogue of the parts; inter-Lutheran and interchurch drawing back (Galesburg Rule)

IV. 1900-1950
   (a) America comes onto the world scene, growingly secular,
       growingly pluralistic; heyday of denominationalism, Roman
       Catholics, mainline, conservatives
   (b) The Conciliar Movement ascendant (1908, Federal Council of
       Churches; 1948, World Council of Churches; 1950, National
       Council of Churches of Christ in the USA)
   (c) National Lutheran Council, 1917; Lutheran World Federation,
       1947. ULCA, General Synod pulls back from the FCC;
       development of the representative and confessional principles
       and their application to councils; moving into WCC
       leadership roles
V. 1950-2000
   (a) Radical pluralism and secularism; mainline losses and
       repudiation
   (b) Conciliarism waning; COCU (Churches of Christ Uniting);
       Vatican II
   (c) Full participation in councils — more interest in bilateral
       dialogues (a step backward), seeking full communion, a
       resurgent "catholic" movement.

This essay is a quick look at the relation of Muhlenberg Lutherans to the ecumenical movement over the past 250 years, with a concluding glance at the twenty-first century. Two main theses undergird this analysis: (1) that Muhlenberg Lutherans are best understood as "Birthright Americans"; and (2) that, even though a second more radical pluralism of recent decades calls for new patterns of cooperation among Christians, some form of conciliarism will be vitally important for the twenty-first century.

Birthright Americans

What does it mean to say that Muhlenberg Lutherans are Birthright Americans?[1] It is to distinguish them, as stemming from the eighteenth century

---

1. For elaboration of this birthright theme, see F. K. Wentz, "Birthright Americans: The Shape of the Muhlenberg/Schmucker Tradition," *Seminary Ridge Review* (Lutheran Theological Seminary, Gettysburg) 1, no. 3 (Summer 1999): 12-27. See also a shorter version, "A Contrast Between Muhlenberg Lutheranism and Midwestern Lutheranism," in

with their main roots in eastern America, from "immigrant" Lutheran groups emerging in the nineteenth century with mainly midwestern roots.

In 1923 Henry Eyster Jacobs, for decades a leader of the General Council from the Philadelphia Seminary, declared:

> The Lutheran Church of America is no exotic, transplanted from a foreign shore, but is a native of this continent. . . . Its position is not that of a naturalized citizen, but one which rests upon a birthright.

This assertion appeared in Jacobs's introduction to Abdel Ross Wentz's textbook, *The Lutheran Church in American History*. Wentz himself used the birthright idea in introducing later editions of this work. The book became the standard textbook in the field for fifty years, wielding unusual influence. This is his affirmation:

> The position of the Lutheran Church in America rests upon a birthright. It is not an immigrant church that needed to be naturalized after it was transplanted from some European land. It is as old as the American nation and much older than the American republic. The Lutheran church in America is an integral and potent part of American Christianity. The people in the Lutheran churches of the land are a constituent and typical element of the American nation.[2]

The birthright idea goes beyond the claim that there were many Lutherans and an organized Lutheran synod on hand in the colonies when the nation was formed. It encompasses a remembered and revered history, i.e., a tradition that assumes and builds upon an original citizenship at the nation's birth. From this, flow decades of a particular faith-posture, psychology, and attitude toward the surrounding world that can be contrasted with an immigrant stance and consciousness and that can be traced within the patterns of Lutheran history and the actions of Lutheran people.

It is first of all a matter of identity — a self-understanding and a way

---

The Periodical (Lutheran Historical Society of Eastern Pennsylvania) 43, no. 2 (October 1998): 15-17.

2. In 1955 this textbook was reworked and retitled *A Basic History of Lutheranism in America* (Philadelphia: Muhlenberg Press), p. v. In 1964 it was revised and updated. These editions shortened these paragraphs from the Preface into the form quoted. In the original 1923 edition, see p. 3.

of relating to others. It involves the confident assumption that one belongs, that one's roots and ancestors are here, and that those around one are peers, fellow citizens, in some way brothers and sisters. This contrasts with the sense of newness, perhaps insecurity, of immigrants, including a "set-apart" feeling towards others, perhaps even distance and distrust. The birthright United States citizen is relaxed about one's loyalty — it can be taken for granted — and can be open toward one's surroundings and neighbors.

Such a confident sense that we belong has led the Muhlenberg tradition of Lutherans into ready cooperation and participation in public or civic life. It has meant an assumption of friendship and common concerns with people of other denominations while remaining careful to maintain a distinctive confessional identity, echoing Muhlenberg's practice of being selectively friendly toward other churches.

Emerging Conciliarism

In the nineteenth century, in the face of a growing number of denominations often engaged in unlovely conflict, and particularly through the leadership of Samuel Simon Schmucker and the General Synod, people of the Muhlenberg tradition entered into nondenominational and interdenominational organizations that could better face the public and could better render services in civic life than could a single denomination. Schmucker's 1838 *Fraternal Appeal to the American Churches* was a pioneering, influential voice in this trend.

In the twentieth century one of the most significant movements in American church history was the Conciliar Movement, the formation of councils of churches that enabled organized Christianity more effectively to serve the public interest and to wield wider influence upon society. Muhlenberg people participated in many state councils of churches, in the Federal Council of Churches (1908), the National Council (1950), the World Council (1948), the National Lutheran Council (1918), and the Lutheran World Federation (1947). If we can name Muhlenberg and Schmucker in previous centuries, we can mention the leadership of Franklin Clark Fry in the ecumenical movement in the mid-twentieth century.

The emerging eighteenth-century pluralism that led Muhlenberg to develop selective friendliness toward other churches and led Schmucker in the nineteenth century to envision a federation for cooperation brought the

63

Conciliar Movement in the twentieth century as the full bloom of response to the presence in America of a diversity of religious groups. Whoever says "denomination," says "council"; i.e., when we say we are Christians denominated Lutheran and you are our Christian friends denominated Reformed or Methodist, we must have an organized way to face the public as Christians together.

In the early twentieth century Muhlenberg Lutherans became more sophisticated in their selectivity (the Evangelical Principle) and helped councils to be selective in membership.[3] Conciliar involvement is a significant continuity and contribution of the Muhlenberg tradition for two centuries. Surely it is to be celebrated.

Rough Seas

But the Conciliar Movement has sailed into rough seas in the last four decades. Often it is true of movements in history that, after decades of ascendance, they establish themselves institutionally at about the time they are ready to wane as a movement. This has happened to the conciliar movement. What does this mean for ecumenism in the twenty-first century? First a closer look at the idea.

The dream was a noble one. Faced with a cacophony of religious groups and the necessity of separation of church and state, zealous Christian activists sought to shape the morals and social attitudes of the nation and to evangelize the whole world. They developed a generic kind of Christianity called Evangelicalism, which was prominent within many denominations. They also learned to work together in voluntary societies. By the twentieth century, denominationalism developed councils as a form of cooperation (even as they competed fiercely like baseball teams in a league). For 150 years (1820-1970) this dream and its two patterns (voluntary societies and councils) were quite influential in the United States.

There were also dreams of hegemony or dominance among the people. By the twentieth century these ideas were totally unrealistic, though in some circles they remain today. In the late nineteenth century Evangelicalism split deeply between fundamentalists and nonfundamentalists, so that

---

3. See the Lutheran Historical Conference, *Essays and Reports*, vol. 18 (2001), for this author's article on the topic of the General Synod tradition on ecumenism carried into the twenty-first century.

before 1950 there was a counter-council to "mainstream" conciliarism, the National Association of Evangelicals.

Still more deadly for the hope of a common Christian cooperation in America was the steady emergence of a group that could not accept indirect influence through cooperation with other denominations, the Roman Catholic Church, easily the largest group in twentieth-century America. Now there were three main religious groupings. Other forces were at work as well. For example, a worldwide Christian community was emerging, and the people of Africa, Asia, and Latin America were making more radical demands upon rather complacent American Christians.

But the largest force that emerged in the late twentieth century to undermine the effectiveness of conciliarism was the radical new pluralism that swept western civilization. Whereas the earlier pluralism (1750-1950) had a post-Christendom setting, wherein the phrase "under God" still had some meaning for most citizens and was not contested by the rest, the new pluralism was aggressively secular in shaping a society in which religion (of which there was still plenty) was strictly private. With an influx of people from many lands and a free market of religious or "spiritual" ideas, the religious life of the American people no longer assumed biblical roots.

Bilateral Dialogues

In this cultural conglomeration much of the Christian leadership turned inward in a search for the renewal of the church in our midst. For many Lutherans, including those of the Muhlenberg tradition, this meant a rediscovering of Reformation roots and a growing commitment to an evangelical or confessional catholicism as the setting for Lutheran church life. In the 1960s, when Vatican II held up the possibility of a more open Roman church, friendlier toward other Christian bodies, Muhlenberg Lutherans allowed their commitments to a dominantly Protestant conciliarism to fade before a new wave of ecumenical activity — bilateral dialogues. In these new patterns theologians of Muhlenberg background along with other Lutheran theologians entered into meetings — sustained theological discussions over a period of years — with another church body or church family, with Roman Catholics, Episcopalians, the Orthodox, Presbyterians, the Reformed, Methodists, Moravians, and others. There was in each case a search for agreement on a precise theological basis. At the turn of the century this has developed into agreements toward "full communion" between the ELCA (perhaps half of which is Muhlenberg tradition) and Episcopal, Reformed, and Moravian church bodies.

Though not without controversy, this trend toward full communion has engendered enthusiasm and holds out hope. *But it cannot take the place of twentieth-century conciliarism.* Now let this historical survey end in advocacy!

Twenty-First-Century Conciliarism

The conciliar movement, as herein traced, emerged in order to provide a *visibly united Christian witness and service* to the world around us for the competitive denominations that were in our society. They are still there in the twenty-first century. Denominationalism as a pattern (like a baseball league) has collapsed, but denominations remain. The *only* alternative, from the standpoint of our society and its citizens (many of our own children), is sects, each claiming unconvincingly to be the Church.

Bilateral dialogues and full communion agreements *cannot, for decades to come, provide any real, visible unity for Christians* before the citizenry of the United States and the world. They are to be dismissed as creating a larger denomination or sect in a still cluttered, competitive, and unconvincing Christian witness.

For the twenty-first century we badly need some form of conciliarism, broad-based cooperation among many denominations.[4] We cannot, of course, simply renew the cooperation of the previous century. Today the leaders of the National Council of Churches are clear about that. But leaders of the ELCA had better be eager and energetic in seeking new and broad patterns for a common Christian voice in the burgeoning dialogues in a small world that is crowded and radically pluralistic. We need to be dialoguing seriously with all kinds of Christians in order better to enter into all the other dialogues — interreligious, intercultural, international.

Lutheran theology lends itself well to the dialectic processes of true dialogue. In behalf of Lutherans, Franklin Clark Fry made an impressive impact upon the National Council of Churches at its founding. Lutheran leaders should be helping that organization to dissolve and reemerge as a broader structure in the decades ahead.

It would be possible, of course, to say that full communion agree-

4. See *Essays and Reports,* vol. 18 (2001) for further reasons for this conclusion.

ments are adequate twenty-first-century fulfillment for a Muhlenberg tradition of selective friendliness in interchurch relations. Some Muhlenberg Lutherans in effect do that. But for those who recognize the full Muhlenberg tradition as Birthright Americans, with its responsible development over two centuries of conciliar cooperation, a visible witness to Christian unity before the citizenry of this nation and the world is part of our calling.

II. Roots and Seeds for New Plantings

The climax of the celebration of the founding of the Ministerium of Pennsylvania was a three-day Symposium, held at Muhlenberg College, Allentown, Pennsylvania, August 7-9, 1998 — as close as possible to the first meeting of the Ministerium 250 years before. Compared with the initial event at Baltimore in 1997, which aimed at a limited audience of leaders and often scholarly experts, the Symposium was for a larger audience, whoever wished to come. Some 250 persons registered from across the country. Discussion of issues had continued in the interim, at Seminary convocations, local events, and behind the scene, for example, on bilateral dialogues and councils of churches (F. Wentz) or Wagner's pro-Zinzendorf reading of the encounter with Muhlenberg in Philadelphia in 1742.

As focus for the Allentown event, the plenary address stressed Muhlenberg himself, his ministry, and the beginnings of the synod he formed. Attention to worship, the arts, and culture is reflected in Part III below. Three ELCA synods, four church-related colleges, the three seminaries in the Eastern Cluster, and eleven social ministry organizations were officially represented. When opportunity came for attention to "arenas of service" in life, participants could choose from among ten groups, including education, social service, healthcare, business, law and public service, family, leadership in the church, the arts, international responsibility, and the media, each with professionally involved church members leading the discussion. After the closing worship service, many went to Trappe, Pennsylvania, for the dedication of the Muhlenberg family home, newly restored. While congregations still active from Muhlenberg's day were represented in the procession into the Egner Memorial Chapel, attention was also given to African Americans, Hispanics, Russian immigrants, and other groups. Thus the picture included our legacy from the past in the Muhlenberg tradition and implications for a vision of the future, in a new millennium, blossoming on the territory of the old "mother synod."

The Plenary Address reexamined and probed more deeply into Muhlenberg and the Ministerium in the eighteenth century, with respondents taking up subsequent developments and suggestions for the present day.

Muhlenberg's Ministry and Ministerium, Two Hundred Fifty Years and Counting

John Reumann

We celebrate the 250th anniversary, with all its ongoing implications, of the founding of the Ministerium of Pennsylvania, called by August Graebner "the most important event in the history of the Lutheran Church in America."[1] There is much that could be said about Muhlenberg and the Synod. I shall concentrate mainly on the man and his mission, a sense of order in ministry, and some aspects of the day that helped shape subsequent Lutheran history. The keynote address by Robert Marshall, "The Church Still Being Planted" (1997) — and the more I have worked on this presentation, the more I have come to recognize how excellent Dr. Marshall's pages are — provides considerable coverage on links between 1748 and 1998 and lessons for today. But what exactly do we celebrate?

The 250th, but Not Exactly

If Henry Melchior Muhlenberg himself were here, he would remind us that "[t]he united preachers and [*Hallesche Nachrichten* = HN reads 'delegated'] elders and deacons of the United Congregations" met in Philadelphia on Sunday, *August 14,* to dedicate St. Michael's Church, and in the afternoon five German and Swedish pastors (Brunnholtz, Handschuh, Muhlenberg, Hartwick, and Sandin the Swedish provost) ordained John

---

1. *Geschichte* 313: Eine Begebenheit von so hoher, weitragender Bedeutung war darum jene Synodalgrundung vom 26 August 1748, dasz wir dieselbe wohl als das wichtigete Ereignisz in der Geschichte der amerikanisch-lutherischen Kirche des siebzehnten [sic] Jahrhunderts bezeichen durfen.

Nicholas Kur[t]z, "with three Reformed preachers" as "witnesses." Then on August 15 "the first [HN: general] conference [HN: or synod . . .]" met (*Journals* 1:201-2). But these were "Old Style" dates; New Style the synod met August 26 (*Documentary History,* 3; Tappert 1975: 49; Marshall 90).[2] Cf. *Journals* 1:18, where Muhlenberg writes that April 17 was "April 7 according to the old style English calendar" — for Muhlenberg, after Easter, which he had celebrated on March 25 in Germany, but in England it was still the week before Palm Sunday; and 3:517 (Nov. 25 = Dec. 6, 1742).

What's more, we cannot speak of an organization that met regularly thereafter from 1748 on. The *Documentary History of the Evangelical Ministerium of Pennsylvania and Adjacent States* was published in 1898 (on its inaccuracies, see *Journals* 3:44 n. 1), with Roman numerals assigned for each annual meeting. But for the years 1755-59, 1764-65, and 1767, it is admitted ("These conventions exist . . . only upon paper" [43]) no evidence is available (83). Muhlenberg himself did not record attending in 1774, 1775, 1776, 1779, and 1782-87; H. L. Nelson 83 therefore speaks of the synod's "fitful beginning." Lack of meetings is not totally surprising, given exigencies like the French and Indian War and the American Revolution. Further, H. E. Jacobs, no less, wrote that 1748 was but "the temporary foundation" of the Ministerium of Pennsylvania; the year 1760, when it was revived at the urging of the Swedish provost, Carl Magnus Wrangel, "may be regarded as" its "permanent" foundation (*History* 260); H. L. Nelson 206-9 characterizes the Ministerium reconstituted in 1760, compared with the organization of 1748, as "theologically more inclusive, more pastorally dominated, and it met more regularly . . ." (206-7).

Also noteworthy are earlier predecessor efforts in North America. Salute the Danes! From 1665 on, in the Virgin Islands (Jens Larsen, *Virgin Islands Story: A History of the Lutheran Church in the Danish West Indies* [Philadelphia: Fortress, 1968]; Tappert 1975: 4). If Greenland counts as part of North America, H. P. Egede, a Norwegian pastor who had studied in Copenhagen, went to Greenland on his own when neither bishop nor king was interested in ministering to earlier settlers; he and his wife, Gertrud

---

2. When Pope Gregory XIII reformed the Julian Calendar in 1582, the correction involved a jump of ten days; between 1700 and 1800, eleven days. See Hans Lietzmann, *Zeitrechnung der römischen Kaiserzeit, des Mittelalters und der Neuzeit für die Jahre 1-2000 nach Christus,* Sammlung Göschen 1985 (Berlin/Leipzig: De Gruyter, 1934), p. 5. The Gregorian calendar was introduced in Germany in 1700, but not adopted in England until 1752. Cf. *Correspondence* 1:xxi and 22 n. 3.

Rask, labored in Greenland among the Eskimos from 1721 to 1729, when there were the first baptisms. Dutch Lutherans were in New Amsterdam as early as 1643 but never had freedom to organize under Dutch Reformed hegemony and Governor Peter Minuit; yet it was for ministry in New York that Justus Falckner, from New Hanover, Pennsylvania, but previously educated at Halle, Germany, was ordained in 1703 by three Swedes (Andrew Rudman and two assistants) in Philadelphia (Tappert 1975: 6-10, 13-14). In 1725 William Christopher Berckenmeyer (1686-1751) came to New York with "impeccable Orthodox Lutheran credentials" (H. L. Nelson 93 n. 2; see also the publications of H. J. Kreider) on behalf of the Lutheran Consistory in Amsterdam. He and later colleagues (like Michael Christian Knoll, arrived 1732, or John August Wolf, 1734) came from the quite orthodox Lutheran Consistory of Hamburg. At one point, in 1735, Berckenmeyer attempted a meeting of clergy and lay representatives to solve a church quarrel at Raritan, New Jersey, but this "classis," to use the Latin term from Reformed polity, led nowhere (Tappert 1975: 14-16; H. L. Nelson 155-57).

Lutherans from the Church of Sweden — actually many of them Finns, like Pastor Lars Lock — settled on the Delaware from 1638 on. They built churches, even with organs, showed interest in evangelizing Indians (Campanius), but never had much freedom from the Consistory in Sweden to develop in the American scene. Magnus Wrangel, who was in America 1759-68, hit it off well with Muhlenberg; for their touching interchange of letters late in the life of each, see *Journals* 3:620-27. Muhlenberg lamented in 1784, "Concerning the Reverend Missionaries from Sweden . . . they shun our friendship. It is no longer like it was in former times . . ." (3:627). Had Wrangel not been forced by the Consistory to return to Sweden, Lutheran history in the Mid-Atlantic colonies might have turned out very differently.

There had also been attempts at organization beyond local congregations by irregularly ordained, often fly-by-night itinerants, men of dubious credentials, who prayed and preached and preyed upon Lutheran settlers (Lehmann 1998: 65-68). For example, before Muhlenberg arrived, Valentine Kraft, once a pastor but deposed from the ministry in Zweibrücken, Germany, had plans for a "grand presbytery of Pennsylvania," a special one in Philadelphia, and a consistory of which he himself was president, claiming ties with the Darmstadt Consistory in Germany. He tried to get the newcomer Henry Melchior to assist him at the ordination of a schoolmaster and then sought to isolate Muhlenberg by "assigning" him to Providence and New Hanover. Muhlenberg confronted him at a German inn in Philadelphia just seven days after he landed in Philadelphia on December 1, 1742. By Third Christmas Day Muhlenberg had secured his position in the United Congregations, and old Pastor Kraft retreated to Lancaster (*Journals* 1:65-74, esp. 68-69, 70-71, 74; Riforgiato 93-94). Two Philadelphia laymen, Peter Koch, a Swede, and Henry Schleydorn, German, sought a union of Lutherans in the early 1740s (H. L. Nelson 85 n. 2, citing Jacobs, *History*, 237-39; *Documentary History*, 9). John Christopher Hartwick claimed the Duke of Saxe-Gotha "had sent him here as superintendent to exercise supervision over Lutheran congregations in America," a claim on which Muhlenberg commented, "This is apparently the reason why he has wandered around America all these years, building castles in the air, etc., etc." (*Journals* 3:273). Later Muhlenberg made a pun on this "title," when Hartwick sponged on him for a meal, by writing "superintendent" as "Supper intend" (3:291; cf. 383, 453, 720-21, 734; the caption from Tappert and Doberstein at 3:291 refers to Hartwick as "a rolling stone"). But one may say that Lutheran unity was "in the air" as Muhlenberg came on the scene.

To put matters into historical perspective: we celebrate the 250th anniversary of the *first* meeting of the Ministerium of Pennsylvania, oldest Lutheran church body with *continuing* (but not continuous) existence on the North American *mainland*. There had been earlier efforts to organize beyond the scattered preaching points, however, and German Lutherans began coming in increasing numbers, perhaps 80,000 to over 100,000 in Muhlenberg's lifetime (Tappert 1975: 36-37). But Germans were Johnnie-come-latelys and lacked a European government behind them. The Dutch Reformed had been organized in New York and New Jersey since 1637; the Reformed Church in America thus celebrated its 350th anniversary of continuous ministry in 1987. German Reformed congregations in Pennsylvania organized a coetus on September 19, 1747 under the Rev. Michael Schlatter, a friend of Muhlenberg.

Among Muhlenberg's predecessors we note particularly John Casper Stoever, Sr. and Jr.; the latter's complicated relationship with Muhlenberg was the subject of a play at the Symposium concerning a fictional encounter August 14, 1748 (below, "A Twisted Cord"). The father (1685-1738) and the son (1707-1779), who was a teacher and an organist (Muhlenberg's *Journals* record his death, while still in harness, 3:242-43), each had some theological study in Germany before coming to America in 1729. (Some of Stoever, Jr.'s library went to St. Michael's, Philadelphia, at his death, 3:260.) The father was listed at arrival as "Missionaire" and the son as "Theol. Stud." (Winters 15). By 1729 both began to baptize, preach, and officiate at the Lord's Supper and weddings from a base near New Holland, Pennsylvania, in that state, Maryland, and Virginia (on Stoever, Sr., note 3:202). The definitive monograph of Stoever, Jr., is by Roy L. Winters (later Home Missions Secretary for the Ministerium of Pennsylvania, under whom I did door-to-door surveys for new mission sites in 1947-49).

Stoever, Jr., seems to have been ordained in 1733, perhaps at Trappe, by John Christian Schultze, himself "probably not ordained" but who officiated in Lutheran congregations, including Trappe, for about six months (Winters 23-27). Pastor Daniel Falckner in Raritan had earlier declined to ordain Stoever, Jr. (Winters 24). Tappert 1975: 47 says of Stoever, Sr., "privately ordained." John Casper Stoever, Jr., traveled tirelessly, doing pastoral acts (twenty-four localities in 1735, Winters 137; some eighty-five for his career, pp. 108-10; Muhlenberg in 1776 noted eighteen changes of residence for himself in his thirty-four years in America, 2:720; p. 734 lists twenty-one moves), though the Hill Church (Berg Kirche) at Quitophila ("Quitobehel," *Journals* 1:555, 3:111), four miles northwest of Lebanon, and a fortress-like parsonage and mill nearby were home base. He was designated by Kraft to be "assessor" in his proposed consistory. Stoever's gifts had more to do with establishing churches than remaining as pastor or developing much organization. Winters spoke of Stoever's "Pecuniary Propensities." The Ministerium in 1748 referred to him and three other preachers as people "who care for nothing but their bread" (*Documentary History*, 11). As a miller and landowner, Stoever knew how to make money.

John Casper Stoever, Jr., has been placed among the "orthodoxists" in theology (Tappert 1975: 63) or "orthodoxy . . . seasoned by pietism" (Winters 128-31). An orthodoxist bent is indicated by the insistence of Stoever and others on the adjective "true" in the formula for administration in the Lord's Supper, "This is the *true* body of Jesus Christ," ". . . *true* blood . . ." — a wording to which Muhlenberg acceded in the Liturgy of 1748 (Winters 130; Oldenburg 64-65; *Journals* 1:193). One difference between the two men was that Muhlenberg the devout pietist believed Stoever too lax personally in morals. Still another was that Stoever was a more polemical defender of the Lutheran faith, both by temperament and his experiences. He and his father had fled Germany because of Jesuit oppression of Reformation believers (Winters 14, 131). In the Ephrata area Stoever encountered Sabbatarians and cloistered mysticism, akin to the Wissahickon hermits[3] who had settled in Philadelphia in 1694 under

3. The chaplain of this Theosophical Society, Heinrich Bernhard Köster, deserves

Baron Johannes Kelpius (Justus and Daniel Falckner were among them). If we use their earlier name, Brethren of the Rosy Cross, or Rosicrucians, we see their attempt to combine "the rose" (for science) with "the cross" (Riforgiato 62) and a movement that reached deep into the Prussian government, including Friedrich Wilhelm II (cf. Winters 41-44). John Casper Stoever, Jr., had a nose for heresy and so, as Winters put it (133), "organized citadels of orthodoxy on four sides" of the Cloister at Ephrata — namely at Muddy Creek, New Holland, Warwick, or Brickerville, and Lancaster (Winters 44-58). Thus the Lutheran church was being planted against *Freigeisterei*. The threat from such groups was no idle one, for Muhlenberg's father-in-law, Conrad Weiser, was for a time swept into such views (Riforgiato 88); the influences came through Peter Miller and Conrad Beissel. Riforgiato speaks of the Moravians as "the threat from the left" for Muhlenberg, and "New York Orthodoxy" as "the threat from the right," but things were even more complex.

Roy Winters's summary on the earnest but often incompatible John Casper Stoever, Jr., pays tribute to his "indefatigable missionary efforts which attempted to keep religion alive during the irreligious colonial period" (154). But more than a crusader was needed at this stage of the church's life, or someone whose divisiveness lingered on even after Stoever was dead (3:377). It was time to establish "congregations into a corporate body" (101). Muhlenberg and Stoever were "not conflicting but complementary" (100).

To be most precise, we celebrate not just a two-day meeting in Philadelphia in 1748 but an event where Muhlenberg and others, standing on the shoulders, or reaping the results of the work, of predecessors and contemporaries, were doing ecclesiology beyond the three United and other scattered congregations.

The beginnings of the Ministerium have something to teach us about continuity, before and since 1748, and how we too stand on the shoulders of many saints and sinners. Perhaps Muhlenberg was right that the synod need not meet every year. ELCA synods have less and less become meetings for deliberation and decision. Some have experimented with skipping an annual session for economic reasons. The ELCA Churchwide Assembly, it has been proposed, should meet only every third year. Pastors and elders and deacons are less and less the decision-makers.

---

mention for holding Lutheran services in 1694 at the home of the Mennonite Van Bebber family.

Many tasks are in the hands of what can be called, in a good as well as a bad sense, a bureaucracy. The relation of the local to the more-than-local church in a democracy is still being worked out.

Muhlenberg's Mission

Though he knew Latin better than most of us, Muhlenberg does not seem to have used the preferred phrase in recent American Lutheranism, *missio Dei* — even if we add "God's mission *through the churches.*" For in Germany, as elsewhere in the eighteenth century, mission work was the task of societies and institutes like those at Halle rather than the state churches; in England, the SPG (Society for the Propagation of the Gospel in Foreign Parts) and SPCK (Society for Promoting Christian Knowledge). Muhlenberg visited the house in London where the *Societas de Propaganda Cognitione Christi* convened (*Journals* 1:21), and he knew English preachers supported by the *Societas de Propaganda Fide,* founded in 1701 (*Journals* 1:154, 282, 297, 324, 355, 619; 2:269, 370, 646; because of its grants Anglican congregations did not need to depend on collections to support pastors, 3:663 696). The *Societas de Promovenda Cognitione Christi,* founded in 1698, numbered among its corresponding members the court preacher Ziegenhagen in London, Prof. A. H. Francke in Halle, and Rector J. A. Urlsperger in Augsburg, the champion of the Salzburgers. It supported German work such as the charity schools in New Hanover and elsewhere and Lutheran pastors like Bol[t]zius at Eben Ezer (*Journals* 1:73, 309, 518, 646; 2:557, 575, 600, 642, 659-60, 668, 676; 3:93, 103, 123). Muhlenberg long had correspondence with its members (125); the place in Providence intended for "worn-out Lutheran preachers or poor widows" was to be "under the *trusteeship* and *administration* of . . . the aforesaid English Society in London" (600 and n. 1; 664). For Sweden, the "Society pro Fide et Christianismo" is noted in Wrangel's letter to Muhlenberg in 1784 (*Journals* 3:620-21).

Muhlenberg's call from the three United Congregations, "to the Lutheran people in the province of Pennsylvania . . . on trial for a few years," was broached to him at a meal on September 6, 1741 by Gotthilf August Francke at Halle (*Journals* 1:6-7). His acceptance of the call went to the court preacher in London, Ziegenhagen, who worked out details. Muhlenberg had to be released from his call at Grosshennersdorf and the orphanage by his patrons, the twenty-fourth Count Reuss and Count Henckel (*Journals* 1:7-8). "The church," in the sense of Consistory (as at Leipzig, p. 5) or "Landeskirche" for some territory or principality, was *not* involved. (Cf. Mann 21-23, 26-27; Riforgiato 26.) The one contact Muhlenberg had in this time with Hannover church authorities involved a reprimand for "holding pietistic conventicles" in Einbeck (*Journals* 1:11-14); a "sharp rescript against the missionary, Muhlenberg . . . from the Consistory in Hannover" and the threat of imprisonment were compared by Muhlenberg to "the Spanish Inquisition where they first cut off the head of the accused and afterwards inquired what his crime was" (*Journals* 1:13; cf. Mann 30-32). Once in America Muhlenberg often exhibited his call and referred to his "letter of instruction from the Rev. Court Preacher" Ziegenhagen as source of authority and purpose (*Journals* 1:72, 74, with Tranberg, the Swedish minister). Thereafter Muhlenberg regularly referred to Ziegenhagen and the reverend fathers in Halle as his ecclesiastical superiors.

On more than one occasion Muhlenberg declined to involve himself in a situation because it was not the focus of his call and work in the United Congregations. He insisted, e.g., that he had "no instructions with regard to Germantown," only the three United churches (*Journals* 1:66). Similarly with a request from Monocacy, Maryland, to "remain and be their pastor" (*Journals* 1:157). Or with a schoolmaster wanting Muhlenberg to ordain him (1:87-88). The catechist, not Rev. Mr. Roth, was to take care of the New Hanover Church "until orders came from Europe" (1:575, in 1762).

Sticking with his call gave Muhlenberg a view of mission narrower than we might wish. Jeff G. Johnson, in the Helmut Lehmann Memorial essays on *The Roots of 250 Years of Organized Lutheranism in North America* (1998), has deplored the lack of any "discernible plan" on Muhlenberg's part to establish a "relationship to African Americans" (23) or to propose "a solution" to slavery. The response by Michael Cobbler seems to me better nuanced: Muhlenberg was a man "not afraid to meet people where they are, whether they are black or white," and not afraid to minister to them.[4] The matter is similar with Indians and Jews. Muhlenberg engaged

---

4. In addition to the references in Muhlenberg's *Journals* cited by Johnson and Cobbler (1:57, 58, 721; 2:674-75, Johnson's chief text; 362, a mulatto baptized; 638, 567), see 1:63, 105, 209, 223 (slaves worked the land to support the pastor in a German church in Virginia developed by J. C. "Stoever" [Sr.], where a later pastor took special interest in them, 3:203); cf. also on Eben Ezer, Georgia, 2:374, 515, 614, 616, 622, 628, 649, 656, 671, 674-75, 677; 1:301, 441, 466 *nigers* (loan word sometimes used by Muhlenberg, italicized as other "English" words in the standard translation); 1:321, 330 a manumitted Negro is said to have willed land to the Lutheran congregation; 342; 367, 442; 484 Provost Wrangel had a *Niger* slave; 569 Wrangel instructed and brought grace to two Negro prisoners, whom he

in a ministry of one sort or another, as possible, when he met Native Americans or Jewish individuals, but they were not his target audience.[5]

---

accompanied to their execution, as also at 2:7, a *niger* who "was hanged for murdering a child" but received Baptism from the Provost; cf. 2:11-12 Muhlenberg judges the man to be a sinner "actually saved," and "hoped that the elder son, Luke 15, will not be envious or critical" because God forgives — though "orthodoxists call this fanatical and enthusiastic if it does not appear to agree with the post-Reformation *consensus patrum recentiorum* [consensus of the more recent fathers]"; 372 Swedish was "too good and sacred" a language, a Swede said, for a Negro slave to speak; 439 Muhlenberg baptized "two *niger* children" and "[u]nited the Negro Richard Sloan and the Negress Martha in marriage." At 1:669 a mulatto/Negro baptized earlier by Muhlenberg brings his infant daughter for baptism. Christ Church (Episcopal), Philadelphia, had a "catechist to Negroes," 2:104 n. 3. Further 2:340, 564, 586 a German family in Georgia ran a plantation "without the use of black slaves"; 593, 594; 636-38 members of the Eben Ezer congregation have little success giving Christianity to young Negroes they have purchased; 658 fear of Negro slave rebellion in the South; 664, 683 the Moravian mission, one man thought, converted slaves who thereby became "exceedingly useful" for their masters; 701, 714, 732, 759, 766; 3:34, 39, 53, 135, 215, 258-59, 295, 301, 303, 425, 462; 552 John Peter Gabriel Muhlenberg had three Negroes (cf. also 573-76, 578-82, 599-600, 660); further, 571, 630, 632, 634, 739. Some of the references in later years are simply to "the Negro" of Martin Brooks (2:723, 725, 735) or of someone else, but others record rumors that the British would free Negro slaves so as to have their help in defeating the Americans (3:13, 78, 105 along with "a regiment of Catholics"). References continue to pastoral acts by Muhlenberg: 3:120 "I have for a long time been baptizing children of these two Negroes"; cf. 213, 270-71, 556, 595. See further H. L. Nelson 192-203, who concluded Muhlenberg was increasingly "assimilating American racial values" (or prejudices).

    5. Muhlenberg's father-in-law, Conrad Weiser, advised in 1747 that any missionaries to the Indians would have to live among them and adopt their manner of life, "translate our revealed historical and dogmatic truths into their language," and learn their melodies (*Journals* 1:168). Lutherans did not engage often in work among Native Americans as "French papist fathers" did in Canada or even as the Moravians attempted, until much later (cf. F. W. Meuser, in E. C. Nelson, *Lutherans* pp. 283-84; e.g., Rocky Boy mission; Wisconsin Synod Apache work; little note has been taken in the U.S.A. of German missionaries like Moritz Bräuninger [† July 22, 1860] martyred on the Western plains by Indians). Some early efforts with Indians turned out disastrously (cf. *Journals* 1:386, 703, 705, 728; 2:18, 19, 22, 84, 88. H. L. Nelson 182-92 sees Muhlenberg at first "somewhat objective about Indians" and wishing their conversion, but later more negative about them, as were many colonials; pp. 192-203 on his assimilation of social attitudes of the period in America.

    Some think that because Muhlenberg once considered working in a mission to the Jews (*Journals* 1:4), he should have continued special efforts with any Jewish person he met. He noted in 1749, "There are only a few Jews in this country and these few may fairly be counted amongst the practical atheists" (1:139). Again such work was not in the hands

The Latin phrase *ecclesia plantanda* has often been taken as Muhlenberg's mission aim, "The Church Must Be Planted" as his motto. This Latin phrase served as the title for the magazine of the Board of Home Missions in the United Lutheran Church in America, and the Philadelphia Seminary's 1997 Convocation on Muhlenberg took the words as its theme, with the subheading, "The church has not already been planted *(plantata)* but must continuously be planted *(plantanda)*." H. E. Jacobs's *History of the Evangelical Lutheran Church in the United States* (1893) used the concept in introducing Muhlenberg: "his favorite motto . . . not simply congregations but a church . . . ; congregations had been planted, but a church was to be planted" (210). A. R. Wentz *(History)* and others repeated this view (even the *Encyclopedia of the Lutheran Church* 2:1672; details in H. L. Nelson 42).

But Theodore G. Tappert (1953; 1975: 56) made clear it was a description, not a motto, meaning "a church that still had to be planted," in contrast to the church in Europe "that had already been planted" *(ecclesia plantata)*. Muhlenberg was contrasting the isolated Lutheran congregations he found upon arrival, *plantanda* or *colligenda* ("being combined or united"; *Journals* 2:87, 366, 391, 494, 542; 3:205, 340 n. 1 renders *colligenda* as "still to be gathered"), with the *ecclesia fixa* in Germany. The *ecclesia*

---

of the church but of what Muhlenberg thought an excellent model, the Institutum Judaicum at Halle (founded 1728, under J. H. Callenberg [1694-1760] for education of missionaries to Jews and to "Mohammedans," the former with some success, the latter with little in results); it worked through itinerant evangelists *(Journals* 2:390-91). Occasionally Muhlenberg met Jews in America. His *Journal* 1:167 records an altercation between a Lutheran cabinetmaker and a Jew residing at the home of deacon Philip Barndt in New Hanover. In some instances he discussed religion and even baptized the person (a Jew from Surinam, 2:251, July 8 and 10; 263, 264 with Wrangel, 266). 3:123 speaks of a converted Jew at Upper Milford who took in a destitute pastor. Sermons, like Wrangel's (recorded in 2:1-2), wrestled with "the difficult matter of the hardening of the hearts of the Jews" (cf. also 2:261). On one occasion (2:196-97), in dealing with John 5, the paralytic at Bethesda, the qualification is made that "the Jew" (John 5:15) "here cannot mean the whole nation . . . but the council or Sanhedrin"; and the explanation was offered that the ex-paralytic, in disclosing the identity of his healer, "was attempting . . . to get himself out of danger" — an explanation more generous than that in the exegesis of the passage in *Proclamation 6* in 1997. 2:685 records debate over Isaiah 7:14; see 3:584, 586-87 for "ecumenical" pastoral care (Muhlenberg and the Anglican John Wade) of Israel Israel, a child of an Episcopal mother and father who was "a Jew outwardly," the child baptized by Muhlenberg thirty-eight years earlier, now under Wade's pastoral care (March 7, 26 and 31 entries). Cf. *Correspondence* 1: pp. 13, 54, 55; 2:311-13, 315 n. 13.

plantanda was in 1745, he said (1:102), "at a very critical *juncture* here," due to lack of strong ministerial leaders. (Cf. also *Journals* 1:445, 597; "our poor *ecclesia plantanda* in North America; 2:295, 313.) In an eloquent contrast, Muhlenberg wrote in 1778 to Pastor Kuntze, "You were brought up in the *ecclesia plantata*, which is protected by walls and hedges, you have not yet experienced any such soul-destroying, satanic, heart-breaking, and almost irreparable dissensions as I" at Lancaster, Philadelphia, Eben Ezer, etc. (*Journals* 3:202). The list of references in H. L. Nelson 42 n. 3 is more complete than the index in *Journals* 3:763, but several references belong under *colligenda*, not *plantanda*. Most accurate is perhaps the phrase at 1:701, *ecclesia colligenda* and *plantanda*.

As to a motto, Muhlenberg recorded on November 1, 1742, "I chose for myself the motto of the Danish missionary, Daniel Zeglin: 'If Thou desirest me dead, here am I, my God. If Thou willest that I should live, I submit to Thy will'" (*Journals* 1:63, repeated Dec. 31, 1776, 2:770). Zeglin, from Stettin in Pomerania, went to Tranquebar, India, in 1740. Had Muhlenberg learned of his motto through reports from Malabar to Halle or earlier in Halle personally? There are numerous times when one can see Muhlenberg reflecting this motto (e.g., 2:686).

Muhlenberg's sense of churchly mission can also be seen in his use of scriptural and other analogies for his work. The imagery of "the word as seed" was common. On October 11, 1742 Muhlenberg wrote, concerning Bol[t]zius and the Salzburgers in Georgia, ". . . a fine harvest is to be hoped for, because the living Word of God is taking root among them like a seed and is growing, even though thorns and thistles are not lacking" (*Journals* 1:62; cf. 60, "The German people listen to the Word of God . . . and it appears as though it will burst into fruitage"). That was said of an enterprise that envisioned plantations, a mill, churches, and an orphanage (1:60-63). In examining people, prior to receiving the Lord's Supper, to lead them to repentance by using law and gospel, he said, "[W]e dig around and dung the old trees and plant and water, and then ask God for the increase" (1746; 1:119; cf. 3:116, God "allowed us to be digged about and dunged. Now what about the fruits?" Christmas 1777). A little later, "One hoes and digs and dungs these twice-dead trees, but the vice of drunkenness smothers it all and there is little hope" (1747; *Journals* 1:176). Tares among the wheat were common experience (e.g., at *Journals* 1:443, of the Swede, Paul Bryzelius, whose conventicles were adjudged by some "watchmen on the walls of Zion" to be "tares which the enemy had sown among the good seeds"). Muhlenberg, at Easter 1786, hoped "some of my very numerous descendants to be fruitful seed . . . in some future seeding in this western wilderness" (3:705).

While Muhlenberg, at the first meeting of the Ministerium in 1748, could refer to the newly dedicated church building as "only an external structure" for the "hearts of all hearers" as "holy temples of the living God," and referred to the business at the August 15 session as "only the external scaffolding of the spiritual edifice" (*Journals* 1:201-2), he suggests that such reflections of 1 Peter 2 should not cause us to overlook the way even Old Testament figures could be woven in to show how we ". . . strive that stones and mortar be prepared, the walls of Zion built, and the Kingdom of our blessed Redeemer extended in this western wilderness" (*Journals* 2:505). He continues in the same passage, combining 1 Corinthians 3:6-10 and 12:14-25: "Many and varied laborers are required to build a temple or house. Some must dig in the ground where the foundation is to be laid. Others must cut the rough stones and make mortar out of lime and sand. Surely the dirty hodman and lime-daubers are not despised and rejected because they are not also skilled to do the work of carpenters, joiners, glaziers, sculptors, painters, etc. Every member of the body has its own special function; the foot cannot be an eye, nor the eye a foot, yet even the meanest part is necessary for the whole."

A vivid analogy compared churches to beehives. In Philadelphia by 1764 there was need for a second Lutheran church besides St. Michael's, "for the first church is just like a beehive where the bees are crowding one another and ready to swarm. And if the young swarm departs and the keeper is careless and fails to have a new hive ready, the first, second, and third swarms will go out and be lost" (*Journals* 2:4, cf. 6; Zion Church was therefore built in 1769). Similarly at the "Peikstown beehive" (2:511).

Several images from Scripture are combined in the maturing judgment expressed in 1753 about how America differs from Europe: "If the seed has not yet taken strong and deep root and gained the upper hand, it is in danger of being rooted out or of being smothered by the weeds of erratic opinions," from competing religious groups, far more prolific than in Germany. America, as an elder said to Muhlenberg, was like Israel in the time of the judges: "In those days there was no king in Israel, but every man did that which was right in his own eyes" (Judg. 17:6; *Journals* 1:376).

Muhlenberg was needed not so much to plant congregations as to bring them together. Laypeople had been there before Lutheran clergy came. These people built churches. Muhlenberg's mission had to be bringing order instead of contention and chaos in congregation after congregation and somehow bringing them together in a cord that would not break, bees that would not swarm so readily into strange hives. The jump from three congregations in 1742 to eighty-one associated with Muhlenberg and the synod in 1771 (A. R. Wentz 1964: 44, cited in H. L. Nelson 105 n. 2) was not the result of pioneer evangelism work on Muhlenberg's part but of networking the points of light that other Lutherans had brought into existence.

Sticking to his call gave Muhlenberg direction: to gather together existing congregations — three of which already called themselves "united" in summoning him — into a more than local expression of the Lutheran Church. H. L. Nelson (53) describes Muhlenberg's work as "supra-congregational." That is a possible term, provided, as the Commission for a New Lutheran Church insisted in the 1980s, we do not regard anything beyond the local community as somehow more the church than the parish church where the word goes forth in preaching and sacraments. We may well call Muhlenberg's mission "extra-congregational."

Order, Ecclesial and in Society

We shall never understand Muhlenberg's world without recalling how the structures of society continued in his day to reflect Aristotle's model of household and state within the cosmos. This was a view brought into the later New Testament books and the Christianity of the Roman Empire and thence into the Middle Ages, and not least as a part of Luther's thought, expressed for example in the *Haustafeln* or "Table of Household Duties" in the Small Catechism (Tappert et al., *Book of Concord* 354-56; Kolb/Wengert 365-67). Thus for January 1, 1763, Muhlenberg recorded, "For the new year prayed for the three estates of Christendom" (*Journals* 1:583), i.e., the home, the state, and the church. Only with the American Revolution and more violently the Revolution in France, would this society be shaken, though not in Great Britain or Germany.

We further misunderstand Muhlenberg if we think of his outlook as only "individualistic" or just "congregational" in a caricature of pietism. It was also institutional — Halle provided a model. The orphans' home in Georgia — the 260th anniversary of which fell in 1997 (Tappert 1975: 72); there was also the hope for a school for girls (2:668-69) — was a dream for the Ministerium (*Journals* 1:121). So were a retirement home for pastors and spouses (*Journals* 2:550), schools, and a seminary; the prayer was vivid at the 1769 Synod meeting "for a *seminarium* which is yet to be established,

Song of Solomon 8:8, 'We have a little sister and she hath no breasts'" (*Journals* 2:401, 547, 763). Kuntze did begin such a school, which lasted only from 1773 to 1776; note also Hartwick's plans for a school for mission to the Indians (Tappert 1975: 73).

How global the outlook was can be appreciated when we find Muhlenberg reading reports about Halle missionaries on the Malabar coast of India (*Journals* 1:348, 519; 2:374, 376, 401, 433), edifying accounts to be shared with others in America — or not so edifying, when Tippu Sultan took vengeance on the British (3:651, 660; Muhlenberg refers once to "the so-called Black Hole of Calcutta," 3:166; Madras destroyed, 3:454; Tranquebar saved, 563). Did missionaries in India, one wonders, read about Muhlenberg's work in America? The 107th continuation report on India apparently arrived at the same time as the 11th on Pennsylvania in 1770 (*Journals* 2:440). Muhlenberg at times made comparisons between America and India (2:713, about when enemies attack establishments). The peace treaty settling the American Revolution had global aspects (3:533-34). "The world is the field" (Matt. 13:38-40; 3:660).

For church as well as society, a sense of order was an innate part of Muhlenberg's heritage. For the church, 1 Corinthians 14:40 loomed large: "All things done decently and in order." For the state, Romans 13:1-7 set the tone (*Journals* 2:19, with Wrangel; 680, 735; 2:746-47; 3:5, 28, 34). Muhlenberg knew the view, through Thomas Pyle, an Anglican commentator, that Paul was cautioning Jewish Christians in Rome against insurrection such as Judas of Galilee and other Jews were prone to (2:55-56; cf. 3:92 about God's way of ruling through "Heathen Governments," where 1 Peter 2:13-17 is also cited, as also at 3:124). Further, 3:257, "tribute to whom tribute is due"; but see his reservations at 3:278 about "a sworn account of income, expenditures . . ." etc., but he paid it (279; also 3:124 and 222). In 3:103 it is to be noted how Muhlenberg, in his 1777 defense of his neutrality in the Revolution, added to Romans 13:1 the words "for the time being" — "Let every soul be subject unto the higher powers which have authority over you and protect you p[ro] t[empore], or for the time being" — as H. L. Nelson notes, in his discussion (229-35); but Muhlenberg may simply be reflecting an apocalyptic bent there, as he goes on immediately to cite Daniel 2:21, about God removing kings. God "is a God of order," Muhlenberg wrote in 1765 (2:200) and in 1768 (as also in the 1751 articles of reconciliation for New York, 1:293; cf. article XI there, against "disorder"; 3:165, voiced by laity to Muhlenberg): "Whoever fears Him, loves order for God's sake. If we wish to be Evangelical Christians and congregations, we must hold to and observe Christian, Evangelical order" (2:358). The motif of (good) order appears again and again for parish affairs (e.g., 1:83, 120, 481; 2:654; 3:7-8, 286; cf. H. L. Nelson 45-54). The unity that Halle preachers displayed, even opponents "were forced to admire" (1:174). Moreover, English law insisted on "laws, rules, and order" for churches (as Justice Delaney put it in New York, 1:281; cf. 561), though Muhlenberg, like other Germans, was not always familiar and comfortable with English procedures (2:388; 1:617, swearing an oath). English laws, he felt, were sometimes too lax, as on marriage (1:314, 354-55, 653); slander against the Bible was punishable but not against Luther's exposition of Scripture (2:235; cf. 1:323).

It is not surprising therefore that Pennsylvania German Lutherans wished, at least in theory and out of their heritage, that church life be as well ordered as their households, farms, and businesses. But this was not the case in many a quarrelsome congregation, prior to Muhlenberg, let alone in extra-congregational life. As reasons, one may begin with the nature of the immigrants themselves, generally peasants unaccustomed to ordering things beyond farm and family. There were few from the nobility or upper classes. "Prince" Carl Rudolph, supposedly a Lutheran pastor, was actually a "whoring . . . swilling . . . charlatan" (1:154). The aristocracy of "Baron" Henry W. Stiegel — manufacturer of glass and iron products, who gave land for the church in Manheim, Pennsylvania, for which "one red rose" was to be given every June — was uncertain (2:312, 391-92, 415, 423, 466-69; Tappert 1975: 60, 75). The picture in Marianne S. Wokeck's essay is generally negative. Her subtitle, "The Desert Is Vast, the Sheep Are Dispersed," is disputed by John Kleiner when he stresses on the bright side that, in the *corpus permixtum* of wheat and tares that made up Lutheran congregations and environs, "the Wonderful Gospel" was "spreading." Negative factors included the need for the immigrants, in their poverty, to scratch out an existence economically, so that there was little time for things beyond local survival, plus the often bewildering new freedom America brought, especially in William Penn's colony. Before looking at the lack of educated pastoral leadership as a further aspect, we must note some things that "order" did *not* imply for Muhlenberg.

One was (in spite of proverbial use of Judges 17:6 or 21:25; 2:759; 3:122) a king at the peak of the social pyramid (cf. 3:393). Germany was a land of petty states, lacking nationhood and king such as Great Britain, France, and Sweden had. While Muhlenberg could take a certain pride in George II and III as Hannoverians (3:123), eventually he came to distinguish "King of England" from "Hannoverian ruler" (e.g., 2:680, in 1775), and the younger generation made this transition away from the British monarch even more rapidly. Other Germans knew well, but were sometimes fleeing from, Prussian, Austrian, or other rulers, and ecclesiastically the consistories of various cities and territories. More important, German Lutherans knew no system of bishops as in the Church of England (which, however, kept its episcopal sees at home, not in America), nor a system such as Presbyterian and Reformed churches brought or created. Lutherans had no two- or threefold "orders" of ministry and so could adapt to American egalitarianism, though, as we shall see below, they did espouse confessionally one *Predigtamt* or pastoral-proclamatory ministry that distinguished them from congregational free churches. While espousing "good order," they had no one church polity that their Confessions regarded as divinely mandated. Of the several models available, that of Lutherans in Holland proved most helpful. Muhlenberg and compatriots were influenced by developing American democracy — or, more properly, republicanism, for the nation born in Muhlenberg's last years was by no means a full democracy. But Lutherans did not derive their pattern for their church's ministry and polity from it. H. L. Nelson (373-74) emphasizes how German settlers, "despite the voluntaristic, pluralistic, congregationally oriented religious climate of the Middle Colonies . . . clung to their German views of the pastor and his office."[6]

In general it can be said that subsequent American Lutheranism, like the Ministerium from its outset, has prized good order highly, but has shown ability to adapt to changing needs. The judgment of J. J. Mol that Muhlenberg's pietism was more suited to the American scene than Berckenmeyer's orthodoxy can be termed more a sociological judgment (Reumann 1979 = 1987: 229 n. 74) than a theological one; it emphasized openness and independence from Europe (cf. H. L. Nelson 157-58, who puts his emphasis on the "individual personalities" of Muhlenberg and Berckenmeyer; 157 n. 4 for other comments).

Of political involvement, Muhlenberg was personally wary, as were Pennsylvania Germans generally. He knew that politicians, when they "get into a tight corner," want to make use for their own purposes of preachers "who at other times are only disgusting creatures" to them (2:678). Faith E.

---

6. That this was true generally of colonists in the region is noted by Jon Butler, "Power, Authority, and the Origins of American Denominational Order: The English Churches in the Delaware Valley 1680-1730," *Transactions of the American Philosophical Society* 68 (1978): 8-75.

Rohrbough has attempted to see development and "maturation" in the pastor from Grosshennersdorf; he became the immigrant in America, and then "the troubled retiree" who remained "an agonized neutral" at best (Tappert 1942b) or was still a supporter of the king (H. T. Lehmann). But in the end, she says, Muhlenberg remained "a part of the old world which is slightly out of place in the new" (53). Samuel Zeiser's "Comment" astutely questions the term "maturation" and urges us "to separate Muhlenberg's political skill as a church leader from his guarded political stance in affairs of state" (59). Muhlenberg seems to have taken the required oath of allegiance to the United States on May 27, 1778, just before the June 1 deadline (*Journals* 3:157, 159, so Glatfelter). This oath was a problem not only for Moravians, Schwenkfelders, and others but also for Anglican clergy (3:160).

Any generalization about millions of Lutherans in America since the eighteenth century and politics would be simplistic. But has not traditional "balance" amid such ambiguities — a concern for order but an awareness of change — usually led to *noninvolvement* by Lutherans in the political process (with some exceptions)? Today Lutherans can sometimes be found with the "politically correct left" or the "politically correct right" (but seldom leaders in either camp) or, more often, they are part of the vast middle ground. H. L. Nelson 250 n. 4 notes how Riforgiato (259) concluded that Muhlenberg "operated on the view that church and state were complementary realms brooking no intervention." One needs only an awareness of the "Two Kingdoms" (or *zwei Reiche*) view to understand the first part of that conclusion about complementarity. It would be a long time before an appreciation of "functional interaction" between church and state could arise in American theology.

Pastoral Ministry

The particular form that ecclesial order took for Muhlenberg and the Ministerium of Pennsylvania — note its original name, "ministerium," which was reluctantly given up only in 1962, even though it had long been inaccurate — was the called and ordained pastoral ministry of the Word of God. This was inevitable, given the Lutheran Confessions, the place of the *Pfarramt* in Reformation lands, Muhlenberg's own call, and the chaos he found in America, with ministerial pretenders of various ilks bilking Lutheran congregations.

Muhlenberg was an "orthodox pietist"[7] who, with the Lutheran Confessions, held to the one office of pastor/presbyter, which exists by divine right *(jure divino)*. Here bishops are pastors who do exactly the same things as pastors but in a larger jurisdiction; anything more for bishops is a human creation *(jure humano)*.

The case is instructive, beginning in 1779, of the proposed ordination of an Episcopalian, John Wade, by the Lutheran Ministerium for service in the English Church in the Blue Mountains. Muhlenberg examined him and suggested (3:255-56, cf. 253-54; 422, 425, 427-28, 450-51) ". . . it is my humble Opinion, that in the present critical Junctures an Examination and Ordination of a regular Protestant Ministry may do as an episcopal one. And since there is as yet no Episcopal Jurisdiction established by Law in the independent States of North America, why should Congregations be left destitute of the necessary Means of Salvation, be neglected and destroyed, only for Want of an Episcopal Ordination? which is but a piece of pious Ceremony, a form of Godliness empty of Power, and may be of Service, where it is established by Law, tho it does not appertain to the essential parts of the holy Function itself. In the primitive Christian Church the Ambassadors and Ministers of Christ could impart extraordinary Gifts of the Holy Ghost unto believing Candidates, by prayers and laying their hands upon them, but this Prerogative is not continued, and we may controvert for ever about apostolical and Episcopal Succession. Experience shews too plain, that neither Episcopal, nor Ministerial or Presbyterial Ordination doth infuse any natural and supernatural Gifts or Qualities, otherwise we should not find so many counterfeited Ministers, refined Hypocrites, and grievous Wolves in the Christian Church on Earth, instead of true and faithful Shepherds." Upon request of an Episcopal vestry (3:405) and Wade himself (411, 502, 503-4, 510, 534, 539-40, 547), he was examined by the Ministerium at its convention in 1783 (*Documentary History*, 187, 189; he was subsequently ordained, *Journals* 3:549, 550, 557; other frequent references in Muhlenberg's *Journals* are to visits from Wade, and once Muhlenberg records that he admonished him; cf. H. L. Nelson 343).

---

7. So A. G. Roeber, in the Helmut Lehmann Memorial Volume, p. 12. But see my critique of Roeber's description of "[t]he preferred church order" according to the Confessions in "The Priesthood of Baptized Believers and the Office of the Ministry in Eastern Lutheranism, from Muhlenberg's Day to Ours," in the *Proceedings of the Lutheran Historical Conference 1998*, 202-4; cf. *Journals* 1:323; 3:286.

The Wade case was an exceptional one, during an "emergency" situation for Anglicans in the United States. In the case of Isaac Rawling, a member of the Episcopal Church, connected with "Wesley's disciples," caution was shown and later concern (3:495, 533, 567). Henry Melchior Muhlenberg knew that, under Anglican polity, to minister in a colony like Virginia, where the Anglican was the state church, one had to receive ordination from a bishop in England (*Journals* 2:374-75; 536 n. 2, on Peter Muhlenberg; somewhat different and more complicated was the case of Frederic Daser in South Carolina, *Journals* 2:580-84, 603, 651; 3:164; Mann 459-63). But in Pennsylvania there was no such requirement, and Lutheran ordinations could continue to be by pastors, as in Amsterdam or by a German Lutheran consistory (or even by permission of the Consistory in Sweden). The ordination of J. N. Kur(t)z indicates Muhlenberg's preference for having a group of pastors, not just one, ordain a pastor.[8] Consider also the letter from German Lutherans in Nova Scotia, taken up by the Ministerium (*Journals* 2:370-72), about the Swedish-German pastor Bryzelius, who had now appeared in Lunenburg. For a time he used Lutheran forms, but eventually showed he was, *sub rosa*, "neither a genuine Lutheran nor a genuine Reformed pastor" but now a government-supported Anglican. Cf. 2:372 and note the story about a boastful *clericus* in New York on "the succession . . . from the apostles' time to the present."

While Muhlenberg and the Ministerium laid strong emphasis on call and ordination, much more important in church life was the rich understanding of what ministers of Christ are and "how they are to be appraised and used," as a sermon on October 14, 1764, spelled out (*Journals* 2:131-37, within an ecclesiology from 1 Cor. 1–4). Clergy are faithful stewards who minister and are not just used by the congregation for its interests. The whole section is worth reading, even today, about men "made free in Christ through repentance and faith by means of the Word and the Spirit; learned in divinity . . . regularly ordained to teach God's Holy Word . . . rightly administer the Sacraments, and be examples to the flock" (134).

For all the involvement by laypeople in building and running congregations that Muhlenberg found in American voluntarism, he never subscribed to an *Übertragungslehre* or theory that laity voluntarily hand over a portion of their power to a minister who would then do their bid-

---

8. Cf. Reumann 2003: 204-5; *Journals* 1:202; 3:358, 496-97; C. H. Glatfelter, *Pastors and People*, vol. 1 (1980), pp. 262-63.

ding. He was not a Free Church congregationalist. In the same sermon for the funeral of Pastor Johann Friedrich Handschuh (1714-1764), Muhlenberg dwelled on how the church was built by Paul in Corinth, a church with several divisive, harmful parties. He included the "Pauline party" (1 Cor. 1:12), which Muhlenberg likened to many after the Reformation "who called themselves Lutheran and orthodox, made a shibboleth of the article of sanctification, and persecuted . . . genuine Christians who refused to put aside what Christ, Paul, and Luther had joined together!" (132-33; that he means "justification and sanctification are inseparably connected" by God is indicated in Muhlenberg's entry at 2:684). Muhlenberg waxed eloquent on how "Paul, Cephas, Apollos, Johann Hus, Luther, Chemnitz, Arndt, Spener, . . . Bengel, or Whitfield or Wrangel . . . are yours if you . . . remain true members of Christ and have no cause for envying, strife, and divisions" (134). Then Muhlenberg launched into how people should treat their pastors (135-36, really how *not* to treat them):

1. Not as "mere *opera operata*" or sacrament machines (my phrase), administering the Lord's Supper when someone is about to die.
2. Not as devout witnesses to God while you follow your own lusts.
3. Not as the butt of ridicule. Muhlenberg knew what it was to be slandered (1:217, 405; 2:692-93; 3:44), accused even of sex scandals. When he lost his voice, as frequently (2:217-18, 432, 435-36), he appeared "a speechless rider . . . on a stiff old horse" (1:247), plodding on through snow or swollen streams, lest, if he fall, people would claim he was drunk or not up to his tasks. One opponent even suggested Muhlenberg was the dragon of Revelation 12 (1:257; cf. 1:265). In 1774 a note was left at Muhlenberg's door, signed "Tacitus," about possible irregularities with bequests from Europe (2:556). Cf. 2:688 for a lampoon of clergy; 3:190-91 for a lampoon of doctrine. Muhlenberg was threatened with death by the Doane gang of outlaws in 1783 (3:560), as Wrangel had been on occasion (3:623).
4. Not as preachers who simply attract big contributions in the collection plate when they should be proclaiming the gospel of "righteousness, peace, and joy in the Holy Ghost" (Rom. 14:17).
5. Not as objects of flattery, but rejected when they apply the truth of the gospel. Muhlenberg illustrated this with the story of a man who told him, after Muhlenberg had preached, "I felt just as though I was listening to *den lieben Gott im Himmel* himself." But later when

Muhlenberg took him aside and urged leaving his sinful life, repenting, and finding peace, the man exploded, "Who is this devil's priest to give me advice? This is a free country!" (136).

One may recall Muhlenberg's earlier judgment in 1742, about this land where "[e]verything depends on the vote of the majority[:] A preacher must fight his way through with the sword of the Spirit alone and depend upon faith in the living God and His promises, if he wants to be a preacher and proclaim the truth" (1:67).

The real ministers of Christ, who set forth God's word, Muhlenberg said, were often accused by Quakers of being mere hirelings (a paid clergy), and by sectarians as "priests of Baal." Unchristian lawyers preferred those who caused lawsuits. As Muhlenberg concluded the sermon in 1764, he recalled the three deceased pastors who had sojourned among his hearers (the Dane Brunnholtz, from Schleswig, pastor in Philadelphia 1745-57; Heinzelmann; and now Handschuh) and gave the verdict: they were sinners with many human faults, but also "pardoned, justified, God-disciplined sinners"; educated scholars (though Muhlenberg deplored the desire of some to have university "*magisters* instead of *ministers*," 2:138; cf. 1:147 and 3:695), but also "scholars of the heart who actually experienced . . . justification. . . ." They had "a regular call," toiled among you, feeding the lambs and sheep with the "sincere milk of the Gospel" and then "stronger meat" (1 Cor. 3:2), building "upon the Christian Evangelical foundation with gold, silver, and precious stones" (1 Cor. 3:12). The pastor speaks in Christ's stead (2 Cor. 5:20; *Journals* 1:449). H. L. Nelson finds an interesting reflection of the importance of the *Predigtamt* for Muhlenberg in the list of "modes of Christ's presence" in *Journals* 2:174-75: the Spirit, the Word, Baptism, the Lord's Supper, Christian assemblies ("the mutual consolation of the brethren"?), and Christ's "laborers in the office that preaches the atonement" (= 2 Cor. 5:18). The closing appeal of the sermon was (2:137), Receive with meekness the Word: "Obey your teachers and follow them as they follow Christ" (Phil. 3:17, cited on p. 136).

Many features evident in this funeral address can be said to characterize much of later Lutheranism in America, to the present day. There is the desire for an educated, called, ordained pastorate, persons with the experience of salvation and lives to match (one might speak here of an eighteenth-century "Expectations" statement for clergy). They are to be ministers in accord with the Confessions (*Journals* 1:91, 156, among many references), and a laity with them and for them in a united church. Muhlenberg lifted up Luther's counsel about what makes a pastor a good theologian — *oratio, meditatio, tentatio* (prayer, meditation, experience) (2:677); his description of Anna Barbara, the wife of Pastor Rabenhorst, is worth recalling too: "a Mary in faith and a Martha in charity" (2:677; 3:348). Many things the Ministerium of Pennsylvania stood for continue to be much needed nowadays in the self-understanding of pastors, amid what can still be termed, in Joseph Sittler's phrase, "the maceration of the ministry." Riforgiato (151-52) is correct in stating that, for all his background in pietism, Muhlenberg "did not emphasize, as did Francke and Spener, the doctrine of the priesthood of all believers" (cf. Reumann 2003). For the many "earthly callings" of laypeople Muhlenberg admitted he lacked wisdom to provide rules (1:377). But for all, piety was a way of life, one of the factors that could abet growing into a united church in the new world of America.

Piety

Muhlenberg stood at the intersection of three forces in *Geistesgeschichte* (spiritual and intellectual history): Lutheran orthodoxy, the widespread pietist movement, and the emerging Rationalism of the Enlightenment or *Aufklärung*. The interaction of these three trends can be seen vividly in the first stirrings of what became "biblical theology," namely the inaugural lecture by Johann Philipp Gabler at the University of Altdorf (near Nürnberg) in 1787, the year of Muhlenberg's death.[9] The disputes between orthodoxists and pietists were soon to be influenced by the biblical criticisms to which Rationalism gave birth. Some effects were already being felt in Muhlenberg's day. Note his wish (3:130) for "a moral theology rationally based upon a sound exegesis of the higher revelation"; on feeling and reason, compare the Latin at 3:203 ("Feeling takes the place of reason. Believe one who knows from experience") and 224 ("I am more readily convinced by reasons than exclamations"); 3:613, where the caption is in Doberstein and Tappert, "From Pietism to Rationalism." The three currents were assessed by T. G. Tappert in the ULCA's *Christian Social Responsibility* series in 1957. He reached the judgment that "Orthodoxy and Pietism had passed

---

9. J. Sandys-Wunsch and L. Eldridge, "J. P. Gabler and the Distinction between Biblical and Dogmatic Theology: Translation, Commentary, and Discussion of his Originality," *Scottish Journal of Theology* 33 (1980): 133-58. Cf. *The Promise and Practice of Biblical Theology,* ed. J. Reumann (Minneapolis: Fortress, 1991), pp. 2, 6, 53-54, 100.

their prime by Muhlenberg's day" but "Rationalism was in its ascendency" (H. L. Nelson 28, cf. 2-29).

Muhlenberg's emphasis on the Lutheran Book of Concord (not just the Unaltered Augsburg Confession) can be judged an influence enhanced by Protestant orthodoxy, but more likely stemmed from the Reformation itself. Influence from Rationalism is harder to chart (H. L. Nelson 28), but Muhlenberg's use of the books by J. D. Michaelis (1717-1791), whom he knew at Halle and who was later professor at Göttingen, is one illustration (*Journals* 1:462, but why "*late* famous Professor Michaelis"? 2:761; 3:50, 72, 82, 85, 575). H. L. Nelson (24-29) sees the period of almost two months that Muhlenberg spent with Ziegenhagen (and Michaelis) in London in 1742 as, ironically, a time when rationalistic influences were at work on Muhlenberg (*Journals* 1:18-20; *Correspondence* 1:16 n. 26; 20, 21).

As for pietism, it is specifically the Halle variety from Spener and Francke that marked Muhlenberg. He had had his "conversion experience" while a student at Göttingen (*Selbstbiographie* 5-6; *Journals* 1:3; cf. Mann 8-10; Roeber 2, 6-9, who stresses its "covenant-oriented nature," p. 8; Marshall 93; Muhlenberg reported a vision at Christmas 1776 of the Savior sustaining his disciples in Pennsylvania and New Jersey, 2:767; references to dreams and visions and portents seem to grow more frequent in his later years). This turn in Muhlenberg's life occurred under the influence of Prof. Oporin, for whom he was amanuensis. It centered on his own depravity (cf. Sattler) and Christ crucified, "the sinner's Friend." (The christological title, Jesus the *Philanthropos*, "friend of the human race," appears at 2:187, 195, 260, etc.). Muhlenberg's account of his earlier years probably blackens his past, about "boozing, brawling, and all kinds of evils." One result of the conversion experience was involvement "with two upright theological students . . . to instruct the poor, ignorant beggar children in that place in reading, writing, reckoning, and especially in the Catechism." Muhlenberg got into trouble over this program with the authorities in Hannover (4). But the venture flourished. When he revisited Göttingen in 1742, Muhlenberg was pleased to find the charity school now supported by a noble benefactor, faculty, and church. Roeber terms him "throughout his life a moderate pietist within the bounds of confessional Lutheranism" (6).

What may seem strange and almost offensive to us today in Muhlenberg's pietism was the way in which he confronted sinners and rebuked sin. He may seem to us priggish and pharisaical when, for instance, he condemned the cursing and swearing on the ship to America (when he wasn't seasick) (*Journals* 1:25-26, 27, 30, speaks of passengers who were

Protestant in the sense of "protesting against God and His holy Word"; 33, 34-35, and passim). The ship from New York to Amboy in 1752 was to Muhlenberg "like Sodom and Gomorrah"; his complaints were fenced off by the rejoinder, "Do not act too piously" (1:346-47). Wedding receptions were a trial because they could get out of hand (1:136-37, 449-50); funerals too (1:317-18). But then one may recall Muhlenberg's unchurchly contemporary in Philadelphia, Benjamin Franklin, who was rather priggish in the way he claimed to master one virtue after another in his *Autobiography*. For Muhlenberg it was simply natural to ask about a person's spiritual condition, much as a physician might ask about physical condition (1:406). Once when he asked a seventy-year-old man, "How far have you come?" he had in mind not "a quarter-mile" but "how far on the narrow way that leads to life" (1:408).

Perhaps in later years Muhlenberg mellowed ("maturation"?) and became less aggressive in such matters. Taverns could be acceptable, if orderly (1:314, but cf. 369). There are more than passing references in the *Journals* to drinking beer (1:392; 2:115, 725; 3:727), wine (1:481, 562; 3:279, "for sick persons"; 3:532 for medicine; 589), and coffee (1:582; 3:426); tea, often. The Muhlenberg family's "sensual gratification" at eating sauerkraut (recorded at 2:591; cf. 3:450, 512, 513 cabbage; 551 Germans compared to sauerkraut; 630, 633, 635) is one of the bits of evidence that led H. L. Nelson to conclude, Muhlenberg "used Christ's example, the overall teaching of scripture and theology to support his appreciation of moderate sensuality" (239). Some Hallensians were more pietistically inclined than Muhlenberg, others less so. And not all who ministered in the Ministerium were pietists. It can be argued that the real home for inclinations that many associate with pietism, such as no alcohol (contrast Lehmann 1998: 68-69, Muhlenberg's stein, pipe, wine glass, and decanter) or keeping Sunday as Sabbath, came to roost in central Pennsylvania and the Seminary and College at Gettysburg.

Whatever we may mean by "pietism," its features long kept a hold on many subsequent Lutherans in America. American Lutheran pietism had an "activist heritage" in such matters as "ecumenism," sabbath observance, temperance, peace, and abolitionism (e.g., S. S. Schmucker; the Franckean Synod, begun 1837), a heritage that was subsequently lost (Kuenning). In any case its moral reflection of Christian commitment is a trait greatly to be desired today. Indeed, if the Muhlenberg heritage had continued and developed its piety in positive terms, discerningly, amid changing conditions, there would be a rich way of life among us and less need for a frantic search for "spirituality" and "spiritual formation," the latter a term originally from Roman Catholic sources and with all sorts of dangers from the stamp of uniformity that pietism in its individualism resists. But the "spirituality movement" has moved far beyond Roman Catholic and even Christian categories to cover nowadays almost everything under the sun, from various world religions to "New Age" syncretism. As Henry Bagger, pastor of Holy Trinity, Lancaster, synod and seminary president in the twentieth century, often remarked, there's a lot to be said for piety, which we can recover to our advantage.

Piety included one's personal experience in the faith. (Note the reference at *Journals* 3:529, to a treatise "On the Value of Feelings in Christianity" — a pointer toward Schleiermacher?) The element of experience has been raised in our day by feminist and liberation theologies[10] to a place of authority, sometimes superseding Scripture, church creed and confessions, and reason. Muhlenberg helps us see a place, but not an exclusive role, for personal experience in religion, including in Bible study (cf. Marshall 95-96).

Crisscrossing through Muhlenberg Lutheranism

Just as Muhlenberg went *kreuz und quer* across the Pennsylvania countryside, so we may now jump around to touch on some remaining aspects of the patriarch's life and the synod's history, in Eastern Lutheranism and the broader picture.

Relating to Other Christian Groups

Thus far we have followed themes agreed upon in the outline for the Muhlenberg Tradition series, as in Dr. Marshall's initial survey. His final

---

10. One should not read our changed social world and "cultural wars" into Muhlenberg's day any more than we should use material from his era to "solve" our problems in these areas. "Liberation" for him had to do primarily with forgiveness from the bondage of sin, and he had to wrestle long and hard, often disapprovingly, with the political results of the colonies' revolt against Great Britain. He lived in a period when a dispute between a pastor and his wife included the clergyman's disapproval of the fact that his wife had changed the dirty diapers of their child *in his presence*. He also refers to a divorce case where the wife thought — erroneously, it is added — that "man was created for the sake of woman" (3:427). There was also the instance of a woman claiming to be Jesus, 3:736-37, cited below.

point, "Ecumenism," uses a modern term, brought into our vocabulary in the late nineteenth-century as a Protestant equivalent, from the Greek *oikoumenē*, for the traditional term "catholic." That Muhlenberg was what we call "ecumenical" may be substantiated in a negative way by the fact that Graebner (322-23, 327, 382-85, and 440) charged him with "unionism," a term sometimes employed by Lutherans against other Lutherans (cf. Jacobs, *History* 277-89; H. L. Nelson 341-42, who himself speaks of Muhlenberg's "Ecumenism of Word and Sacrament," 341-39).

In his day Muhlenberg did know of Protestant church reunion schemes. There was not only that of Count Zinzendorf (see below) but also that of the Anglican rector in Philadelphia, William Smith, president of the Pennsylvania Academy (and University of Pennsylvania) 1754-79 until the "Presb[yterian] *politico-Christiani* . . . drove Prov[ost] Sm[ith] from his office and home" (3:625; cf. 546 and 551). It was Smith's hope to unite Lutheran and Anglican churches in America, with Smith as bishop, a scheme in which the SPCK charity schools were a pawn (Riforgiato 187-90, 197-98, 215-18; H. L. Nelson 171-78, who shows how Muhlenberg abetted the schools without receiving the blame Michael Schlatter did among the Reformed; for Muhlenberg's positive assessment of Smith, see *Journals* 3:625-26, 665).

Muhlenberg's language was noteworthy in inviting leaders to a meeting (about a lawsuit) on October 11, 1764. He addressed the ". . . Ministers of the English, Swedish and German protestant catholick Churches in Philadelphia" (*Journals* 2:125; cf. "catholick Protestant Zion" at 2:301). During the 1769 meeting of the Ministerium, Zion Church in Philadelphia was dedicated. At one service English Episcopal and Presbyterian clergy and a Baptist pastor were present (2:402-3). There was discussion of a current plan for English Presbyterian, the Dutch Reformed (with their Canons of Dort), and German Reformed to unite in one *corpus,* supported by money from Holland. Should German Lutherans join in and "allow themselves to be 'reformed' or [should they] unite with the English Lutherans [footnote: the Anglicans or Episcopalians] in order to preserve the balance"? (2:412). Actually, since Lutherans had evenhandedly invited Presbyterians as well as Anglicans for the occasion, "everything became quiet again" (2:412), and the plan never eventuated. Muhlenberg observed that, for the dedication service, the assembly sang only the second stanza of the hymn (by Nikolaus Decius), "Allein Gott in der Höh sei Ehre," as the Gloria in Excelsis. Muhlenberg added wryly, "I should perhaps have chosen the first stanza, but I am always afraid that the words, *'All Fedh hat nun ein Ende'* might be misunderstood in the church militant." For "all feuding" had *not* come to an end in the church on earth, even if Christ's cross ended hostility between God and humanity (2:400).

Dr. Marshall speaks rightly of "selective openness with other churches" on Muhlenberg's part (97). His closest ties may have been with the German Reformed (especially with the Rev. Michael Schlatter; cf. 3:198 on a collection for him among Lutheran congregations in 1778, gifts to be left, among other places, at Wissahickon Road, Chestnut Hill; cf. 3:385) and with Presbyterians (but there could also be disputes, 3:308, 321). Muhlenberg's *Journals* frequently note the doctrine of absolute election or eternal decrees *(absolutum decretum)* as an unresolved difference (1:219, 298, 300, 330; 2:57; 181, Presbyterians whom Muhlenberg otherwise much admired "push the doctrine of absolute predestination . . . too far, and their pastoral staff is tipped with steel"; cf. 2:681; 3:254, in the Thirty-Nine Articles, the Anglican John Wade could not accept #17 on predestination). But there is no evidence that Muhlenberg had ever read Luther's "Bondage of the Will," which might have disposed his outlook differently, H. L. Nelson claims (346 n. 3). Muhlenberg looked to a time "when our higher theologians have more clearly discovered the axis around which nature and grace turn and enlighten us concerning it" (1:298). The 1997 *Formula of Agreement* between the ELCA and three Reformed churches dealt with such matters under a principle of "complementarity." But the real solution of tension about predestination lay more in the fact that the Presbyterian churches in the USA had in 1903 "disavowed" the Westminster Confession on double predestination (*A Common Calling* [1993], 54).

Something of Muhlenberg's relations with Anglicans has already been noted. There is an interesting description of the Church of England as "Catholick Spirited and indulgent," with the explanation that she "has never yet forced or pressed any Protestant Denomination into her Jurisdiction"; this was asserted by Muhlenberg during his appeal in 1775 for Eben Ezer's building to be recognized as a Lutheran church not under Anglican jurisdiction, as a mistake in the grant had made it (2:675-76). At points (3:247-48) a sort of Lutheran-Episcopal "pulpit exchange" existed. William White, who was ordained in England at the same time as John Peter Gabriel Muhlenberg, attended the 1781 meeting of the Ministerium (3:427). During his lifetime, rumors abounded about the patriarch. Once, when he sat in on an Anglican synodical meeting, the report went around that the President of the German Synod had subscribed the Thirty-Nine Articles (1:456). In 1774, when Muhlenberg visited Georgia, "slander deluged me, and it was said that I fled to England and that, since the king had become [Roman] Catholic, I had surely been made his chaplain" (3:102-3, cf. 124; 2:692-93, 697). The impression that "our Germans were papists" was not uncommon (1:418). Subsequent family history includes the fact that William Augustus Muhlenberg (see below) became an Episcopal clergyman.

There has been a major change on the Anglican side since Muhlenberg's day. He had to give attention, in what he called "the High Church," to "apostolic succession" (1:323, the theory that "through deep mud during the dark ages," through the succession "the water had been conveyed through a canal and had remained pure, etc." — a real "pipeline theory"; 3:255-56). But "the historic episcopate" had not yet been articulated as a *sine qua non* for Anglicans and as necessary to have licit clergy and a valid ministry. That came formally only with the Quadrilateral of 1886 and subsequent restatements about the historic episcopate.

The Moravians appeared to Muhlenberg as a particular kind of ecumenical threat (Riforgiato 77-107). The reason that Muhlenberg again and again advances for his opposition is seldom noted. The Lutheran-Moravian ecumenical agreement for full communion, *Following Our Shepherd to Full Communion,* only hints at it (p. 14) and does not really deal with the results of the meeting between Count Zinzendorf and Muhlenberg on December 30, 1742 — probably in Benezet's home on Market Square, Germantown — for the dialogue's narrative breaks off at that point (p. 15; see *Journals* 1:76-79 for Muhlenberg's version; none seems to survive from Zinzendorf, for whom, at the time, Muhlenberg was probably just a minor inconvenience to his plans). H. L. Nelson 143-45 speaks of "an inquisition conducted by the Count." One may ask how much social class played a role in self-understandings of each at that time. The Zinzendorf meeting with Muhlenberg can interestingly be compared with John Wesley's encounter with Zinzendorf on September 3, 1741 and their clash over sanctification (recounted in *The Journal of John Wesley* 2:467 = Forell xvii-xix; Forell is too contemporary with the 1960-70s in calling Zinzendorf a "Jesus freak," p. xxx). In both encounters Zinzendorf was the interrogator.

What Muhlenberg often objected to in Moravianism, in its *Sichtungszeit* or "Sifting Period" (1743-1750), was "the Plan" (or "the *Plans,*" 1:247; the term is not in the index to the *Journals*). Zinzendorf (1700-1760), who had revived the *Unitas Fratrum* of the Hussites from dormancy, envisioned an ecumenical "Congregation of God in the Spirit," an *ecclesia* made up of many *ecclesiolae* or *tropi,* such as Lutheran, Reformed, Anglican, and even Catholic tropes. To achieve this, Herrnhutters or "Moravian brethren

. . . offered their services to pastorless flocks, externally conforming to the dogma and liturgies of their particular denominations, but working all the while to effect an ecumenical union of churches" (Riforgiato 80).

Muhlenberg criticized the fact that the Moravian Brethren "have never come forward sincerely and honestly with a complete confession of faith, as did our fathers in the Augsburg Confession" or Anglicans in the Thirty-Nine Articles. At most "they have occasionally published some writings of their teachers according to how the wind happened to be blowing." The result is "a contradictory give and take . . . which falls short of, or conflicts with, or goes beyond God's Word." So even with some of Zinzendorf's hymns (1:160). This allowed Moravians to pose and feign the type of Christianity where they were trying to gain converts. As Muhlenberg spelled this procedure out (1:159), "When the head, namely, Count Zinzendorf, and his brethren are in Russia, their faith is in exact accord with the articles of the Greek Church. When they are in Catholic lands, they believe and live as the Pope and Councils teach. When they are in Switzerland, they believe and live in accord with the Synod of Bern. When they are in Sweden, they believe in accord with the Augsburg Confession, and when they are in England, they believe and live in exact accord with the Articles of the Episcopal Church." This is the principle of *cujus regio ejus religio* carried to the ultimate, all things to all peoples. Muhlenberg added, "I hate their crooked ways and corrupt methods" (1:159). He complained of "Moravian Jesuits" (*Correspondence* 1, 98).

Moravians, well organized and financed from the Zinzendorf institutions in Bethlehem, were in the 1740s constantly trying to get into and take over Lutheran congregations (*Journals* 1:108). Riforgiato 95 stresses their mobility and "central authority" in Bethlehem for this task. They made the gate of salvation "too wide," Muhlenberg charged (1:219), through a "sweet doctrine of all too universal grace without repentance and faith," providing "a shorter road to the Saviour" (1:242). On their "*intrigue* and snaky crookedness with the authorities in London" and New York, see 1:257, 282. Muhlenberg in 1745 wished for a *responsum* from Halle, the universities like Tübingen, and Sweden on the question, "Do the Moravian Brethren of the present day come so close to us Lutherans in their doctrine and practice that we can unite our ministry . . . ?" Muhlenberg added, ". . . we have reason to believe it cannot be" (1:109). Eventually Muhlenberg got a rescript from the Archbishop and Supreme Consistory of Uppsala that called "the Zinzendorf doctrines . . . utterly false" (1:169).

"The Plan" went so far as to include discipline on whom to marry and when. Muhlenberg sometimes had to deal pastorally with former Zinzendorfers who had been put "under the ban" for going contrary to the Moravian plan (1:182, 184, N. Deyling, Jacob Lischy). On L. T. Nyberg, from Sweden, as really a Moravian (which he denied to Muhlenberg) and the intrigues in Lancaster, see Riforgiato 100-102.

By 1748, however, the Moravian threat had peaked and passed. Zinzendorf never came back to America after the 1742 meeting with Muhlenberg. Riforgiato (102) attributes change also to the Moravians having abandoned "their *tropos* scheme" so they could form themselves into a church. Later (1775) Muhlenberg referred in Georgia to "two newly arrived Moravian missionaries [MS: so called]" as "Lutherans after a fashion" (2:666). Subsequent Moravian historiographers have offered the criticism of Zinzendorf that he was no church organizer, as Muhlenberg proved to be.[11]

Clearly Muhlenberg found affinity with "church people" (Reformed, Presbyterian, Episcopal), but discomfort with unchurchly sects. There is frequent defense of (infant) baptism, against German and English Anabaptists and Quakers (*Journals* 1:86, 134-35; 208-10 on the essence and accidents of baptism; 723-24, sermon; 2:164-66, Wrangel's address on the topic;

---

11. John R. Weinlich, *Count Zinzendorf: The Story of His Life and Leadership in the Renewed Moravian Church* (Nashville: Abingdon, 1956; repr. Bethlehem: The Moravian Church in America, 1984), pp. 165-69, sketches the opposition in Pennsylvania to Zinzendorf's ideas not only by the Lutherans who followed Muhlenberg but also by "the strict Calvinists" and "Separatists." His meeting with Muhlenberg is barely mentioned (p. 168). The impression is given that Zinzendorf stimulated spiritual life among all Christian groups and that "Muhlenberg's coming was in direct response to the challenge raised by Zinzendorf's efforts to organize Lutherans in Pennsylvania" (in December 1741; p. 169). But the United Congregations had been formed as early as 1734 to seek pastors from Germany (Tappert 1975: 30). A. S. Lewis, *Zinzendorf the Ecumenical Pioneer: A Study in Moravian Contributions to Christian Mission and Unity* (Philadelphia: Westminster, 1962) speaks only of "Lutherans" in describing the Seven Synods held under the Count in January-June 1742 and opposition by them and Calvinists and Separatists (pp. 144-48). While the Moravian Church was formally organized in North America October 12-16, 1748, Lewis dates only in 1859 "their independence of the German benevolent despotism" and movement "into an area of denominational development" (p. 148 n. 1). Cf. George Forell's introduction to his translation of Zinzendorf's *Nine Lectures on Important Subjects in Religion* (1746; Iowa City: University of Iowa Press, 1973). The Bibliography in the 1984 reprint of Weinlich lists theses by Mary Elizabeth Forell and Joan Mau on Lutheran-Moravian matters.

2:161-63, should a Presbyterian woman be baptized again by Baptists? Note *"actio passiva"* on our part in baptism [162]; more polemically, 2:499-500 and H. L. Nelson 334-36). A critique of Quakers in 1777 touches on their rejection of "the whole Gospel, Baptism and Holy Communion" as well as political authority (3:75-76). On one occasion, Anna Maria Weiser Muhlenberg, his wife — that "woman of grit" (Lehmann 1998: 62-65) — weighed in against an Anabaptist who called infant baptism "a superficial sprinkling which children know nothing about when they grow up" with the reply, "David knew very well when he was grown up that he had been circumcised in infancy, and . . . that Goliath . . . was uncircumcised" (2:114). Lutherans encountered strange religions which the New World could spawn, like the "Butler sect," founded by Eva von Buttler (1670-1717): in South Carolina Jacob Wäber was regarded as God the Father, Peter Schmidt as the Son, and "a godless colored preacher" named Dauber, the Spirit (2:577-80; the latter two were murdered, for which Wäber was hanged). There was a turbulent group called "The Newborn," who claimed visions and sinlessness (1:149-50, 375-58), and another group calling itself "the *Stillen im Lande*" (1:151). Lutherans were sometimes confused by sects and joined themselves to them (3:420, 571, 572). Sometimes they resisted the fanatics, among whom what Luther called "the black devil and the white devil have been having their sway" (3:543). Muhlenberg included Schwenkfelders as seducers into error (3:563) and makes reference to Swedenborg's works, then appearing in English, as contrary to the Formula of Concord (3:719).

American Lutherans have continued as church people to seek fellowship with mainline churches and subsequently Roman Catholics, a contact impossible in and long beyond Muhlenberg's day (only occasional conversions are mentioned by Muhlenberg, e.g., 3:140, 693; but the Roman Catholic priest in Lancaster was to be one of the trustees of Franklin College in that city, 3:725). An extreme example of the sectarian perversions involved an English woman from Rhode Island who in 1787 was "giving herself out to be Jesus of Nazareth," accompanied by two "apes of Satan" claiming to be the two witnesses of Revelation 11:3 (3:736-37); they set up shop for a time at a Schwenkfelder home in Skippack. H. L. Nelson 349 sees "Muhlenberg's basic ecumenical principle" toward these churches as "hospitality," but it did not include "intercommunion." Subsequent Lutherans have, like Muhlenberg, expressed similar bewilderment over, and avoided, sect groups.

Some Ministerium Characteristics

We turn finally to some observations about the Ministerium in Muhlenberg's day, characteristics that continue to some degree or another to the present.

1. *Poverty* and hence *poor support for the church,* locally and beyond. In 1747 Muhlenberg lamented (1:142) that Quakers, Mennonites, and others had come "in the earlier, good times when land was still very cheap." He went on, "Our German Evangelical settlers in Pennsylvania are, for the most part, the most recent immigrants to this province." The rich land had been snatched up. Lutherans could not afford it. Many "had to be slaves for several years to repay their passage" and then struggle on poorer land. After a few years many moved on to opportunities further west or in Maryland and Virginia (1:141-42). By 1784 Muhlenberg was advising Europeans, "Stay in your own country, and get along somehow" (3:581), for even those of some intellectual gifts, like teachers, could not find adequate work (3:616, 630).

Complaints about congregational debts and lack of church endowment dot the pages of the *Journals* (e.g., 1:116). From one struggling church after another, committees came asking for contributions from Muhlenberg, the Ministerium, and the somewhat established congregations (e.g., 3:688). As Mark 14:7 says, "You always have the poor with you," *pauper ubique est* (2:160, 248; 3:229, "There is want everywhere"). There were subscription lists, but people didn't always pay (1:292). The Muhlenbergs often found his salary spent almost as soon as it was received (2:168). Mrs. Muhlenberg's inheritance supplemented his income for three years (1:518; cf. 2:713, her "widow's mite" was used toward the house in Trappe, over 1000 pounds, according to 3:673), but on occasion they had to ask for an advance (1:718) or borrow money to pay bills (1:117, 448, 517, 579, 708; 2:1, 34, 241). In the *ecclesia colligenda,* where the United Ministerium had undertaken to minister to "the poor, the forsaken, and scattered sheep," perhaps one needed itinerant pastors with no *salaria fixa,* like those engaged in mission to the Jews in Europe (2:390-91). On another occasion in 1780 he considered what amounts to "worker priests," preachers who carried on "an honorable trade on the side" (3:369). Pastor Carl Solomon Fri[e]derici had such large debts that friends feared he would be imprisoned (2:451, 455, 547; 3:228-29). Muhlenberg complained in 1762, "I am expected to minister and run to the assistance of our poor churches everywhere, and to do this at my own expense, although I can hardly raise enough money to supply my needs and those of my poor children" (1:501). The Ministerium did not elect a treasurer till 1804, though it earlier had a limited treasury (e.g., 2:703). Was it merely *captatio benevolentiae* when an appeal to the authorities in Philadelphia about buying land for a new burial ground in 1775 spoke of our "Mites of Penury" and how as German Lutherans "we were too bashful and shy to importune our Munificent Patriots"? (2:708). Shades of Lake Woebegone, which in some ways suggests early Pennsylvania German Lutheranism in Norwegian guise!

Marianne Wokeck counts the poverty of the congregations among the impediments to Muhlenberg's fulfilling of his mission (86, 88-89, 92-93). Once Germans were successful in business, they often "joined the meetinghouses and churches of their Quaker and Anglican partners in efforts to further their . . . careers" (93). Attending a Lutheran church often meant "no fancy church buildings, bells, organs and music that might draw Lutherans in Europe" (95). Being Lutheran might draw opprobrium from Quakers and the sects because they had to pay their pastors. Poverty had its consequences. Lutherans said, "We're too poor to do this or that." Union churches sometimes ingrained a notion of needing to give only every other week, for just half the cost of shared buildings and a pastor shared with other congregations. Such an attitude long marked much of Pennsylvania Lutheranism. G. Elson Ruff is said to have called Berks County, in terms of financial giving, "the Death Valley, statistically, of the ULCA."

2. This poverty helps explain why *hopes for institutions* like an orphans' home (1:121), residence for retired pastors and wives of pastors (2:550), and a seminary (2:627-28) were *slow in being realized*. H. L. Nelson heads one section in his treatment on Muhlenberg, "Many of His Visions Were Unfulfilled" (91-92). Muhlenberg thought highly of Presbyterian endeavors such as William Tennent's "Log College" in Neshaminy (2:295) and more important Princeton. In 1765 he wrote that the Presbyterian Church "is growing so rapidly among the English in America that in a few years it will spread and surpass the Episcopal and all the rest. This *progress* is due to the fact that they have established seminaries in various places, educate their ministers, keep strict discipline, and tolerate no ministers except those who have good moral character and the ability to speak, and who are content with small salaries and able to endure hard work" (2:181 — what church leader would not covet presbyters like that? cf. 1:631, 689; 2:295, 576). And of course they could fund such enterprises. Muhlenberg's own "unprejudiced doubts about the proposal of a free school" (*Hochschule* or

seminarium in Philadelphia) is a model of realistic caution, to count the cost before trying to build a tower (Luke 14:28; 2:527-29). In 1785 he lamented the lack of means and of "suitable men" for schools such as the "Episcopal and Presbyterian church bodies" have (3:687).

At times Muhlenberg wished for a church tax and government support for church institutions, as in Germany, but realized that, if instituted under British rule, it would benefit Anglicans primarily (2:192, 367, 374, dissenters had to contribute to the support of the established church in Virginia; 2:605-6; 3:125, a desire to introduce the tithe; 3:202). Besides, it was said (3:660) a poll tax for clergy salaries would "make laborers in the kingdom lazy and slothful"; Muhlenberg agreed. He was disappointed that Quaker Pennsylvania provided no support for churches and that the new, emerging United States did not provide funds for religion (2:740-43; Maryland considered it in 1785, 3:660). Lotteries were occasionally used (2:469; cf. 1:429, 466, 562; 2:232; Bible verses were originally chosen in the Herrnhut *Losungen* by lot, 1:481, cf. 399; 3:1, 77), but he realized that freewill giving was needed (2:143). Yet with pledges it was "easier to secure promises than payments" (2:494, cf. 500). Hopes for contributions in the collection purses by Anglican guests at Zion, Philadelphia, caused misunderstanding (2:412) and Muhlenberg's ironic comment that "English people have such tender sensibilities that they have conscientious scruples about handling money during divine service" and "are unwilling to soil their fingers with money" (2:442). At Pikestown Muhlenberg scotched an Anglican-Lutheran accord because of fears that contributions to a new building from neighbors (at St. David's Episcopal Church, Radnor) would give them "a right and share in the church even if they contributed only 20 s." (2:695).

3. Besides poverty, which arrested church development, we may also suggest inferiority in *social class* and a sense of being *cultural outsiders* as a mark that all too often and for too long has characterized the sons and daughters of the Ministerium. Societal structures, their own circumstances, and often a lack of educational opportunities readily caused them to look to others as their "betters" and to avoid the arenas of the upper classes and culture. A "Dutch countryman up in New York" wanted his son baptized "Hans," not "Johannes," because, as he put it, "I don't want to make a *gentleman* out of him. I'm raising him for the plow and the farm" (2:669). The country life was rough for refined people (3:559).

An example of how Muhlenberg felt, even after he had been in America for thirty-two years, is the way he responded when William

Tennent invited him to preach in a large Presbyterian congregation "composed of [MS: the most] influential citizens." He said no. Next week? Only at the afternoon service? "I declined, pleading my illness and hoarseness and that I was not capable of preaching in English to a congregation with such a refined and delicate taste, that they would be offended by my harsh pronunciation and I would only become a byword, etc." (2:570). He did so, however, on September 25, 1774, but the results were not ideal, in part because "the darkness at the pulpit . . . prevented me from seeing my outline notes clearly" (2:571). On another occasion there is reference to his difficulty in visiting those in big houses (2:101); Provost Wrangel could, but Muhlenberg did not expect "to find our Saviour, the sinner's Friend, in such a stately house."

How upward mobility led Lutherans into other churches with more status has already been noted. Often, too, attaining new cultural levels led them to leave the churches of Germans whom Benjamin Franklin characterized as "Palatine Boors" (cited in Riforgiato 185; German *Bauern?* H. L. Nelson 170-71 cites *The Papers of Benjamin Franklin,* ed. W. Labaree et al., vol. 4 [New Haven: Yale, 1951], 483). Muhlenberg himself once said of the immigrants, "Whoever was not accepted in Europe found a place here" (Wokeck 91, citing *Korrespondenz* 1:101; see also 1:353, 455; her use of the letters illustrates many aspects of the nature of the immigrants; apparently Muhlenberg's "remarks concerning German emigrants to America" drew criticism in Göttingen, 3:586). For all of this, Henry Melchior Muhlenberg committed the Ministerium and its churches to the English language; as H. L. Nelson shows, language was "a Medium [for the mission of winning believers], not the Message" (161-69), and Muhlenberg even tried to persuade the Consistory in Sweden to ease up on the instructions for its Mission "to preserve the Swedish language" (see Suhr 1940: 82).

Muhlenberg's own sons illustrate the ability of immigrants in the second generation to go far in scholarship, politics, and society. But John Peter Gabriel did not remain in the ministry (nor did Frederick Augustus Conrad, though Gotthilf Henry Ernst did, at Lancaster). By the next generation Frederick Conrad Augustus's son, Henry William Muhlenberg (1772-1805), had prospered as a wine merchant, and his son, William Augustus (1796-1877), no longer speaking German, grew up with his mother's people, in the Episcopal Church, attending Quaker schools, Philadelphia Academy, and the grammar school and college of the University of Pennsylvania. He continued the family involvement in ministry, studying under Episcopal clergymen, before beginning a distinguished career in the Episcopal

Church, as rector of the Church of the Holy Communion, New York City. He was also a journalist for a paper called *The Evangelical Catholic* (which lasted from 1851 to 1853). In 1853 W. A. Muhlenberg introduced a memorial to the House of Bishops for the Episcopal Church "[t]o become a central bond of union among Christians," in part by extending ordination to potential pastors from other church backgrounds without their surrendering "all the liberty in public worship to which they have been accustomed" (Skardon 215-16). This proposal for a broader "ecclesiastical system" with what were termed "Sunday Presbyters" had no immediate results (235-36), though it is cited in preamble to the 1886 Quadrilateral (*Quadrilateral at One Hundred,* ed. J. R. Wright [Cincinnati: Forward Movement Publications, 1988], 11). At the restoration of Augustus Church, Trappe (for which W. A. Muhlenberg and his sister provided the funds), he was invited to preach. On this occasion he proposed rapprochement by reviving an order of "evangelists," a "preacherhood" not dependent on apostolic succession (234). An institutional bent is to be seen in his creation of the "Society of St. Johnland," on Long Island, as "the church's answer to Socialism" (246-56). H. E. Jacobs, in "A Commonplace Lutheran," *Lutheran Church Review* 21 (1890): 117-29, argued that many of W. A. Muhlenberg's ideas came from Lutheran sources. While "historians of the Episcopal Church" have "generally accepted" this view, Skardon (262-63) finds little of Lutheran origins, though there were parallels in the Lutheran Church. In any case, to rise to new cultural levels was for people of Lutheran background a not uncommon experience — but often outside the Lutheran Church.

Subsequently the lack of involvement by Lutherans in political life and leadership has often been lamented. Norman A. Graebner, in the bicentennial essays edited by Groh and Smith (1979), speaks of "paranoia" among Lutherans, Germans especially, "toward American political and social life" (12). Lutherans proved to be "less active politically" than most denominations, with John Peter Gabriel and Frederick Augustus Muhlenberg the major exceptions (so J. W. Albers, "Review Essay" on the volume, in *The Cresset* 44 [1981]: 35). The same volume also deplores the absence of Lutherans in the top ranks of scientists or Nobel Prize winners (Bruce Wrightsman [84], citing only Norman Borlaug as an example). The picture for U.S. Lutherans in science, society, and U.S. politics is not bright, for Eastern Lutheranism or generally. Often reasons are sought in doctrine (the "Two Kingdoms" teaching was not understood, and so Lutherans were not inclined toward political involvement). But should we perhaps look more to sociological and cultural factors for explanations?

4. But what of *theology?* John Kleiner objects that "Professor Wokeck's rather negative portrayal of Muhlenberg and his attitude toward the German Lutheran immigrants is due to an insufficient appreciation of his theology" (109); he then cites Muhlenberg's optimistic view of the eighteenth century as "a remarkable time" when the gospel is spreading and "the cause of good is advancing" (*Correspondence* 1:312, Letter #60 to his patroness, Baroness Wilhelmina Sophie von Münchhausen, 20 February 1747; see further, Kleiner 1990). Lutherans generally, and the Ministerium heritage in particular, have, not without some warrant, taken pride in their theology — confessionally, biblically, and practically applied.

Muhlenberg himself as a theologian has been variously assessed. Oddly enough, Lutherans like E. P. Pfatteicher (*Journals* 1:v), Tappert and Doberstein (*Journals* 1:xvii), and A. R. Wentz "tend to discount his prowess," but non-Lutherans like Robert T. Handy (*A Recent History of the Churches in the United States* [Oxford: Clarendon, 1976], 98) and Riforgiato rate him more highly (more references in H. L. Nelson 270-71). Riforgiato stresses his theology (135-57) to counter the common view of Muhlenberg as "a pragmatic, opportunistic organizer" (11), though he also recognizes him as "the Compleat Politician," in the church, if not in civic politics. H. L. Nelson, who views Muhlenberg primarily as one who sought to save souls, not just organize churches, has also given us a picture of his theology, both as objective, Trinitarian, christological doctrine (*fides quae creditur*, 282-349), and as subjective response (*fides qua creditur*, 349-62). One suspects that the pendulum will in time swing again to reflect current nontheological moods in the churches.

My own reading is that Muhlenberg had decent theological training in the Germany of his day and constantly used aspects of it in his missionary work. He is confessional, pietistic in the later Halle style, and at times reflects a place for reason. The *Glaubens-Lied,* twelve stanzas that he put into English poetic doggerel for a sixteen-year-old girl "who desired to take the Lord's Supper with us, but did not know the German language," may be the most interesting piece from Muhlenberg. It sets forth the *Ordo Salutis* — one stanza on God and providence; one on Adam's "turn" to wrath and death; three on Christ; two on the Spirit, two contrasting children of the Spirit and those who reject the Spirit, plus the last three admonishing us to rely on God, Christ, the Spirit, and means of Grace (1747; *Journals* 1:146; in manuscript vol. PM 95 Z4, pp. 201-4, cf. 200 for other versions of verse six; H. L. Nelson 279-80; see *Journals* 3:428-29 on its genesis and revision by Kuntze). To illustrate, stanza 8 runs thus:

They that by Him in truth and fact
repentance, faith and love do act
are children of the Spirit born
cannot be damned or be forlorn.

In Muhlenberg's own theological expression, particular emphasis was placed on the doctrine of Providence (also the place from which many of his letters were written, cf. 3:587), the covenant(s), especially of grace (3:77), and later in his life apocalyptic millennialism. On "the prominence of the covenant," stressed by Roeber, see also H. L. Nelson 313-20. Amid the events on the eve of the American Revolution the mood was widespread, especially among sectarians, that "the millenium [sic] is now at hand and that they will reign completely," 2:699. But exegetes in Germany, like J. A. Bengel, struck the note that the second beast and third woe in the Book of Revelation were "imminent," 3:406, 410; cf. 3:420 on the "fierce heat" of Revelation 16:9; 548, 567, 722; 749 Bengel and C. A. Crusius (1787) suggest "changes" in nature and church to come in 1788 or 1836. Muhlenberg thus reflects at times, from his Scripture studies, the outlook of the books of Daniel and Revelation as part of his biblically oriented thought as well as from the American environment.

Muhlenberg's Ministerium set certain standards for pastors theologically. But in the ups-and-downs of subsequent centuries the level of achievement, in synod life, college, or seminary, seldom matched that of the mother churches in Europe. The Ministerium has produced theologians, but concern for theology has often been more apparent than actual accomplishment in the overall theological scene.

Summing Up

As we celebrate 250 years of heritage, it would be contrary to the nature of Lutheranism and to Muhlenberg's often-gloomy realism to wax triumphalistic. Our situation has seldom been all-glorious. Muhlenberg once explained why he had to take on the care of more than the three original United Congregations, by comparing "our church in Pennsylvania with the man who fell among thieves" (1:624). We've been at times half dead, congregations battered by self-styled pastor imposters. There have been neighbors who needed help. In 1763 he wrote, "Things are going very much the way they did before the destruction of Jerusalem, as the old adversary is perpetuating his *diaballein* [slanders], and the Judgment may well be near at hand" (1:652; 3:727, of the inner and outer temple). Problems with fly-by-night ministers and counter-synods did not cease with formation of the Ministerium; e.g., the "addled vagabond" Götz, or John George Butler's "synod" at Carlisle, 3:699-703; Hörner at Falckner's Swamp, "ordained" by an English general in Canada, 3:741-42. The planting of the church goes on — and on, and on, with ups and downs.

We mark, then, (1) *Muhlenberg and the Ministerium,* but *much more,* the efforts of many, on whose shoulders we stand, but not triumphalistically.

(2) It goes, almost without saying, that Muhlenberg's perpetual concern was to proclaim the Word of God. The Evangelical, gospel-centered nature of his ministry and life is readily apparent. H. L. Nelson stresses "the primacy of soul-saving" so as to relegate emphasis on the church. He describes Muhlenberg in his summary "as a man who sought to save and edify (especially German) souls by providing what he took to be the divinely established means of word and sacrament in the American wilderness" (396). But this gives too little attention to Muhlenberg's concern for what we might call "the whole person" and not just "souls" (recall his efforts at medical treatment of people, in the Halle tradition);[12] his proclaiming of law as well as salvation (unless that be taken as part of "edification"), and too little reflection of the ministry and the church as locus for word and sacraments. It is simply fact that Muhlenberg was not primarily a pioneer evangelist but more a gatherer of people in existing congregations and an organizer of Lutheranism that went beyond the local assemblies.

These efforts produced a *church, supra-congregational, extra-congregational.* It is still not only growing, with new plantings, but also being joined together anew in unity, within the synods and with other Christians, amid the cultures of America. There was already a cultural pluralism in Muhlenberg's day, all sorts of frontiers to cross, cultures that Lutherans at times could embrace and at times wisely opposed. The relationships between Christ and culture are many. "Church and culture" is a never-ending task of discernment and at times of battle. Cultural Protestantism is not our model. The art of practical theology may involve when to affirm and what to oppose in our surroundings.

(3) The Ministerium heritage has often shown *openness to new needs and emphases,* particularly in *urban* areas where new waves of immigrants

---

12. Cf. John N. Ritter, "Muhlenberg's Anticipation of Psychosomatic Medicine," *Lutheran Church Quarterly* 19 (1946): 181-88.

came. Philadelphia in Muhlenberg's day was the third largest city in the British Empire, ranking only after London and Calcutta. Of all U.S. cities, it is probably the one with the greatest percentage of Lutherans throughout its history, though more recently Lutherans have tended to leave the cities and not be replaced with immigrants from Lutheran lands or by converts, so that few large cities have kept up their Lutheran population. *Social ministry* programs have been a feature of this sort of Lutheranism. These were often begun by groups of people who belonged to Lutheran congregations, but the society they created to do the work was not formally part of synod structures. The pattern has been for the church to become more institutional but at times to spin off programs and even institutions to the civic realm for government to carry through.

(4) Ministerium Lutheranism, for all of Muhlenberg's *confessional* emphasis, became less confessional after his death. Muhlenberg spoke after the Revolution of people wishing to be "*independent* from God and his revealed word and will" (3:707; the "reformation" going on in other American churches is described; e.g., Massachusetts Episcopalians dropped the term "Trinity" and the Nicene Creed; faith became "rational"). All this was the work of the Antichrist (3:720). But the confessional revival in Germany beginning in 1817, with the 300th anniversary of Luther's posting of the Ninety-Five Theses, found particular resonance in the Ministerium. Here was an example of openness to a new trend, not at the moment dominant in American Lutheranism. One reflection of this confessional revival was, at last in 1864, the founding of a seminary in Philadelphia. The synod's heritage kept the Ministerium from abandoning the Confessions or from going overboard into hyperconfessionalism.

(5) Ditto for *liturgy* that is historically Lutheran. At the 1748 meeting of the Ministerium an Agenda with an order for worship was adopted as a unifying factor (Oldenburg 61). The Constitution of 1779 required each minister to use the "Liturgy which has been introduced" (*Documentary History,* 175; so also in the model constitution for congregations in 1762). In a way perhaps strange to contemporary liturgical variety, where congregations have been encouraged to have different worship styles, the early Ministerium believed, indeed prescribed, discernibly uniform worship. H. L. Nelson (380 n. 3) thought this "remarkable since the Augsburg Confession Article 7 allowed freedom in these matters," but is it not simply an attempt, as in any territorial or national European church of Muhlenberg's day, to have an agreed liturgy? This was the more necessary in the face of the variety, indeed the chaos, of the New World. The Ministerium and its

seminary, especially in the latter part of the nineteenth and early twentieth century, reflected the liturgical renewal in Germany, along with confessional revival (Marshall 94-95). Its heritage has kept it, often, from treating liturgics cavalierly or as a new toy that becomes the center of the universe. By now the principle of sound confessionalism and sound liturgy has been become a commonplace for Lutherans generally.

Much the same thing can be said of *hymnody*. Lutherans, like the German Reformed and Moravians, sang their faith. Mark Oldenburg (68-69) has detailed almost 250 hymns mentioned in Muhlenberg's *Journals* (note 3:147-48 on Kuntze's publication in 1778; cf. 3:448, 524-25). The Hymnal of 1786 came into existence late in Muhlenberg's life (Oldenburg 70-76). Commitment to the use also of English led to hymnals by Lutherans in English as early as 1795 (H. George Anderson 1975: 89).

We do not always realize how singular was what we take for granted. Presbyterians of the time sang mainly metrical psalms, like those by Tate and Brady. The Reformation in the Church of England "produced no great hymns" (Skardon 31). In 1778 Muhlenberg recorded an observation that "singing was hardly tolerable any more among the English people because it is so little practiced among them . . ." (3:143); contrast the emphasis by Helmuth on a "Singing School" (3:719-20), and the "Uranian Society" (3:737). Episcopal Bishop William White in Philadelphia "never permitted hymns to be sung in the United Parish [Christ Church, St. Peter's, and St. James] except at Christmas and Easter, and then only one or two" (Skardon 33). The American Book of Common Prayer in 1790 included only twenty-seven hymns. It was William Augustus Muhlenberg who led a fight against Bishop White's position and produced *The Hymnal of 1827* (or 1828, p. 37), with the argument against use of psalms only: "Are we always to be Jews?" (34). Eastern Lutheranism long has lived the expression of its faith through songs, right down to a new hymn commissioned for this Symposium.

(6) Along with its deep roots and long history, a certain *balance, breadth, and catholicity* can be said to characterize Eastern and other Lutheranisms related to the Ministerium. Along with all the familiar references in Muhlenberg's writings to the Evangelical, i.e., gospel-centered, church, he also kept a "catholic" heritage in view. In 1763, for example, he wrote, "We indulge in a great deal of talk about universal love and brotherly love and of the great necessity of harmony between preachers, but when the mind of Christ, self-denial, and the *catholique spirit* is lacking and, each one looking out only for his own skin, how can there be any real

harmony?" (1:679). The Reformed minister at New Hanover, Nicholas Pomp, preached in a manner, Muhlenberg said of a Whitmonday sermon, that was "apostolically catholic and convincing, pleasant, and edifying with respect to dogmatics and exegesis" (2:697), and he went on to refer to "an affectionate harmony among the German Protestants in this and other places."

Riforgiato is not wrong to use *"moderation"* to describe Muhlenberg the missionary. But while outspoken on some matters, Ministerium Lutheranism has often *lacked* the fire of *exuberance*. Perhaps that is the result of being the next thing to a *Volkskirche*, a "people's church."

(7) This anniversary points us finally and unabashedly again to *the church*. Shaping up *the local assembly*, as with the Constitution for St. Michael's, Philadelphia, in 1762, which some feel was one of Muhlenberg's great contributions to posterity,[13] and *the extra-congregational church* — these were the areas of Muhlenberg's achievement. Churchly confessions, churchly piety, churchly liturgy, ecclesial ministry of pastors.

As the second Christian millennium draws to a close and a new one beckons, it is the doctrine of the church that is in the forefront of Faith and Order discussions and a new round (XI) of Lutheran-Roman Catholic dialogue, in terms of "koinonia ecclesiology." Muhlenberg reminds us of a heritage richer than we have often suspected: a visible church, not ultimate but vital in setting forth the Word of God (1:118-19). "The high and mighty look upon our Evangelical Church as a dead and discarded lion near the vineyards of Timnath," Muhlenberg wrote in an elaborate metaphor based on Judges 14 and Samson's riddle (1:353; 3:54 alludes to the same passage): "as long as they pass by without investigating the matter, it remains a riddle to them. But there are still some among the masses who find pleasure on the path upon which those whom the world reviles as fools do not go astray, and on this path they find meat coming forth out of the eater and sweetness out of the strong."

In this Symposium I may be the only speaker born and bred in the old Ministerium of Pennsylvania and Adjacent States, likely one of the few here with its name on my ordination certificate. Yet I am part of a stream

---

13. Cf. Beale M. Schmucker, "The Organization of the Congregation in the Early Lutheran Churches of America," *Lutheran Church Review* 6 (1887): 188-226; Mann 370-71 on the constitution as a crowning glory; Tappert 1975: 55-56; *Journals* 1:561-64; H. L. Nelson 209-21, who notes the involvement of both men and women in the vote of confidence (212; *Journals* 1:561) and the balance among preachers, elders, and members (1:545).

of people who came later into the Ministerium, people the Synod welcomed, people who in turn enriched it. That is as it should be. Not everyone honoring the Muhlenberg and Ministerium heritage need be from Philadelphia or Berks County. For the Ministerium has long had an ability to reach out and embrace others and find agreement from others with regard to what it has stood for in its long history.

My testimony is that I have found strength and security for theology and witness in this synod. No frantic searching for a "real church" outside Lutheranism. *Ecclesia plantanda* is precisely a church of God being planted in our midst, as a vehicle of and response to the word of God. In honoring our past, we join with many others, in a vision for an Evangelical Lutheran Church of North America, within the world mission scene, a vision of the word still being sown and a believing community planted and united extra-congregationally.

Responses to "Muhlenberg's Ministry and Ministerium"

The three responses to the Plenary Address by John Reumann came from Lutheran historian-theologians from different parts of the country, each teaching at an ELCA college or seminary. The common thread was looking ahead, extending the Muhlenberg/Ministerium or Eastern Lutheran heritage over the decades to and beyond the present day. Each lifts up aspects of the work of Henry Melchior Muhlenberg but moves into new areas of life today, as he or she saw fit. The responses precipitated further discussion, formally and informally at the Muhlenberg College event, as they may also now in printed form.

Carrying on the Muhlenberg Tradition and Mission

Darrell Jodock

Professor Reumann's solid introduction to Henry Melchior Muhlenberg has provided an excellent foundation upon which to build, as we seek ways to "carry on the Muhlenberg Tradition and Mission."

The task of respondents is to explore the connections between Muhlenberg's work and church life today. The goal will be to *extend* what the presentation has started — to draw out some aspects that we think apply today, with each respondent to pick up on different themes suggested by Muhlenberg's life.

Introduction

Before identifying three main points, allow me to describe one image I have of H. M. Muhlenberg. I never have been a fan of *Mad Magazine*, but my younger brother used to like it. I remember lots of cartoons in the issues of that magazine in which something would be going on in the foreground (say, two people talking) while all sorts of chaos would fill the background — none of which had anything directly to do with what was occurring in the foreground. My image of Muhlenberg is of a person with a pretty clear sense of what he is doing and where he is going, working his way through a chaotic time. In the background, all sorts of things are going on.

- Political battles are raging in Pennsylvania.
- Wars are being fought; the French and Indian Wars directly affected German immigrants to the west, near Shippensburg, Pennsylvania; later the American Revolution affected those to the east as well.

- Socially, there is a lot of mobility. In 1747, Muhlenberg laments that in the previous five years over half of the immigrants in his congregations have already moved on — some to "eternity," but most to "distant parts" (*Journals* 1:142).
- Socially, what is happening in one part of the colony has little to do with what is happening in another.
- Some individuals have little contact with anyone. Others form groups that try to give some sense and order to their little corner of this chaotic society.
- People have come from Europe and are bewildered by the new terrain, the new laws, the new language, the diversity of their neighbors, and the unfamiliar situation of the church.

It is a time of *social dislocation*. Somehow Muhlenberg has to bring order to the church life of German immigrants, but it cannot be the same order that prevailed in Germany. He can rely on none of the structures and institutions that were in place there. He has to adapt and adapt and adapt, but to adapt in such a way that his Lutheran identity and his Christian faith are not lost.

Many differences separate our day from his, but one striking similarity will undergird virtually everything we say. *Ours* is also a time of *social dislocation*. Today's dislocation, however, is not caused by people moving from one country to another. It is happening because of drastic changes within our own society. These changes are so great that many of us who have grown up here often no longer feel at home. Thus, the church of today often faces conditions more similar to Muhlenberg's setting than to conditions during the 250-year interim. Whatever the case during the interim, we now face a new round of *social dislocation*.

Community

Of the three interlocking themes I would like to address, the first is *community*. When the German immigrants came to Pennsylvania, they did not settle into villages (where they had lived in Germany) but scattered throughout the countryside. Houses would be built in clearings in the woods. Muhlenberg's *Journals* offer report after report of families traveling many miles to attend a service or of others unable to make the long trip. Yes, they traveled such long distances because of their need for spiritual renewal, but they also sought contact with other human beings. The church was a *community* of believers — a place where individuals could find support, encouragement, and solace.

Muhlenberg recognized the importance of gathering people, of organizing congregations, and of convening that yet broader association of clergy and congregations known as a synod. He knew full well that communities need some sort of structure, and he knew — or very quickly discovered! — that they can be hard to hold together. Factions and disputes were as common in his dealings with congregations as were muddy roads on his journeys!

Between Muhlenberg's day and our own, fairly stable neighborhoods formed. And the church functioned as a thread woven throughout the fabric of those neighborhoods. Today, however, those seemingly stable local communities — whether urban or rural — have begun to unravel.

- For one hundred years economic enticements have beckoned wave after wave of young people from rural communities to urban centers.
- For fifty years, people with enough affluence have sought to escape their old urban neighborhoods. They have moved out, and then moved out again.
- Not only have they attempted to get away from the problems of the city, they have followed new career and job opportunities from one metropolitan area to another.
- And all of this has been reinforced by an outlook that incorrectly regards freedom as being unencumbered by ties with others and establishes as priority #1 looking out for my own career, my own needs, and my own individual happiness.

Our communities have unraveled because we have not paid enough attention to them.

Part of the ongoing mission of the church is to gather isolated individuals into communities of faith. The task was difficult in Muhlenberg's day. He had to ride day after day throughout eastern Pennsylvania, central New Jersey, and northern Maryland. The task has new difficulties today — because a myriad of distractions camouflage, from people themselves, their need for community. As they sit in front of a television set, a video game, or a computer, they do not recognize their own isolation.

Not only have stable neighborhoods been undermined, but, for reasons I do not really understand, Americans have also been withdrawing from "secondary communities" — that is, from those groups that regularly bring them together for face-to-face contact. To illustrate, let me turn to an article by Robert Putnam, in 1995, titled "Bowling Alone: America's Declining Social Capital."[1] The first part of that title comes from Putnam's observation that between 1980 and 1993 the number of people who bowled increased by 10 percent, while the total of those participating in bowling leagues went down by 40 percent. In other words, more people were bowling but more were "bowling alone." Because a bowling league brings people together face-to-face on a regular basis, it is one example of a secondary community. And, lest one think that bowling is a trivial example, he points out that 80 million people bowl each year — one-third more than voted in the 1994 congressional elections and about as many as say they attend a worship service in any given week.

This still leaves the question: Is the trend toward "bowling alone" indicative of anything? Putnam did some digging. His discoveries:

- Participation in church activities: down, according to his estimates, by about one-sixth.
- Membership in the PTA: down from 12 million in 1964 to 7 million in 1994.
- League of Women Voters: down 42 percent since 1969.
- Boy Scouts: down 26 percent since 1970.
- Red Cross: down 61 percent since 1970.
- Lions, Elks, and similar organizations: all down.
- Membership in labor unions: down from 32.5 percent in 1953 to 15.8 percent in 1992.
- People who have attended any meeting dealing with community or schools in the last year: down one-third between 1973 and 1993.

The pattern is clear. And the pattern makes him worried, because participation in secondary communities accomplishes two important things: it builds trust and helps people sort out their response to contemporary events, especially crisis situations. Nonparticipation in secondary communities undermines trust, and in the article he cites studies that document

---

1. Robert D. Putnam, "Bowling Alone: America's Declining Social Capital," *Journal of Democracy* 6 (1995): 65-78; see further, Putnam's *Bowling Alone: The Collapse and Revival of American Community* (New York: Simon & Schuster, 2000).

precisely that decline. The result is diminished "social capital," or an impoverished reserve of social cohesion and established social contacts with which to tackle the problems facing the community.

One purpose of a church is to serve the larger society. So, besides gathering people into communities of faith, churches have another task: to help form other secondary communities. We need to think of ways to get people in our neighborhoods to meet each other and develop trust — and then also to help people from different neighborhoods do the same. In a local neighborhood, block parties may be one way to start, community festivals may be another, neighborhood watch programs yet another. Such activities may not bring new members into the church, but they will improve the health of the society in which we live. They will reduce isolation and suspicion — and in so doing reduce one cause of violence.

Morality

The first theme was community. The second I would like to address is *morality*. A reader is almost startled to observe how often Muhlenberg records a confrontation with a contemporary over his/her behavior. Perhaps, as Professor Reumann says, Muhlenberg was sometimes priggish or pharisaical, but, as Reumann also suggests, this was not the whole story. At the center of his ministry were grace, faith, forgiveness, repentance; yet, alongside this core, a concern for appropriate behavior was never absent. He must have been very interested in encouraging believers to exhibit a pattern of behavior consistent with their Christianity.

If we turn our attention to today, my growing conviction is that in our society the church can live with integrity only if we give more attention to behavior. The kind of attention that I have in mind is best illustrated by the Amish. They have endeavored to find a community-oriented, family-oriented, simple way of living that is coherent at every point with their Christian faith, that is *in* this world but not *of* it. It is striking to meet a young Amish widow with several young children who continues to be supported entirely by the community. What we non-Amish need to take seriously are the reasons they prohibit television sets, telephones in their homes, electric power lines, automobiles, and video games, the reasons they run their own schools, the reasons they use horses and buggies, the reasons they worship in their homes — namely to keep the community together, to keep families together, and to seek greater coherence between their faith and their daily life.[2]

The contemporary church must give greater attention to Christian behavior, because deep down most people know that the patterns our society endorses are not working. Children are being abused or neglected, children are shooting at each other, stress is destroying our health, and our way of life is devastating the environment. The only way the church can witness to the silent disillusionment most people feel is candidly to admit that things are not working and to profess and practice an alternative — a life of fidelity and integrity, of stewardship for the earth and responsibility for others in community, a life with a rhythm that includes time for celebration, a life that resists consumerism and careerism and the reigning attitude of entitlement.

As heirs of Muhlenberg, I believe we can do this without falling into moral*ism* and without getting hung up on the politically charged issues that can easily distract us from the more basic ones.

My second observation, therefore, is that planting the church in our day includes planting the seeds of Christian behavior as well as encouraging community formation.

Adaptability

The third theme I want to discuss is *flexibility* or *adaptability* — that is, a readiness to change without abandoning the basic identity of the community of faith.

Think again for a moment of the many changes Muhlenberg faced:

- People here were scattered.
- Governmental support for churches was missing. Here they had to finance themselves.
- There were no church authorities to whom to refer disputes. Another way had to be found to settle them.
- There were few if any schools, orphanages, or social service agencies.
- There were no sources of clergy in the colonies.

2. One source of reliable information about the Amish, especially those who live in Pennsylvania, is Donald Kraybill, *The Riddle of Amish Culture* (Baltimore: Johns Hopkins University Press, 1989).

- Lutherans here had to compete for loyalty with all sorts of unfamiliar religious groups. They were no longer the dominant denomination in a specific province.

Muhlenberg had to find ways to adapt and create patterns of church life that fit the new circumstances in which Lutherans were now living. Some things could be borrowed from the new surroundings. Others needed to be rejected. Likewise, some things could be borrowed from Germany; others not. The decisions all needed to be made with care.

In only two of the colonies did the government seek to keep out of religion: Rhode Island and Pennsylvania. If Christendom is that societal arrangement that grants Christianity a privileged place, colonial Pennsylvania was already to some extent a post-Christendom society. Ours is even more so:

- There is little cultural support for the church. The image of the church held by contemporary culture as a whole is authoritarian and imperialistic, and thus its value is easily dismissed.
- In most communities the church has been marginalized; it is no longer at the center of the community but on the periphery.
- In Christendom most people growing up used to have some contact with a church. From attending funerals and marriages, at least, they gained some idea of what went on inside its doors. Today the number with absolutely no knowledge of the church, or what it is, is growing rapidly. About three or four years ago I was surprised to learn that 20 percent of my introductory class in Western Religion had never set foot inside *either* a synagogue *or* a church.
- In Christendom, clergy were accorded authority by the entire community as spokespersons for its deepest values and aspirations. Today clergy have little social standing. The image of clergy held by those outside our churches is largely that associated with discredited TV evangelists.
- In Christendom the mission field was across the ocean; now it is right outside the door of the church.[3]

Once again adaptation is needed. New patterns of church life need to be devised to fit a post-Christendom society.

3. See Loren Mead, *The Once and Future Church: Reinventing the Congregation for a Mission Frontier* (Washington, DC: Alban Institute, 1991).

- We will, for example, need to adjust our outreach so that it is directed at persons who have no idea what it means to be religious, much less Christian, to say nothing of being Lutheran.
- We will, for example, be able neither to expect clergy to speak for the church, nor to expect untrained laity to do so. We need to equip laity to serve effectively as the faces and voices of the church, people who are seen, heard, and respected by their unchurched neighbors.
- We will, for example, need to develop behavior patterns associated with a minority status. We need to expect to be out of place in our society and in some fundamental ways out of step with its values and practices. As Christians we cannot fit in to a society
  - that allows ugly urban sprawl to destroy well over fifty acres of farmland every hour (at precisely the time when that farmland is becoming needed to feed the growing population of the world),
  - that turns its back on over 20 percent of its children growing up in poverty,
  - that surrounds many of the other 80 percent with toys but denies them emotional stability,
  - that is not outraged when a corporation pays Michael Jordan more each year to advertise the shoes it sells than it does all its workers in all its plants around the world to make them.[4]

Conclusion

I believe that we, the heirs of Muhlenberg and of Luther, have crucially important things to offer our society. But we can recover and affirm those contributions for our own day only as we are ready to look contemporary problems in the eye, admit that they are real, admit our addiction to consumerism and individual license, and struggle our way through to a new pattern of mission. The new pattern I have in mind is one that fosters community, expects behavior consistent with our Christian faith (and is consequently out of step with society), and adapts itself to serve in an increasingly post-Christendom, socially dislocated society. If our church does these things, it will indeed carry on the Muhlenberg Tradition and Mission!

4. The Nike/Michael Jordan data are cited by Jim Wallis, *Who Speaks for God? An Alternative to the Religious Right — A New Politics of Compassion, Community, and Civility* (New York: Delacorte Press, 1996), pp. 92-93.

Revivalism and "Mainline Churches," Clergy, and Laity

Cynthia Jurisson

The hard work of the Mission Resource Institute and Kenneth Senft in lifting up the Lutheran heritage in such a public way at this Symposium, so as to be accessible to so many, is a blessing to the ELCA. It has been a real pleasure to read and react to John Reumann's paper today.

In the spring of 1742, in anticipation of his imminent missionary voyage to North America, Henry Melchior Muhlenberg, a German Lutheran pastor, was sent to England to spend a few months working under the tutelage of the London court preacher Friedrich Michael Ziegenhagen. After spending two months with Muhlenberg in London, Ziegenhagen sent a sermon evaluation of sorts to the director of the missionary society in Halle, Gotthilf August Francke. The experienced senior pastor was not circumspect in his assessment of Muhlenberg's skills for ministry. His sermons were lousy, his exegesis worse, the theological consistency of his work apparently nonexistent.

> It is with right suffering that I have to inform you that I could understand almost nothing of the whole sermon because it was deficient in clarity, exposition, and nexus from beginning to end. I cannot think of another example to match this one. He is not only weak but totally incapable of conveying a clear idea of a matter to somebody. Therefore I am deeply concerned that all our hope and expenses will be to no avail, because circumstances in Pennsylvania will be much too hard for him. (Strohmidel 1992: 13)

In short, there seemed to be little to commend this second-career student to the ministry, much to suggest that he needed immediate vocational counseling, and nothing to indicate that he would experience even a shred of success in his North American missionary venture. Unless Ziegenhagen was simply dyspeptic, we are led to the conclusion that Muhlenberg did have, to put it euphemistically, a number of rough edges and many significant areas for improvement.

Such a pessimistic view of Muhlenberg is uncommon in American Lutheran historiography, which for the most part has tended toward panegyric, bordering on canonization. But more recently, historians have begun to take a fresh look at Muhlenberg and have, quite helpfully I believe, discovered the flesh-and-blood human behind the ecclesiastical superhero. Their unflinching examination of Muhlenberg's character, words, and work, warts and all, has, among other things, provided empirical evidence for the truth of the longstanding Lutheran conviction that the Holy Spirit can and does accomplish God's work through fallible human vessels like you and me. This is not an insignificant discovery for American Lutherans today. In dispelling the myth of Muhlenberg the superhero, we are led to the conclusion that Lutherans today are no more and no less capable of responding to our mission field every bit as effectively as Muhlenberg responded to his.

Having said that, we should not assume that all we need to do to be successful is to replicate Muhlenberg's work and words in our time. We share with Muhlenberg the challenge of doing ministry on the North American mission field, but the context and the culture in which he ministered are not the same as ours. Furthermore, Muhlenberg's success was due, not to personal heroism, or to having an easier mission field in which to labor. Rather, it was due to a confluence of unique factors, among them individual personality traits, the religious situation in the mid-Atlantic states, the theological foundations of Muhlenberg's ministry — which he located in the Lutheran Confessions, and a variety of social and economic factors both known and unknown to us. An examination of his work provides for us not so much an action plan as a case study, an opportunity to observe a successful minister in a specific context to try to understand the sources of his success as well as the dynamics of some of his failures.

No doubt there were several personal qualities that served Muhlenberg well in the North American mission field. Despite Ziegenhagen's doubts, the facts of history suggest that Muhlenberg must have done a few things right. He may not have had the theological acuity of Jonathan Edwards, or the preaching skill of George Whitefield, but nonetheless he managed to accomplish enormous things in an unfamiliar and challenging environment. I want to focus on three general constellations of personal qualities that I believe helped Muhlenberg to succeed.

First, throughout his career he evidenced a genuine *love and compassion for his parishioners* even to the point of self-sacrifice, and an *integrity of character* that made it possible for parishioners to trust and respect him in return. In short, he was compassionate, mature, and reliable. These qualities are evident early in his ministerial career: his German patrons and congregation in Grosshennersdorf were not happy to see him go, because he was liked and respected. And despite his urgent desire to leave for the mission field, he delayed his departure and refused to commence his mission work until he was sure that his flock at Grosshennersdorf would have adequate pastoral care after his departure (Strohmidel 1992: 9). In many large and small ways, the historical evidence suggests that Muhlenberg's integrity and commitment to his parishioners earned for him their affection and respect.

Muhlenberg's journal attests to the fact that his compassion and love were stretched to the breaking point many times during the course of his ministry. Earlier in his career, he was several times forced to defend the legitimacy of his status as a called pastor before both congregations and other pastors. His journal serves as a running record of the many accusations leveled against him, everything from embezzlement to being a papist, to being the dragon of Revelation 12. He endured innumerable insults and frequent rebukes by his own parishioners, and over the course of his career in many specific instances his pastoral authority was challenged or flatly denied by those around him. Then as now, the pastor was sometimes a lightning rod for people's anger and frustration. But it appears that when he couldn't summon up personal reserves of compassion and love for difficult individuals and congregations, he was at least able to summon forth a sense of professional decorum in order that his commitment to proclaim the love of God not be compromised. His journal contains ample testimony to the numerous occasions when Muhlenberg, confronted with insults and accusations, showed real determination to not respond with the same, so as not to jeopardize his witness to Christ's self-giving love. He knew that there were always people standing on the sidelines, watching "to see whether the preacher will heed Christ's teaching to repay evil with good" (*Journals* 1:257, 264, 265).

A second characteristic that enabled Muhlenberg to succeed was his *adaptability and refusal to wallow in repristination motifs*. No doubt Muhlenberg sometimes longed for the old days of German Protestant church life, the settled and orderly ways of doing ministry there, the deference and authority that well-trained parishioners accorded their pastors, and of course the financial support that the church received from various civil sources. What pastor wouldn't want all that? Certainly Muhlenberg longed, but he did not repristinate. Muhlenberg seemed intuitively to understand that the mission field could bear real fruit for innovators, but render repristinators irrelevant. Early on he exhibited the willingness and ability to adapt and respond effectively to the very different social and ecclesiastical environment of the new country, without sacrificing his theological identity as a Lutheran.

Muhlenberg's attitude toward *revivalistic religion* is illustrative here. Revivalism was a dominant religious paradigm at the time of Muhlenberg's arrival in the colonies, and many would argue that it continues to be a dominant paradigm in North America today. Revivalism served a number of important functions in the developing religious and social life of the colonies, and Muhlenberg certainly was sympathetic to many of its goals as well as aspects of its piety. Among other things, revivalism emphasized repentance and conversion, encouraged individual moral responsibility and accountability before God, reenergized the faithful, and rededicated the lapsed. Far from being the enemy of more theologically orthodox and institutionalized expressions of religious conviction in the early American setting, revivalism may in fact have provided a powerful stimulus to reconnect individuals with local congregations. This was no easy task in the uncivilized, chaotic, even pagan atmosphere of frontier America.

For all its achievements, revivalism also had several weaknesses. One criticism has been that it tended toward anti-institutionalism. Another is that revivalism could lead to fractious sectarianism on the one hand, and on the other, because of its anti-intellectual bent and emphasis on conversion, it could also lead to a blurring of legitimate theological and denominational distinctions. Muhlenberg was open to some aspects of revivalism, even inviting the famous itinerant of the First Great Awakening, George Whitefield, into his pulpit, though he himself was not a revivalist. Muhlenberg's theological grounding in the Lutheran Confessions helped him to avoid several of the problems to which revivalism could lead, yet at the same time allowed him to remain in conversation with the revivalist tradition and thereby benefit from some of its unique contributions to the mission endeavor in North America. He approved of revivalism's emphasis on personal conversion, an emphasis he wholeheartedly shared, yet his grounding in the Lutheran Confessional tradition led him to posit sources of authority beyond subjective human experience. He too emphasized the importance of moral reform subsequent to conversion but did not entertain the possibility of perfectionism, instead remaining convinced of the intractability and inescapability of human sin this side of the second coming. Muhlenberg could rightly be critical of some of the excesses of revivalist practice. But in the New World, faced with a mission field unlike anything he had ever experienced back home, Muhlenberg was pushed to distinguish the essentials of the faith from the nonessentials in order to more effectively serve the gospel. Schooled in the Lutheran conviction that the essence of the church is Word and Sacrament, and possessing a willingness to adapt and innovate for the sake of the gospel, Muhlenberg was able to acknowledge the Spirit's activity in the faithful and earnest piety of many non-Lutheran preachers and parishioners who were more deeply immersed than he in the revivalist tradition. The evidence suggests that these convictions were beneficial to his own ministry. Muhlenberg, along with many other ministers, arrived in North America to begin the task of gathering together the faithful into congregations. Those like Muhlenberg who refused to repristinate but instead responded to the context faithfully, flexibly, and creatively could reap tremendous benefits from uniquely American religious expressions such as revivalism. The revivalist practices of the Great Awakening helped reintegrate many thousands of people, scattered far and wide across the Eastern seaboard, whose congregational ties had been severed in the immigration process, into congregations in the New World. As the research of Jay P. Dolan illustrates, this reintegration process was of enormous benefit to many denominations that were not traditionally revivalistic in practice, including both Roman Catholics and Lutherans.[1]

A third and final personal characteristic that must not be ignored was Muhlenberg's *readiness to contribute to the organization of Lutherans* in North America. Some have argued that Muhlenberg was a brilliant organizer and administrator whose ambition was to transplant the structures of institutional Lutheranism onto North American soil. Others have argued that his primary interest was simply to save souls and minister to individuals. I'd argue that a good part of Muhlenberg's long-term success was in fact due to the way in which he synthesized these two goals with a very functional approach to church organization in North America. He

---

1. Jay P. Dolan, *Catholic Revivalism* (Notre Dame: University of Notre Dame Press, 1978), p. xviii.

recognized that the purpose of any church organization was precisely for the sake of saving souls. Not surprisingly, his main criteria for choosing organizational structures and systems seemed to be whether or not they would effectively further the gospel witness on the North American mission field. In 1748 for example, in his opening address to the First Convention of the Pennsylvania Ministerium, his primary rationale for the creation of the Ministerium was simply the need to convey the gospel message to the children in the Lutheran congregations of the New World (*Documentary History*, 9).

Of all the organizational work to which Muhlenberg contributed, the creation of the Pennsylvania Ministerium was probably his most significant act. However, the significance of his work lay not so much in a particular organizational plan but rather in the appropriateness of the plan for its setting and his diligence in making the plan a reality. The organizational structure of the Ministerium was neither brilliant nor even clever. It was neither complicated nor particularly creative. Quite the opposite; the structure was really rather simple. Its form was determined by its function, so from the start it was task-oriented, flexible, and cooperative in nature, including within its ranks both laity and clergy, with no bureaucracy and minimal hierarchy. Perhaps Muhlenberg knew that if the governance structure was not user-friendly and appropriate to its social and ecclesiastical setting, it was unlikely to survive. Perhaps not. Such a judgment is made more easily in retrospect. For example, Lutheran historian Sydney Ahlstrom has noted how the weightiness of the Moravian missionary Count Nicholas von Zinzendorf's "grandiose ecumenical projects . . ." to unite all German Americans actually hindered the Moravian movement in its attempts to gain footing and influence in the American setting.[2] Muhlenberg was aware that earlier attempts to organize Lutherans had failed, so he started modestly, realizing that it was neither possible nor desirable to enfold all Lutherans under the Ministerium's umbrella. Muhlenberg's cautious determination to create a structure that was cooperative, flexible, and mission-focused proved an enormous boost to the Lutheran witness in North America.

Besides its structural appropriateness, probably another reason for the Ministerium's effectiveness was its commitment to set standards for clerical preparedness and service. Essentially, the Pennsylvania Ministe-

2. Sydney E. Ahlstrom, *A Religious History of the American People* (New Haven: Yale University Press, 1971), p. 243.

rium functioned as a clergy cartel. Not every Lutheran pastor in the colonies, or even in the local area, was a member. From the beginning, the Ministerium sought to promote high standards for clerics as well as to distinguish clearly its members from the Moravian "pretenders" and others who claimed to be legitimate Lutheran pastors but in reality had little knowledge of the Lutheran faith. Muhlenberg and the other charter members of the Ministerium not only articulated specific expectations for clergy who would become members of the Ministerium, but also held themselves to the same expectations and voluntarily placed themselves under a system that sought to ensure compliance with those standards and accountability to one another. They demanded of all members theological continuity with the Lutheran tradition, legitimate preparation for ministry, moral behavior, scriptural adherence, and willingness to be subject to peer review and rebuke (*Documentary History*, 9-11). Creating such a clergy cartel was among the most effective things that Muhlenberg and his colleagues could have done to strengthen the Lutheran witness in the new country. Why? Some congregations in the area had suffered from ill-prepared or self-serving pastors who were unable or unwilling to preach and teach the gospel with integrity. Worse, other congregations had been victimized by disingenuous and deceptive men of no theological training who were only posing as pastors for financial gain. And the trials and temptations of ministry in the New World were enormous, even for the best of pastors. The Pennsylvania Ministerium functioned not only as a clergy consolation and support society but also provided necessary structures of accountability for Lutheran pastors and parishioners. In this way Muhlenberg and other members of the Ministerium were able to provide a sort of "Good Housekeeping Seal of Approval" for Lutheran congregations seeking pastoral service. Muhlenberg's determination to establish the Ministerium in the first place, and his unwavering commitment to sustain and strengthen it, had far-reaching consequences even in his lifetime. Its existence helped to promote trust in the ministerial class, assuring congregations and parishioners that their pastor shared their Lutheran theological convictions, that he could be counted upon to do what he had been called to do, and that he would not take financial advantage of them or substitute some other theological tradition for the Lutheranism to which they were committed.

In conclusion, an unblinking gaze at Muhlenberg and his work does not reveal a man of heroic proportions and mythic qualities. Instead we find a rather average individual whose only remarkable quality may simply have been perseverance. But that perseverance had the salutary effect of amplifying — many times over — the impact of his other helpful but far from heroic characteristics such as organizational skills, adaptability, and concern for his parishioners. We are left, as we noted at the outset, with the inescapable conclusion that Lutherans today are no more and no less capable of responding every bit as effectively to our mission field as Muhlenberg responded to his.

"The Irreligious" and Some Cases in the Carolinas

Susan Wilds McArver

Dr. Reumann's paper illustrates well for us the host of adversaries and difficulties Henry Melchior Muhlenberg faced in his attempt to plant the church firmly in America. The diversity present on that early frontier posed considerable challenges for Muhlenberg's organizational work.

Toward those groups already on the field when he arrived, Muhlenberg developed a variety of responses. With "church people," as Dr. Reumann terms them, such as the Reformed, the Presbyterians, and the Anglicans, he practiced a certain "selective openness." Toward others, such as the Quakers or Moravians whom he felt embodied dangerous heresies, he proved decidedly cooler. But even more did Muhlenberg exhibit discomfort with sectarian groups, those whom he felt were only marginally religious, or those he did not consider religious at all (Reumann, pp. 100-101 above).

It is to this latter group that I would like to address my response, to those whom Muhlenberg and his heirs have sometimes termed the "irreligious": the faithless, the "godless," or even the downright pagan — those who had either turned away from the church of their birth to follow new ways, or those who had never been a part of the church at all. Clearly, Muhlenberg encountered such persons on his travels far more often than he cared to. I think, however, that his response may be instructive to us as we ourselves encounter the "irreligious" of our own day.

As Dr. Reumann has pointed out, Henry Muhlenberg was all too aware of the dangers facing a widely scattered population at the far edges of civilization, people who were not nurtured by an adequate pastoral supply. Pretenders, charlatans, and the merely misguided led large numbers of colonial Americans down fanciful paths, and the pages of Muhlenberg's journals include not only rival clergymen and pious lay people, but also swearing sailors, dancing pagans, New Birth mystics, Sabbatarians, and Rosicrucians, among others. Dr. Reumann's paper, for example, mentions the appeal of certain forms of mysticism so compelling that they could sway the most educated, such as Daniel and Justus Falckner, or even Muhlenberg's own future father-in-law, Conrad Weiser. At least for a time, each found a home within various stripes of German mysticism far outside any traditional teachings of the Lutheran confessions (Reumann, pp. 75-76 above).

Obviously, those with little formal or religious education proved even more at risk. Many in early America had obtained little more than rudimentary schooling at best, and their knowledge of church doctrine extended little further than their knowledge of the alphabet. Left without adequate pastoral care, immigrants who faced the unforgiving landscape of the first American frontier were all too often willingly led astray in their hunger for a spiritual explanation of a world that many found otherwise incomprehensible.

Such spiritual diversity and hunger was not confined to the Germans of Pennsylvania. In colonial South Carolina, the Weberite (Waeberite, Wäberite) controversy, alluded to briefly in Dr. Reumann's paper (p. 101 above), was only one of the more well-known examples of religious fanaticism run wild. Although German settlers, who were nominally Lutheran or Reformed, had pushed toward the central portions of the state since at least the 1730s, it was at least twenty-five years before the first Lutheran pastor arrived to minister to them. Under such conditions, the pioneers were all too often left to their own creative devices. Observer Adolf Nussman wrote in disgust that as a result, "For want of instructors and school teachers they are in utter confusion, and if help does not come soon they will fall back completely into paganism. . . . In the most outlying places . . . blindness, ignorance, superstition and fanatic enthusiasm rage" (Fritz 101).

When Reformed pastor Christian Theus, an acquaintance of Muhlenberg's, accidentally stumbled onto a Weberite worship service around 1761, he witnessed, as he reported later to Muhlenberg, the assembly committing the "most atrocious blasphemies. . . . Groups of both sexes went about unclothed and naked, and practiced the most abominable wantonness." Pastor Theus — who overcame his shock long enough to rebuke the group for heresy — barely escaped with his life. Hearing such reports, Henry Muhlenberg could only shake his head and sadly observe that "the poor people grow up in the country without schools and instruction, and even if the self-appointed preachers do wander in occasionally, it does no good, for the people are wild and are growing wilder" (*Journals* 2:577-80).

American religious historian Jon Butler in at least one way agrees with Muhlenberg's assessment: the religious expression of the Weberites did not prove an isolated incident. Indeed, in his book *Awash in a Sea of Faith: Christianizing the American People,* Butler posits that until the time of the First Great Awakening, early America was probably far less orthodox than our past renditions of the story of religion in America would have us believe. Recent historians such as Butler, David Hall, and Bill Cecil-Fronsman have pointed out that immigrants from Europe brought more to America than their distinctive theological traditions. European settlers, including many German immigrants in both Pennsylvania and the Carolinas, brought to the New World not only their distinctive language and culture, but also Old World patterns of relating to the sacred and a premodern worldview that included a fundamental acceptance of beliefs that the more educated derided as simple superstition. A belief in the use of charms, in the efficacy of certain talismans, and in the power of certain "wise men" and "wise women" coexisted with apparent ease alongside more traditional Christian teachings. Persistent belief in witchcraft, for example, proved only one aspect of acceptance of the supernatural that permeated large parts of early American society long after the infamous witch trials of Salem, Massachusetts in 1692. Many, in fact, often saw no contradiction between their folk belief in charms and witchcraft and their Christian faith. After all, as one contemporary non-German acutely observed, "the Bible was their authority for the existence of witches, and they believed in the one as firmly as in the other" (Scott 99). For many, such beliefs in the supernatural were predicated on an encompassing holistic view of the natural and supernatural world, all operating under the providence of God.

Observing such practices firsthand in Pennsylvania and hearing similar reports from the southern colonies, Muhlenberg regarded such beliefs as nonsense at best, as sacrilege at worst. Muhlenberg dismissed such tales as the idle superstition of the ignorant, and hoped that in time, with proper pastoral care and instruction, such beliefs would wither away. To his dismay, however, he found them prevalent not only among the old, from whom he apparently expected no better, but also among the young: "Many superstitious and godless notions still prevail among the old presumptuous people who have had no instruction in their youth and are unwilling to hear and learn the Word of God in their old age," he wrote. But even worse, it appeared that "most of the new immigrants who are coming annually from various regions are no better; their heads, too, are full of fantastic notions of witchcraft and Satanic arts. Unhappily," Muhlenberg concluded, he had found in frontier America "more necromancers . . . than Christians" (*Journals* 1:349).

Excesses such as these helped convince Muhlenberg of the need for trained, regularly ordained, authoritative pastors. Muhlenberg believed that such superstitious beliefs harmed the simple and caused pain to the ignorant. As Dr. Reumann points out, Muhlenberg proved acutely aware that "'if the seed has not yet taken strong and deep root and gained the upper hand, it is in danger of being rooted out or of being smothered by the weeds of erratic opinions,' from competing religious groups far more prolific than in Germany" (Reumann, p. 82 above, citing *Journals* 1:376).

The diversity of religious experience Muhlenberg reported in the New World of his day reminds us, I believe, of similarities with our own. Sociologists such as Wade Clark Roof and William McKinney foretell the decline of the mainline denominations, to be replaced by newer, nondenominational megachurches, by strident voices from the conservative religious right, or by the individualistic, syncretistic "generation of seekers" who are finding spirituality in an increasing number of pluralistic ways. We face a world where religious belief often appears as nothing more than a "lifestyle choice." As Dr. Reumann has mentioned, the definition of spirituality has come a long way — from the older Roman Catholic idea of "spiritual formation" to the individual, eclectic spiritual quests of the baby boomers and their children (Reumann, p. 95 above). Even a casual perusal of the weekly tabloids and self-help books at the neighborhood supermarket is enough to convince one that Americans continue to dabble in beliefs and practices that cannot be any wilder than those dreamed up by the Wissahickon hermits or the Carolina heretics. Alien space landings, resurrected rock and roll stars, and cosmic predictions of the exact date of Armageddon vie with horoscopes and crystals to put many Americans in touch with the "truth that is out there" — somewhere.

While recognizing with scholar Catherine Albanese that straight lines cannot necessarily be drawn between the mystical practices and beliefs of an earlier day and our own, Albanese (344ff.) rightly, I think, marks parallels that do exist. These parallels point to the continuing hunger for "the sacred," defined differently in different times, linking groups as diverse as the dancing pagans of Muhlenberg's day with the New Agers of our own. New Age mysticism of various stripes, the goddess religion of Wicca, and Tarot cards are often as much a part of some college dormitory life today, for example, as are CDs and computers. The juxtaposition of this most technologically able generation in history with their poignant search for existential meaning rooted in the ancient, serves as a reminder to us all that the search for a connection with the sacred may be our most important point of contact with a world that is becoming, *not* necessarily, I believe, more *secular*, but certainly "differently religious."

Henry Muhlenberg reacted in more than one way to the religious diversity around him. True, as Dr. Reumann observes, he tended to face sectarian groups with "bewilderment" (Reumann, p. 102 above). But Reumann also agrees with Michael Cobbler's recent assessment, that Henry Muhlenberg was a man "'not afraid to meet people where they are' . . . and not afraid to minister to them" (Reumann, p. 78 above).

A striking example of Muhlenberg's openness to those outside his own traditional circles came in his encounter sometime in the 1750s with Anna Manda Müller, an older woman of uncommonly colorful past. "In her younger years," Muhlenberg reported to Halle, "she participated in military actions (in fact, she was present at the battle of Hochstadt and at other skirmishes), had a martial spirit, lived in a coarse manner, and engaged in all kinds of uncouth, sinful practices which, alas, are quite common under such circumstances." Muhlenberg proved less interested in the *fact* of her military service than in the *results* of this service on her soul. "Prominent among her vices were fits of anger, cursing, and drunkenness." Not surprisingly, Muhlenberg reported, these vices "often nullified the workings of the good Spirit." Her "justification," if it could be called that, she found in the merit of her own works, and in her military service to her prince. Despite her formidable appearance, swaggering demeanor, and personal disdain for religion, the woman paradoxically held a "high regard for the evangelical preachers . . . and [she] tried, on her own volition albeit with imprudent zeal, to defend them against all kinds of hostile slanders, and would have been ready to take up the sword in [our] behalf." This, Muhlenberg noted dryly, "did not help" the evangelical preachers' case. Her feisty spirit also apparently provoked other charges against her: her "superstitious and ignorant Pennsylvania neighbors on account of her great size and frightful appearance" accused her of being a witch, and "all manner of knavish rabble submitted her to tests in necromancy" (*Journals* 1:347-49).

Instead of being repelled (or even intimidated!) by this rough woman of no religious training, however, Muhlenberg approached her as an individual, as one, who no matter how "unworthy," was surely still a child of God. To inquire regarding the state of her *spiritual* condition, as Dr. Reumann points out, was as natural for Muhlenberg as for "a physician [to] ask about physical condition" (Reumann, p. 94 above). Muhlenberg understood that "like many others in former times of war, she had been neglected in her youth" and consequently had "gathered no store of divine truths," or even for that matter, been taught to read (1:348).

Muhlenberg began to visit her. At first, "she always wanted to talk at great length about her war experiences," he reported, but gradually, Muhlenberg was able to turn her conversation in a different direction. Muhlenberg and his colleagues supplied her with "edifying" reading, with contemplative books designed to enable her conversion, books that her husband read to her and explained. Toward the end of her life, when she had become bedridden, Muhlenberg visited with her faithfully, answered her questions with gentleness and honesty, read to her from the Scriptures, and interpreted pastorally her visions of the suffering Savior. She died, Muhlenberg wrote, "under His cross, stripped of her own righteousness," and clothed in that of her Savior (1:349).

The story of Anna Manda Müller is a poignant reminder that Muhlenberg — uncomfortable as he may have been personally with her beliefs, her actions, and certainly with her lifestyle — approached this woman, not as an outcast, not as an untouchable, but as an individual "soul," one for whom "the best and truest Friend of man" had died and who was "unwilling that she should be lost" (1:347). We rightly honor here in this Symposium Muhlenberg the organizer, Muhlenberg the patriarch, and Muhlenberg the founder, but we should never forget, as he himself certainly did not, Muhlenberg the pastor. As Robert Marshall has pointed out, "the motivation for [his entire ministry] came from his sense of personal benefit from having received the gospel, and the conviction that all people needed it as much as he" (Marshall, p. 9 above; 1998: 86).

Dr. Reumann observed that Muhlenberg once itemized the ways in which people should treat their pastors. In the story of Anna Müller, we obtain a glimpse of how Muhlenberg believed that pastors should treat their people: patiently, gently, and on their own level. Seen in this light, it does not seem at all out of place or out of character that Henry Melchior Muhlenberg, the grand patriarch of Lutheranism in North America, the originator of 250 years of Lutheran life and work in this country, would take the time to sit down and patiently, carefully, and thoughtfully, compose twelve verses of simple poetry — in a language not his own — for a sixteen-year-old girl desiring to learn about God (Reumann, pp. 107-8 above, citing *Journals* 1:146).

In June 1998, after a consultation at Lutheran Theological Southern Seminary, the Florida-Bahamas Synod of the ELCA prepared a paper titled "Leaders for Tomorrow," designed to stimulate discussion of the ELCA's need for future "missionary pastors." Reading the story of Muhlenberg and Anna Müller, as well as stories of his encounters with many others like her on the frontier, one is struck by the clear points of contact between Muhlenberg's experience and our own.

The Florida-Bahamas synod paper, for example, observed that "the situation in which the ELCA finds itself [today] is so radically altered that new models for the preparation of ordained ministers are necessary. . . . [The synod represents] a changing mission field. Our pastors must increasingly function as missionaries in an unchurched, multi-ethnic culture" (p. 1). Henry Muhlenberg on arrival in the New World also found himself in a radically altered context from his comfortable, European church. Judging from his journals, he surely faced an "unchurched, multi-ethnic culture" — and survived.

The Florida-Bahamas Synod observed that modern Americans rarely know their Bibles or the traditional language of faith, and so "most potential members [today] must learn the faith 'from scratch.' Pastors must know how to teach someone to pray who has never done so before" (p. 1). Henry Muhlenberg's journal is full of stories of his encounters with rough and uncouth men and women who knew little of the traditional faith, and less about prayer.

"Pastors need to leave seminary having received strong personal spiritual formation," wrote the Synod. "They are increasingly asked to be spiritual guides in the midst of the uncertainties of modern life" (p. 1). Henry Muhlenberg was certainly well served by his own training at Halle and proved able to serve as a "spiritual guide" to many who came and asked for instruction — and even for more than a few who did not.

"Pastors must be prepared to walk with seekers and know how to nurture conversion experiences," continued the Synod (p. 1). Henry Muhlenberg knew all about "nurturing conversion experiences"; indeed, he saw it as his primary function.

And finally, "pastors will need specific missionary skills," concluded the Synod, "how to meet people and make themselves known in the community, how to make 'cold calls,' how to proclaim the gospel in everyday language when they are not inside the church building, how to witness boldly in their own personal lives, how to witness to persons of another culture" (p. 2). If Henry Muhlenberg did not know how to make "cold calls" to anyone, anywhere, at any time — in several different languages — it is hard to imagine anyone who did. I am sure the Florida-Bahamas Synod stands ready to issue a call.

I believe, then, that we can still learn much from Henry Muhlenberg's example — not just as founder, organizer, and leader (although he was certainly all of these) — but as missionary pastor in a religiously diverse and changing world. Henry Melchior Muhlenberg faced an audience both similar to and different from our own. His world proved to be filled with "cultural pluralism," as Dr. Reumann terms it, much as is our own world today. For many, the sacred proved sometimes larger than that encompassed by traditional Christian belief systems, in "cultures that Lutherans at times could embrace and at times wisely opposed" (Reumann, p. 109 above).

Dr. Reumann and others have emphasized that the Muhlenberg tradition has moved on when it has needed to do so to adjust to changes in cultural conditions, whether that meant moving westward with the frontier or into new social ministries (see Marshall, pp. 10-11 above; 1998: 87-88, 95; and Reumann, pp. 109-10 above). "The diversity of peoples and the complexity of structures is greater," noted Marshall, "but the need for planting the church in a changing society remains the same" (p. 31 above; 1998: 100). Perhaps what we are discovering in our examination of the past 250 years of the history of the Muhlenberg tradition in America is that in reality, the times have not changed nearly as much as we had thought.

III. Aspects of an Anniversary
in History, Mission, and the Arts

The 250th anniversary of the first meeting of the Ministerium of Pennsylvania was marked by a series of events beyond the opening gathering in Baltimore in 1997 (Part I, above), several seminary convocations, local events, and the Symposium at Muhlenberg College, August 7-9, 1998 (see Part II, above). While five of the seven items that follow in Part III were part of the Symposium at Muhlenberg, two others reflect attention to the themes at a synod gathering and the dedication of the house in which Henry Melchior and Mrs. Muhlenberg lived near Augustus Church, Trappe, Pennsylvania; this happy occasion was a deliberate "add on" to the Symposium in Allentown.

These pages cannot begin to catalogue all the local and congregational reflections of the anniversary, including displays of art and churchly and everyday objects from the past that were brought together, notably at the Lutheran Theological Seminary, Philadelphia (for which a lavish catalogue was prepared, *Henry Melchior Muhlenberg, the Colonial Lutheran Church*) and at the ELCA Churchwide Assembly in Philadelphia, August 14-20, 1997.

The aim throughout these festivities was not merely to revere but also to reflect on the past as it impacts our future. Another, not merely to mark this heritage in fitting ways, locally, regionally, and nationally, but also to stimulate attention to the history of local congregations, institutions, and individuals all too often forgotten and ignored in a changing world. That the celebrations took a variety of forms — and can continue to have an influence — is a tribute to Muhlenberg's many-sidedness and to the creativity of a host of people today.

The Church — Still Being Planted

ELCA Presiding Bishop, H. George Anderson

As a church historian, H. George Anderson has often been called upon to speak and write about Muhlenberg and American Lutheranism, as in the 1975 volume, The Lutherans in North America, *or in a 1992 paper for ELCA bishops meeting in Trappe, Pennsylvania. It was natural that he should speak about "Muhlenberg's Impact on the Church of His Day and Ours" at the convocation of the Philadelphia Seminary, his alma mater, in 1997. For the Symposium at Muhlenberg College, August 7, 1998, he was naturally and inevitably the choice for keynote speaker the first evening. (Illness prevented attendance at the last minute; the manuscript was read by the Rev. Roy G. Almquist, Bishop, Southeastern Pennsylvania Synod, geographical successor to Muhlenberg's Ministerium in Philadelphia and surrounding counties.) Bishop Anderson's address, for a predominantly ELCA audience, reflects "the state of the church" between the 1997 and 1999 Assemblies. While cherishing "the traditions that nurtured us in the faith," it raises concern about the renewed interest in "the Muhlenberg tradition" (or "the Augustana heritage" or any other tradition). History and heritage are never simply benign.*

•   •

Thank you for the opportunity to share in the celebration of the 250th anniversary of the founding of the first continuing synodical body in this country. I have been asked to put this celebration in the context of our present situation as a church still in mission, still being planted after a quarter of a millennium, to use the new unit of measurement in these fast-paced times.

It is a fortunate opportunity to step back and expand our timescale, to think in terms of millennia once in a while. Taking these years in great chunks gives us a perspective that annual reports and quarterly statements do not provide. In fact, they shrink into insignificance. They become mere sound bites in the long conversation that God is having with the world through the church.

Muhlenberg's arrival in America lies closer to Columbus's arrival here than to our own day, and the founding of the Ministerium in 1748 is closer to the date of the Augsburg Confession than to the founding of the Evangelical Lutheran Church in America. So when we think of a 250-year span, we go back more than halfway to the Reformation, which itself was only the midpoint in the millennium that has just come to an end. In that sense, the Muhlenberg tradition, and even the Reformation itself, are relatively recent events in the long history of Christianity.

That perspective is even truer of the short life of the Evangelical Lutheran Church in America. On a millennial timescale it is scarcely possible to detect the brief lifespan of the ELCA. We don't yet have the data to trace ELCA trajectories, constants, and general trends — all the raw material out of which projections can be made. And even if we could try to name a few, how accurate would our predictions be? What sort of future would have been projected for Muhlenberg's Ministerium if there had been a gathering like this in 1758, ten years after its founding? We might note that the Ministerium did not even meet that year; in fact it hadn't met for the preceding three years. No wonder that they hadn't settled on a name for the baby yet. Its chances of survival seemed very slim. So please excuse me if I do not try to see very far into the future; history has demonstrated that such predictions are about as reliable as palmistry and the reading of tealeaves.

It would be an interesting exercise to try to define exactly what we have inherited from Henry Melchior Muhlenberg. He did not found this college that bears his name, nor the Muhlenberg Press. No synod was named after him, as was the case with Hans Nielsen Hauge and Philipp Melanchthon. David and Paul Henkel gave us the "Henkelites" and C. F. W. Walther the "Waltherites," but no one, fortunately, ever tried to use the label "Muhlenbergers." They would certainly have been a tough lot.

In general we have taken the Patriarch's legacy and selected what appeals to us, and then in turn appealed to it as "the Muhlenberg tradition." One could mention confessional loyalty, an ordered ministry, and a common hymnal. Or maybe slogans attributed to Muhlenberg summarize what is important for us: "The Church Must Be Planted" and "One Church, One Book." They have been banners for home missions, for Lutheran unity, and for a single hymnal.

There is a tiny town in Scotland named Rest and Be Thankful. It lies at the top of a long winding grade. The temptation on an anniversary like this is to look backward and marvel at how far we have come in 250 years. It would be pleasant to sit here and rest, panting a bit after all our mission-building and stewardship campaigns, new curriculums and mergers, wiping our collective brow and thanking God for helping us along the way. But the planners of this conference want us to look ahead, or maybe look into our ecclesiological baggage and see what Muhlenberg has packed there for our journey. Before taking a flight we are accustomed to answering the question, "Has anyone unknown to you given you any packages or asked you to carry anything for them?" Well, as a matter of fact, this elderly man in a powdered wig did slip something into our luggage; maybe we had better take it out and examine it.

Of course it wasn't only Muhlenberg; it was all those nameless immigrants who grudgingly supported him because they were hungry for the word of God in a strange land. It was those restless preachers who rode horseback through swollen rivers and bone-chilling snowstorms, convinced that the message and the sacramental ministry they were bringing was as urgently needed as we think medical supplies are today. It was those professors and editors and pastors who argued endlessly over tiny points of theology that could make immense differences in how people understood their relationship to God. It was those movers and shakers who dreamed of institutions of mercy and colleges and seminaries and — despite depressions and wars, fights and failures — incarnated those dreams in flesh and blood, brick and stone. And it was those administrators and executives who saw to it that things got done despite inadequate staff and budget problems, because they believed that the work was more important than the obstacles. What a bundle they have left us! Just compare what Muhlenberg had with what we have been given to work with.

In 1750 there may have been 130 Lutheran congregations in all of the American colonies. Now there are 11,000. Those few early congregations were made up of recent immigrants whom Muhlenberg described as "poor Germans." We now are thoroughly middle-class and estimate congregational assets at over 8 billion dollars. Instead of a few semiliterate schoolmasters, we have a network of twenty-eight colleges and universities, and eight seminaries. Muhlenberg had no place to send orphaned children;

now Lutheran Social Services of America links 250 agencies in America's second largest social ministry system. The ministerium he organized had no funds for common work or cooperative projects. Now the congregations of the Northeastern Pennsylvania Synod, on whose territory we meet, handle 48 million dollars annually.

Correspondence with his home base in Halle took nearly a year; now messages are exchanged with Europe in the time it would have taken him to sharpen his pen. I can travel from my office in Chicago to any of our congregations in the continental United States quicker than Muhlenberg could travel from his home in Trappe to Philadelphia.

It is hard to grasp the instruments we have been given. If the ELCA were a state, it would rank fifteenth in population. Its annual income exceeds 1.8 billion dollars. It operates in every state, plus Puerto Rico and the Virgin Islands. It has representatives in forty-two foreign countries.

Why have we been given all this potential? What does God want us to do with it? How can we employ these resources for the next 250 years as effectively as Muhlenberg employed the resources at his disposal?

When we look at the challenges before us, we lose any sense of triumphalism that the recital of our assets may have kindled. We have a daunting task. We feel it in our bones. We live with anxiety about the future and our ability to cope with the challenges it presents. But we also have this heritage, this long history, and the example of the man whom we remember this year. Such memories give us a certain sense of balance, a perspective that can steady our nerves as we face the future.

First of all, our task may not be so different from his. The more we learn about the situation he faced, the more parallels we find with our own day.

We worry a lot about the loss of status that religion in general, and Christianity in particular, has suffered in recent years. We talk about "the end of Christendom" and "ministry from the margins." Think what it was like for Muhlenberg to move from the state church system of Europe into a country where, as one of his contemporaries put it, "Many thousands of these people concerned themselves so little with religion that it became proverbial to say of a person who completely ignored God and his Word that he had 'the Pennsylvania religion.'"[1]

We worry about mobility. Lutherans seem to be draining away from

1. A. G. Spangenberg, quoted in Donald F. Durnbaugh, ed., *The Brethren in Colonial America* (Elgin, IL: Brethren Press, 1967), p. 280.

their traditional areas of settlement and flowing to other parts of the country. Even in areas where we built new mission congregations forty years ago, freeways and apartment developments have cut up parishes and sent people on to newer suburbs. Muhlenberg faced the same problem. "Our German Evangelical settlers in Pennsylvania are, for the most part, the most recent immigrants to this province," he wrote. "The English and German Quakers, Inspired, Mennonites, separatists and the like small denominations came to this country in earlier, good times when land was still very cheap. These people selected the best and most fertile regions and so enriched themselves that they and their heirs now have firmly established homes and estates. In later years, however, when the poor Evangelicals also found their way and came to this country in great numbers . . . most of them had to be slaves for several years to repay their passage and make shift with the poorer lands and struggle to make a living by the sweat of their brows. But finally, even poor land was no longer to be had. . . . Hence they are moving farther and farther into the wilderness." He noted that during the first five years of his ministry about half the members of his country congregations had moved out of the area, looking for better and cheaper lands (*Journals* 1:141-42).

We are concerned about diminishing denominational loyalty. We cannot count on our members seeking out a Lutheran congregation when they move. Our children seem to be looking for something other than the same old "same-old." Some congregations believe that the word "Lutheran" is a turn-off and should not be used on their signs or in their public notices. Muhlenberg knew the problem that the label "Lutheran" could create. Many of the more "awakened" religious groups ". . . despised the Lutherans and Reformed because not only was there so little vitality to be felt in their services, but also because so much of a disorderly and scandalous nature took place in their life and conduct."[2]

We find that congregational conflict and pastoral misconduct sap our energy and divert our attention from our main task. Muhlenberg also expressed frustration at dealing with what he described as soul-destroying, satanic, heartbreaking, and almost irreparable dissensions in many congregations.

One of our chief decisions will be how to participate in the current stage of ecumenical history. Since the middle of the last century American church bodies have attempted to grow closer together. They have explored

2. Spangenberg, quoted in Durnbaugh, *The Brethren in Colonial America*, p. 281.

a number of paths toward that end. At first it was through councils of churches, where common action could be taken on social issues and some common work done on tasks like stewardship statistics, Bible translation, and the like. It wasn't long, though, before a bolder course was charted. Why not organic union? At first two, then five, and then nearly a dozen denominations explored merger in the 1960s, but by 1970 union seemed beyond their grasp. Meanwhile, Lutherans and some others began picking their way through formerly impassable terrain by means of bilateral dialogues, and in the 1980s they came out on the other side with some new proposals. With the Roman Catholics it was a common statement on justification — a project that led to the international "Joint Declaration on Justification" of 1999. With the Reformed and Episcopalians it was a third way of ecumenical relationship, full communion. Full communion goes beyond the occasional sharing of pulpits or welcoming others to the communion table. It provides for the orderly deployment of clergy when joint ministry is needed. At the same time, each tradition maintains its own identity and governance structures. As we continue the pattern we started in 1997 with the Presbyterian Church (USA), the Reformed Church in America, and the United Church of Christ and extend it to Episcopalians and the Moravians, we will become the link between several long-separated branches of the Reformation.

The cast of characters would be familiar to Muhlenberg, even though their roles have changed dramatically in the course of 250 years.

I don't think that we should ask, "What would Muhlenberg say about this project?" But his spirit could help us in another way. Just as he entered into the formation of the Ministerium with the attitude that it was a trial or test, so we might approach our current ecumenical opportunity in the same open-ended way. Let us see what good can come of it. Like most ecumenical projects, if it is beneficial it will prosper; if it is more bother than it's worth, it will wither and fade.

I realize that some people feel the stakes are too high for that kind of experimental attitude, that we risk losing congregations if we forge ahead. Muhlenberg would understand that kind of risk. He carefully tailored the invitation list to that first organizational meeting for the Ministerium in 1748 to include only sympathetic pastors and congregations. In the end the doubters also came around. They either joined the Ministerium or formed similar groups that eventually merged into a General Synod. If we take the long view, and that's what a 250th anniversary provides, we can count on the healing and cleansing effects of time.

The issues surrounding our ecumenical future bring up another unanswered question before the ELCA today. How fully are we really one church? Do our ethnic traditions, our differing experiences with immigration from European mother churches, and our liturgical convictions drive wedges between us? Have we really gotten our act together? Can we?

I am more than a little curious about the emergence of the phrase "the Muhlenberg tradition." I don't remember it playing a leading role in the history of Lutheranism in this country. It seems to have surfaced more recently when mergers began to make various traditions more self-conscious and nervous about losing their identities. Is it accidental that only a month ago the heirs of the Swedish Lutheran tradition held a reunion at Lake Chautauqua and organized the Augustana Heritage Association?[3] Less than a year ago I attended a big centennial celebration in Minneapolis of the Lutheran Free Church, whose former members are now divided between two church bodies.

Or have you heard people identify themselves as "old ALC," which can mean either the American Lutheran Church, one of the parties to the merger that formed the ELCA in 1988, or — if "old" is really emphasized — the German-background ALC that merged with the Norwegians back in 1960? In such a context, is "the Muhlenberg tradition" really a codeword, a rallying point for another strand of Lutheran history identified with the United Lutheran Church in America?

One has to be careful of this nostalgia, because time can indeed "make ancient good uncouth." About a week ago I attended a country church near Decorah, Iowa, that was observing the annual Nordic festival by using a liturgy out of the old Norwegian hymnal identified, as is often the case, by its color — the "black hymnal." The newspaper ad for the event read, "Old-fashioned service from black hymnal followed by Gospel Sing." It became clear that the old codewords no longer carried the right message when the pastor received several calls wondering who had decided that they would celebrate Nordic Fest weekend with an African American service.

One of the hard lessons we have learned in our ten years as the

3. 1998 Sesquicentennial Heritage Gathering, Chautauqua, NY. For publications from the 2000 meeting in Rock Island, IL, and 2002 in Lindsborg, KS, see Gifford and A. Hultgren, eds., 2006 meeting announced for Chautauqua. The Augustana Heritage Association (1860-1962) also has a newsletter and has announced a comprehensive history in its publication program. See www.augustanaheritage.org.

ELCA is that we are not simply "the new church." During the time of formation we avoided the term "merger" and spoke constantly of "the new church." We had the experience with previous mergers and we wanted to cut the cords to those poisonous "PCBs" — the predecessor church bodies — that had complicated earlier efforts to start anew. So we are indeed a new church, but we rightly cherish the traditions that nurtured us in the faith. We continue to wrestle with diversity from the past at the same time that we struggle to embrace even more diversity in our membership. These diverse strands of tradition can entangle us; or they can strengthen us — in Muhlenberg's image, "a twisted cord of many threads that will not easily break." I believe that the key to whether our diversity strengthens us or divides us will depend on the degree to which we are willing to trust one another.

I close by identifying the most insidious challenge we face as a church. It is not the worship wars, financial meltdown, or any of the social changes I mentioned earlier. In fact it is not posed by any external factor. It involves the soul of the church. That is, it is a matter of faith. Faith in Luther's sense: "trust in God's promises," of being able to say at the end of the Creed, "This is most certainly true." We are in danger of losing that core conviction.

Recent surveys show that many of our members see Christianity as a "lifestyle choice," a way of satisfying spiritual needs that money can't buy — otherwise they would buy it. Religion fills in what money can't. It's the icing on the cake, the final touch on "the good life." We manage all our affairs, handle life's problems, put God on hold, and then — oh yes — if things get too tough, hope that God has stayed on the line and is still listening.

Does Christianity really have eternal consequences, or is it just another good-luck piece in our pocket? When we look at the way Muhlenberg understood the working of God in his life, we understand why he would answer the call to move half a world away. He thought it was vitally important for people to put their trust in God. It is so important that nothing — language, class, age, wealth — nothing could be a barrier to his eagerness to reach them. He talked about eternal things to every soul on that little ship during its 104-day passage to America; he even tried to get through to the Spanish Roman Catholic cook. His conversation always moved to deeper levels, not because he had an evangelistic message to ram down someone's throat, but because he was genuinely interested in that person's welfare, from the state of their health to the state of their soul.

Until we can see the great spiritual vacuum in this culture — until we can feel it in our own lives, sense it in the lives of our co-workers and identify it as the black hole at the center of our most intractable social problems — until our eyes are opened, we will not be able to use the church that Henry Muhlenberg left to us. But if we repent of our pride, our gracious Lord may still have work for us to do.

Hymn for the 250th Anniversary: "Word of Wisdom"

Herman G. Stuempfle, Jr.

The Planning Committee commissioned an original hymn for the anniversary. Its author, the Rev. Herman G. Stuempfle, Jr., Professor and President at the Lutheran Theological Seminary, Gettysburg, Pennsylvania, here explains his thoughts in the five verses. The original tune was the work of Stephen C. Williams, of Allentown.

• •

A celebration of the life and work of the "Patriarch of American Lutheranism" inevitably pushes the mind back to his slogan *Ecclesia Plantanda*. But the church itself is preceded by the Word, the planted seed from which the church springs. I decided, therefore, that the Word should be the governing image of the text I hoped to create.

One cannot meditate on the Word without being drawn to the majestic prologue to the Fourth Gospel. The first verse of the hymn reflects St. John's proclamation that the Word was "in the beginning," the primordial source of all that exists. Verse two moves with John to the announcement of the Incarnation, the Word taking on our flesh in the life, death, and resurrection of Jesus of Nazareth.

With the final three verses, the focus of the hymn shifts to the Word at work in and through the church, the Body of Christ. The verb *planted*, in the opening line of verse three, is a specific reference to Muhlenberg's mission, but points also to the whole company of saints whose witness is part of our heritage. Verses four and five are a prayer for the empowering and sustaining presence of the Word as the church strives to be faithful in its ministry and witness in a world still broken by sin and famishing for the gospel.

"WORD OF WISDOM"

Unison 1. Word of wis - dom, Word of won - der, birth - ing cos - mic time and space;
Unison 2. Word of pro - mise, Word in - car - nate as the Son of God on Earth;
Choir 3. Word well plant - ed Word deep root - ed, sown by faith - ful saints of old;
SATB 4. Word of mer - cy, Word of heal - ing, where the peo - ple cry in pain.
Unison 5. Word em - pow'r - ing Word still bur - ning in your church, a liv - ing flame

light cre - a - ting life un - fold - ing till it formed our hu - man race;
liv - ing dy - ing ri - sing reign - ing send - ing your a - pos - tles forth;
wa - tered by your gra - cious Spir - it bear - ing fruit a hun - dred fold:
Fill the church with Christ's com - pas - sion with your strength her hands sus - tain.
shine through all our work and wit - ness as we serve in Je - sus' name.

Word be - fore all stars and pla - nets we, your peo - ple sing your praise!
Word that sought the lost and lone - ly praise for love that gives us worth!
praise for all who served the Go - spel by their wit - ness clear and bold!
To a world still bro - ken, send us! Make cre - a - tion whole a - gain!
Keep us faith - ful till Earth's peo - ple sing your praise in glad ac - claim!

WORDS: Herman G. Stuempfle, Jr.
MUSIC: Stephen C. Williams

MUHLENBERG
878787

Word of Wisdom, Word of wonder,
    source of boundless time and space;*
light creating, life unfolding
    till it formed our human race;
Word before all stars and planets,
    we, your people, sing your praise!

Word of promise, Word incarnate
    as the Son of God on earth;
living, dying, rising, reigning,
    sending your apostles forth;
Word that sought the lost and lonely,
    praise for love that gives us worth!

Word well planted, Word deep rooted,
    sown by faithful saints of old;
watered by your gracious Spirit,
    bearing fruit a hundred fold:
praise for all who served the Gospel
    by their witness clear and bold!

Word of mercy, Word of healing,
    where the people cry in pain,
fill the church with Christ's compassion;
    with your strength her hands sustain.
To the world still broken, send us!
    Make creation whole again!

Word empow'ring, Word still burning
    in your church, a living flame:
shine through all our work and witness
    as we serve in Jesus' name.
Keep us faithful till all people
    sing your praise in glad acclaim!

*In stanza one, line 2, the earlier version had "birthing cosmic time and space."

Commissioned for the 250th Anniversary of Henry Melchior Muhlenberg's establishment of the Lutheran Church in America. 5/30/97. Revised 1999. Copyright: Herman G. Stuempfle, Jr.

There was precedent in a hymn composed for the Bicentennial Pageant at Muhlenberg College in 1942, marking the 200th anniversary of Muhlenberg's arrival in Pennsylvania. The Bicentennial Pageant, "For God and Country," was presented six evenings prior to commencement; outside speakers included Mrs. Eleanor Roosevelt and Samuel Rayburn, Speaker of the United States House of Representatives. This Bicentennial Hymn, by the Rev. John D. M. Brown, head of the College English Department, was set to the tune of "God of Our Fathers":

> Most Gracious Lord, Who led o'er land and wave
> Through wood and wilderness our fathers brave
> To this new land by faith's unfailing flame,
> In thankfulness we glorify Thy name.

> For all our fathers in the days of old,
> Steadfast and worthy, faithful, true, and bold,
> Servants and soldiers in Thy realm divine,
> Eternal praise and thanks, O Lord, be Thine.

> Sustain us now with Thy celestial aid;
> Fill us with zeal and courage unafraid;
> Give us abundant grace to do Thy will,
> Perfect Thy kingdom and Thy law fulfill.

> Our fathers' God, to Thee all praise we give,
> In Whom the souls of men and nations live;
> With grateful hearts we bow before Thy face:
> Thy strength our glory, and our hope Thy grace.

During 1997-98, local groups sometimes attempted other versions or musical reflections of Muhlenberg's career. Thus one hymn ran, set to the tune of "The Church's One Foundation":

> Ecclesia plantanda, the Church has been planted
> By apostolic prophets, with Jesus at their head.
> It spanned the ancient empires and new worlds far beyond,
> Confessing, suffering, serving, amid the living dead.

> Ecclesia plantanda, the Church is being planted
> Throughout a glorious history of pastors and peoples,

Bringing Christ's gospel into opportunities granted,
By word, in faith, one body, in realms beyond steeples.

Ecclesia plantanda, the Church must be planted
By us sent forth to witness to Jesus and God's grace,
Empowered by the Spirit, a faith ne'er recanted,
True to our wondrous heritage in our own time and place.

Christo et ecclesia, for Christ and for the Church,
The motto of our forebears for mission and in life;
Ours too, today, committed, to grow mid best and worst,
Bring reconciliation, seek peace, and end all strife.

For a congregational celebration, Henry himself was found singing (to the tune "My Favorite Things"),

St. Michael's in Philly,
And old Zion too,
St. Michael's in Germantown and Augustus in Trappe,
New Hanover and Zion, Spring City, these are a few of the churches
I grew.

When the funds dip,
When the road's long,
When I'm feeling blue,
I simply remember the call of my God . . .
And then I don't feel SO BAD!

Or "Must Be Henry" (to the tune "Must Be Santa . . . Santa Claus")

Who planted churches left and right?
Henry planted churches left and right!
Who rode on horseback day and night?
Henry rode on horseback day and night!

Left and right,
Day and night?

Refrain: Must Be Henry . . . Must Be Henry . . . Must Be Henry
Muhlenberg.

Whose middle name is a Wise Man?
Henry's middle name is a Wise Man!
Who for conflict has a plan?
Henry for conflict has a plan!

After seven verses the summary comes (some of it more correct than other parts, but fun):

Scattered hope, Could cope, Sunday School, Gave us rules, Could toast, Good host, God's will, No bill, Barns and boats, Tattered coats, Wise man, Has a plan, Left and right, Day and night.

A Twisted Cord: A Drama Involving
Muhlenberg and Johann Casper Stoever, Jr.

John P. Trump

This play commemorating the 250th Anniversary of the first meeting of the Ministerium of Pennsylvania under the leadership of Henry Melchior Muhlenberg, the official beginning of an organized Lutheran Church in America, was commissioned by the Muhlenberg Tradition Series, 1998.

In research for the play, the author reports that three books were especially useful: the 1980 dissertation by H. L. Nelson; Riforgiato 1980; and Mann 1888.

In the performance at the Allentown event, Muhlenberg was played, as in earlier versions in the Carolinas, by Patrick Gagliano, Chair of the Department of Theater and Speech Communication, Newberry College, Newberry, South Carolina, who is also drama director for St. Andrew's Lutheran Church, Columbia, and Camp Director for Dramarama Camp for At-Risk Youth. Stoever was played by Thomas E. Dalton, Adjunct Professor of Theater and Speech Communication, Newberry College, and Drama Director for Dramarama Camp for At-Risk Youth. Rachel Deal Cooper played the Girl in "A Twisted Cord." A photo of the cast appears in The Lutheran *11, no. 10 (October 1998): 50.*

• •

INTRODUCTION *(to be spoken at the performance and printed in the program)*

The theater is a place of imagination, a place where unexpected ideas and people are brought into action and sometimes conflict with one another. It is a place of exploration and surprise. It is a place of "What if?" What if, this or that had happened? You must imagine, for a moment, a meeting that we know never took place. Muhlenberg kept an exact daily journal. This encounter is not recorded there. However, Muhlenberg was at odds with the Rev. Mr. Johann Casper Stoever, Jr., who was not invited to this first meeting of the Ministerium. Years later he would be invited. Muhlenberg was at odds with Rev. Mr. Stoever because he did not lead a righteous or "pious" life, as Muhlenberg tried to do. Stoever was not theologically educated in Germany. He was involved in the complicated and difficult situation at the church in Tulpehocken, which was split over the issue of who truly was pastor there. What if, by chance — the chance of the theater — they met the night before the first meeting of the Ministerium, at an inn, a few miles outside of Philadelphia? While this encounter may be fictitious, the issues explored and the conflict were real for Muhlenberg. Many remain real for us today. The date is August 14, 1748.

(An inn outside of Philadelphia. It is suggested simply by several rough tables and chairs. There is a man, sitting off to the side. He has books on the table, including a Bible. A "serving girl"/waitress enters, carrying a glass/ mug of ale.)

GIRL: Here you go, sir. We don't brew it ourselves. There's a fellow across the way does that. It's a good brew though.

STOEVER: Yes, it's good. Very good, especially on a hot night like this.

GIRL: Yes, it's hot, isn't it? Though, I guess, for August, it's pretty typical. You've been traveling.

STOEVER: A little ways. I'm used to it though.

GIRL: You're a preacher?

STOEVER: Yes.

GIRL: I haven't seen so many books in this place before.

STOEVER: You've seen this one, I hope.

GIRL: Oh, the Bible? Sure, just not in this place.

STOEVER: Why, we're just outside Philadelphia. Surely, many a preacher has been through here.

GIRL: Only when they're stuck. Usually they try to make it all the way to Philadelphia without stopping. I don't blame them. Still, stuck. Like you.

STOEVER: Actually, no. I am not stuck. I choose to stay here. I didn't want those in Philadelphia to know that I was coming.

GIRL: A surprise.

STOEVER: I hope so. You have a warm place.

GIRL: I try.

STOEVER: I'm Pastor Stoever. J. C. Stoever. I thought you might recognize the name.

GIRL: Sorry.

STOEVER: I believe I've been here before. But I recall a man. . . .

GIRL: My father, but he died, oh, two years ago or so. Pneumonia. Winters are harsh here.

STOEVER: A young woman like you shouldn't be running an inn by herself.

GIRL: What am I to do? Go back to Germany? What do I have there? Here at least, I have a roof and a garden. Besides, who wants to travel that ocean again?

STOEVER: You're right there. But there are more coming every day from the homeland.

GIRL: That's what I'm hoping. And I figure, out of all those men, one has my name stamped right on his forehead.

STOEVER: Oh, I'm sure many a man has tried for your hand . . . or . . . something. . . .

GIRL: Or something. I believe that you are concerned for something more than my soul, Pastor, . . . if I didn't know better.

STOEVER: You might know perfectly well.

GIRL: Drink your ale, Reverend.

STOEVER: To that man, with the stamp upon his forehead!

GIRL: Holler if you need me.

(HE RETURNS TO HIS WORK, READING. SHE EXITS TO THE "KITCHEN.")

STOEVER: *(READING HIS OWN PAPERS)* Jesus said that he would tear down the temple. He had no time for institutions and formalities. He had no time for the hypocrites of the faith. He charged his disciples to carry no purse, no rod, but simply go with the shoes on their feet and the spirit of God. Why, then, must we burden God's spirit with the weight of an institutionalized, gathered church? No . . . , why then, why must YOU burden God's spirit with the weight of an institutionalized church? Consider the lilies of the field . . . yes . . . , consider the lilies of the field. . . .

(HE GOES BACK TO HIS BOOKS. FROM OFF STAGE THE GIRL CALLS:)

GIRL: Did you want me?

STOEVER: No, no . . . , just talking to myself.

(HE GOES BACK TO WORK. AS HE DOES, MUHLENBERG ENTERS. STOEVER SEES HIM, AND HIDES IN HIS WORK. MUHLENBERG DOES NOT REALIZE WHO HE IS. MUHLENBERG ENTERS, BUT NOT SHYLY, FOR HE IS USUALLY NOT SHY. HOWEVER, THIS IS NOT THE PLACE HE WANTS TO BE.)

MUHLENBERG: *(TO STOEVER, SIMPLY BEING POLITE, NOT RECOGNIZING)* Evening.

STOEVER: *(KEEPING HEAD TURNED, UNDER BREATH)* Evening.

GIRL: *(ENTERING, TO STOEVER AT FIRST, NOT EXPECTING MUHLENBERG)* I couldn't hear you . . . , did you . . . , oh . . . , can I help you?

MUHLENBERG: Unfortunately, yes. It seems my horse has thrown a shoe. Is there a blacksmith nearby?

GIRL: There's one. Thomas. About a half mile, but he won't do it yet today.

MUHLENBERG: But I must get to Philadelphia.

GIRL: It will be there tomorrow.

MUHLENBERG: What if I offer him double his usual fee?

GIRL: I know Thomas. It will not matter. You are stuck, sir.

MUHLENBERG: Do you have a horse I could borrow, and I'll leave mine?

GIRL: Sir, I have none. You are stuck.

MUHLENBERG: Could you send someone at least, to this Mr. . . .

GIRL: Thomas.

MUHLENBERG: To Thomas, and take my horse so that he can get to her at first light?

GIRL: I will get the boy next door. He'll do it for a small price.

MUHLENBERG: Let it be done.

GIRL: You will have to rest the night here.

MUHLENBERG: I suppose I will.

GIRL: We have rooms. And dinner if you'd like. They're clean and bug free, both of them, the rooms and the dinner.

MUHLENBERG: That's appetizing. Yes, yes, have the boy take my bags. Give me a room, and something to eat. Some bread maybe, and some cheese?

GIRL: Sit. You look weary.

MUHLENBERG: Weary? No, not really. Thank you. You are kind.

GIRL: It's my job. If I am not kind, I am not paid.

MUHLENBERG: That hasn't stopped many of our preachers.

GIRL: You too? *(SHE LOOKS AT STOEVER WHO INDICATES TO HER NOT TO REVEAL TO MUHLENBERG HIS IDENTITY AS A MINISTER.)*

MUHLENBERG: Too? What do you mean?

GIRL: Oh, it's just that, um, a um, Anglican brother passed through, uh, not long ago. . . .

MUHLENBERG: Of course. Anglicans like their ale.

GIRL: No more than others.

MUHLENBERG: Unfortunately, you are right. Many of our pastors enjoy their ale too much. It is a spice of life. But for many, it is a staple, when the staple is to be the Gospel.

GIRL: For me, it is simply a living.

MUHLENBERG: I understand.

GIRL: I will get you that bread and cheese.

MUHLENBERG: Thank you. *(SHE EXITS. HE PULLS OUT SOME PAPERS. TO HIMSELF:)* . . . Now, these examination questions for Mr. Kurtz. . . .

(STOEVER GETS UP AND, WITH ALE IN HAND, COMES BEHIND MUHLENBERG.)

STOEVER: Rumor has it, Reverend, that Dr. Luther enjoyed his ale, and even brewed it.

MUHLENBERG: *(WITHOUT TURNING AROUND)* Sir, it is true that Luther enjoyed his ale. But Luther was no Christ and certainly had his flaws.

STOEVER: *(UNDER HIS BREATH)* Unlike you.

MUHLENBERG: As to brewing, I believe that was his wife, Katie, who did so to support his ministry.

STOEVER: So, if I, in an act of kindness and friendship, and as a show of support to a pastor, purchased for you an ale, would you drink it with me?

MUHLENBERG: *(TURNING)* Sir, I appreciate your kindness but . . . Stoever! Herr Stoever.

STOEVER: Muhlenberg, Herr Muhlenberg. *(PAUSE)* If this does not

convince us that God in his heaven has a sense of humor, nothing
does.

MUHLENBERG: What are you doing here?

STOEVER: What are you doing here?

MUHLENBERG: You are as impudent as ever.

STOEVER: Me? Herr Muhlenberg, from the moment you landed in
South Carolina, your impudence, your arrogance, has permeated
this land like the poor German immigrants you have come to save.

MUHLENBERG: You have not answered my question.

STOEVER: I am a simple traveler, stopping like you, along the way. Like
you, I have books to read. Sermons to prepare.

MUHLENBERG: You know where I am going. What is your destination?

STOEVER: Let me see, you are heading to Saint Michael's for the dedication.

MUHLENBERG: And for the meeting of the Ministerium.

STOEVER: Ah yes, your Ministerium. Your gathering of Lutheran clergy
and humble laypeople from far and wide, your assembly of saints
for the business of the church. That is an oxymoron.

MUHLENBERG: It is not MY Ministerium. You twist words. Maybe you
can do that with uneducated farmers and peasants, but you cannot
with me, Herr Stoever.

STOEVER: I do not twist words. You are the one who would mince and
chop words to set your agenda and your goals. Even the word of
God.

MUHLENBERG: The word of God? I stand on that word. While you,
you pick and choose from it as you will.

STOEVER: I . . . , I never . . .

*(GIRL ENTERS WITH BREAD, CHEESE, AND ANOTHER ALE FOR
STOEVER.)*

GIRL: Here is that bread and cheese, and another ale for you, sir.

STOEVER: I didn't ask for one. . . .

GIRL: That's alright. I see you two do know each other. I thought it
odd, two preachers in one night. I don't often get one preacher, let
alone two. So, two preachers. I thought, this should be a reverent
and quiet night.

MUHLENBERG: Thank you. But be careful who you see as a minister of God, and who you do not. There are wolves in sheep's clothing.

STOEVER: Miss, I am glad that you, and God, are gracious, for indeed, many of His servants are not.

GIRL: I will be in the kitchen. It isn't quite as hot in there. Call if you need me.

MUHLENBERG: You have yet to answer me, Stoever. You have no church that you serve in this area, unless you seek, once again, to misguide a new fellowship.

STOEVER: Or am I working again to begin yet another congregation? I have begun many.

MUHLENBERG: You begin them but do not stay. . . . You begin them for what purpose, and to what end?

STOEVER: I am a minister of the Lutheran Confessions, am I not?

MUHLENBERG: So you claim.

STOEVER: So you know!

MUHLENBERG: If only your life reflected it.

STOEVER: My confessions, my convictions, reflect it. You are so quick to condemn. Have you not read your gospels?

MUHLENBERG: I have read them, and I seek to live them! You must also live them, Herr Stoever. If you do believe them, you must live them.

STOEVER: I preach the word. I administer the sacraments. I have ministered to more souls than have you. I know this new land better than you. Well beyond the Susquehanna, I know it.

MUHLENBERG: But I know the word, Herr Stoever. You know the allegations brought against you. Do you deny them?

STOEVER: Allegations by you.

MUHLENBERG: Allegations by others, that I have merely repeated and respected and asked you to recant.

STOEVER: What, that my life is not as pious as yours? That I am not as holy as you? Three cheers to that. Let me buy you an ale. . . . Miss . . . , miss!!

MUHLENBERG: I do not want . . .

STOEVER: As a peace offering. . . . Miss!

GIRL: *(ENTERING)* What would you like?

STOEVER: Another ale. For my colleague.

MUHLENBERG: I have no desire . . .

STOEVER: Do not listen to him. Bring him an ale.

GIRL: I will bring it. I am sure one of you will drink it. *(SHE EXITS.)*

MUHLENBERG: I will not drink with you, Herr Stoever.

STOEVER: You would refuse my generosity?

MUHLENBERG: This is not generosity. And you are not simply traveling through. You cannot be trusted, Herr Stoever.

GIRL: Here is your ale, sir. You might try it. On a night like this, it cools you.

MUHLENBERG: There are hotter places than this that I am worried about, Miss.

GIRL: Yes, and I don't think they have ale there, so you might enjoy it while you can.

MUHLENBERG: I trust that I shall not worry about that. God has procured my salvation and given me the gift of heaven.

GIRL: I don't think there's any ale there either, so I would still enjoy it while I could. But that's your matter, Reverend. *(SHE EXITS)*

MUHLENBERG: She has a sharp wit.

STOEVER *(GESTURING):* But a round and smooth . . .

MUHLENBERG: Herr Stoever, must you debase one of God's creatures? You sit and drink, and lust. . . .

STOEVER: Oh, Herr Muhlenberg, come now. Drink!

MUHLENBERG: I will not drink with those who harm God's word and God's church.

STOEVER: Ah, now we are getting somewhere. God's word AND God's church? Or is it, God's word OR God's church, in juxtaposition and even opposition? Or IS it God's word despite God's church? Or even better yet, is it God's word, and Muhlenberg's church?

MUHLENBERG: You are mad. You are mad, because you know that you have failed. You have failed to live the Gospel you have weakly proclaimed. The company you keep. The drink you drink, the women you have . . . , and now there will be a church, a church by whose authority such behavior will be judged.

STOEVER: Yes! That church! With your precious order. Your organization. Sometimes it is the enemy of the Spirit!

MUHLENBERG: What are you doing here?

STOEVER: As I said, traveling.

MUHLENBERG: Where?

STOEVER: I plan on attending the meeting of the Ministerium.

MUHLENBERG: You are not invited.

STOEVER: By whose authority? That of a Ministerium that is not yet formed?

MUHLENBERG: You refused my invitation. I graciously wrote to you to offer you my friendship, to bring you into the fold of pastors who would attend.

STOEVER: Ah yes, your letter. You offered me your friendship IF I should acknowledge the countless mass of sins which I have heaped up. If I should experience genuine conversions of heart, and amend my lifestyle. You also went on to recommend that I read certain theological works, reform my preaching techniques, and bow out of Tulpehocken completely. IF I did all this, then you would consider inviting me to the Ministerium. What is left? Sacrificing my firstborn? I was not invited. Not truly.

MUHLENBERG: No, you truly were. You simply refuse to change, and admit your sins.

STOEVER: Christ said those who are not against us are for us . . .

MUHLENBERG: And he said, "Cut down that tree, for it does not bear fruit."

STOEVER: But the farmer pleaded, one more year . . . , one more year.

MUHLENBERG: And in my letter to you, I was offering you that year, that chance of repentance, and you have not. You remain embroiled in the church at Tulpehocken, where they are left not knowing who is their true pastor, who is truly called to lead them. There is no church authority to restore order, order that you do not understand.

STOEVER: It is Tulpehocken, not my lifestyle, which burns you.

MUHLENBERG: Your presence there hurt those people. They did not know who to trust, where to turn. You claim to be their pastor, but so do others. Some people side with you. Others do not. It is places like Tulpehocken which should convince you of how desperately we need the church to be organized, so that people know who is their true pastor, who represents the true church. They are like sheep without a shepherd, and wolves will come.

STOEVER: Am I a wolf?

MUHLENBERG: You threaten to invade the Ministerium, and you are not invited. You threaten to work to destroy that gathering of the sheep.

STOEVER: It will fail of its own accord, as have others before it.

MUHLENBERG: They, rightfully so. It was not God's time.

STOEVER: But you are so sure that this will take hold?

MUHLENBERG: God's church will take root. The church being planted, is to grow.

STOEVER: Ah, yes, the church being planted. And you are the farmer?

MUHLENBERG: A worker in the vineyard, Herr Stoever. Many are called but few are chosen. You are still not invited.

STOEVER: Christ was uninvited at the temple, yet he preached there and even overturned tables.

MUHLENBERG: I should have expected this of you. You, so-called ministers like you, are the very reason we need a Ministerium desperately. To protect the people from false prophets, from false preachers, from those who corrupt God's word, for no purpose other than their own. With the Ministerium, we can work to have preachers who preach pure doctrine, lead upright lives, and guide their hearers to salvation and blessedness.

STOEVER: I have led many and have served that word faithfully. Even if, as you claim, my life has not been as pious and as holy as yours and your other Halle Institute brethren. As if you alone, as if those who claim one school, one seminary, understand what it means to live as a Christian. Did not Peter and Paul argue?

MUHLENBERG: To experience true rebirth? To live an upright life? Is that so hard?

STOEVER: Luther himself would not be accepted by you.

MUHLENBERG: Were Luther's teachings the end of God's revelation?

STOEVER: Oh, so you speak for God?

MUHLENBERG: I strive to follow God's word, as simple as that.

STOEVER: And the Confessions?

MUHLENBERG: Don't start that, Herr Stoever. Better theologians than you have attacked me, and other students from Halle, on that ground. Since you cannot attack my life, you try to attack my Confessions, as if somehow I was not a true Lutheran. You know full well that I stand by the unaltered Augsburg Confession. You know that in our Ministerium we shall expect loyalty to those Confessions as true understandings of God's word. But we shall also expect upright lives. Doctrine and practice must be pure, but doctrine and practice have come to be hated on account of the wretched conduct of our preachers. We must expect more.

STOEVER: You expect, you expect. You are expecting like a woman about to give birth.

MUHLENBERG: Yes, we are! Birth to a new church.

STOEVER: What makes you think that you will succeed where others have failed? Did not Valentine Kraft try to organize just such a gathering of Lutherans? I was ordained at such a meeting by John Schultze, back in 1733, at Trappe.

MUHLENBERG: Maybe, but you would not have been so at this Ministerium.

STOEVER: Are you so sure? And your precious Kurtz, he will measure up? *(INDICATES PAPERS BEFORE MUHLENBERG ON HIS TA-BLE.)* Are these the questions you will ask him at the Ministerium to see if he will be ordained?

MUHLENBERG: Yes.

STOEVER: Ask me.

MUHLENBERG: Return to your ale.

STOEVER: Ask me. Ask me the questions that you will ask at his ordination examination. What text will you give him to exegete? What, are you afraid?

MUHLENBERG: Afraid? Of what?

STOEVER: That I will answer as well as he might. That you would have to ordain me!

MUHLENBERG: I have little doubt, Herr Stoever, that much of what we ask Kurtz you could answer.

STOEVER: And his text?

MUHLENBERG: Luke 16:9.

STOEVER: Sixteen nine?

MUHLENBERG: Yes.

STOEVER: Let's see, Luke 16, the parable of the steward, the dishonest yet wise steward.

MUHLENBERG: Verse nine. "And I say unto you, Make to yourselves friends of the mammon of unrighteousness; that, when ye fail, they may receive you into everlasting habitations."

STOEVER: How interesting for us to consider.

MUHLENBERG: Why?

STOEVER: Here we are, you accusing me of all that you accuse me, of dishonesty, yet Kurtz is about to be asked to exegete a passage about a shrewd but dishonest steward. If I was to exegete, I might consider that God seeks results, not methods. That God will accept almost any means by any steward, as long as his kingdom is built.

MUHLENBERG: You forget the very next verse: "whoever is faithful in very little is faithful also in much, and whoever is dishonest in a very little is dishonest also in much." You, Stoever, you and your friends think that you can be dishonest, unfaithful, in little ways in your lives, a little ale, a little lust, a little lie, and expect the larger matters to correct themselves. It will not be so. We must be faithful in all things, in even the smallest portions of our lives.

STOEVER: A fine pietistic interpretation. The Halle Institute fathers would be proud since ultimately this will be a Halle, a German, ordination.

MUHLENBERG: It will be an American ordination.

STOEVER: As was mine.

MUHLENBERG: No! It was a charade.

STOEVER: Is my ordination a charade?

MUHLENBERG: You must answer that. But you could not stand before your fellow clergy, as will Kurtz, and answer as will he. He will be asked to give an account of his conversion experience. Kurtz will give an accounting for his life. Could you?

STOEVER: You would have us believe that once converted, there is no longer room for doubt? To be a Lutheran is to believe but also to doubt! Let us be honest. You will ordain Kurtz at this blessed gathering because you need Kurtz. You need him to be your TRULY called pastor at Tulpehocken, to give authority to his call in that place. If you needed me, it would be different.

MUHLENBERG: Kurtz is qualified, and called.

STOEVER: You need him!

MUHLENBERG: He can account for his academic and theological training. You have almost none. He will be asked to give reasons for his ministry. He will preach for us a sermon.

STOEVER: Which I could do better than he.

MUHLENBERG: Better? You would entertain the people, and amuse them for a time. God save us when our church simply seeks to amuse. Would your word be true?

STOEVER: By whose measure?

MUHLENBERG: By God's!

STOEVER: But who speaks for God? Your Ministerium? Your church? How can you be so sure?

MUHLENBERG: How can you be sure it does not?

STOEVER: Ah, there's the rub, that makes calamity of so long a life.

MUHLENBERG: Yes. Upon that, we agree.

(GIRL ENTERS) GIRL: I brought you more bread and cheese.

STOEVER: Maybe she can tell us.

GIRL: I don't think I can tell you much.

MUHLENBERG: Do not toy with her, Herr Stoever.

STOEVER: I do not. I am simply asking her, if she can tell, by speaking with us, from waiting upon us . . . which one speaks for God.

MUHLENBERG: Stoever, I warn you.

GIRL: Sir, if I could tell you that, I would not be waiting on each of you, but would rather tend to one, and ignore the other. And that would be bad for business.

STOEVER: Ah, business. An honest answer. It usually does boil down to business, doesn't it?

GIRL: Some things do.

STOEVER: So you would serve even the devil?

GIRL: Undoubtedly I already have. *(SHE EXITS)*

MUHLENBERG: You should not toy with her.

STOEVER: She is not weak.

MUHLENBERG: You do not care what impression she has of you? And therefore, of the church?

STOEVER: The church is much larger than us, Herr Muhlenberg.

MUHLENBERG: In this place, we are the church.

STOEVER: But you seek to define it much more narrowly. To have your Ministerium THE church.

MUHLENBERG: Kurtz will be called to recognize the authority of the Ministerium.

STOEVER: You see, authority. That's what the Ministerium is really about. Authority.

MUHLENBERG: It's about God's church being planted in this land. It's about saving souls.

STOEVER: Which one is it?

MUHLENBERG: You cannot have one without the other.

STOEVER: Church, yes? But this order, this structure that you seek to impose upon the spirit. I have seen the church. I have planted more seeds of faith in more people, have planted churches, in Lancaster, York, in many places. . . .

MUHLENBERG: But what has become of them? You have worked in the vineyard. I will grant you that. You have preached a form of the word, and even awakened people to God. You have baptized, and given the Lord's Supper, and despite the broken vessel, the sacraments are true. Yet, what becomes of it? Are there any roots? This Ministerium shall be like the pole, next to the plant, to support it as it grows. Without authority the church crumbles, and souls are lost.

STOEVER: You seek your own power, and your own authority.

MUHLENBERG: I seek souls! And for souls to be saved, yes, this church must continue to be planted. Planted in this soil, of this land. A new church.

STOEVER: Your church! And anything else is heathen.

MUHLENBERG: Why do you fear a church that would have respect and authority after what others have done to God's mission? Other clergy. People like Kraft.

STOEVER: Kraft is my friend.

MUHLENBERG: He should not be! A sixty-three-year-old man, planning on marrying a seventeen-year-old girl! All the while, he has a wife in Germany, and has expressed interest in a widow in Lancaster. You call him a friend? Is this the kind of minister you want in your church?

STOEVER: Better than Zinzendorf.

MUHLENBERG: I would not align with him either. Kraft has no morals, and there are many like him. But Zinzendorf is one of those wolves in sheep's clothing. A Moravian, indeed, he called himself a Moravian Bishop, while claiming himself Lutheran and acting as the authority of our church. But what is the church to Zinzendorf? He thinks it is a polite gathering, a social affair that gathers, yes, in the name of Jesus, but what is the church if it does not gather around word and sacrament? What is our church if it is not clearly Lutheran? Don't you see? The people need leadership to walk between these two great walls of water . . . those who would have no confessions on one side, and those who bear no fruits of repentance on the other.

STOEVER: And you are their Moses?

MUHLENBERG: Someone is needed to lead these people, any one, who serves the Gospel and not his own pockets. How can the church stand when we have so-called ministers running from household to household, from church to church, charging for baptisms, charging for communion. We have become no better than Tetzels, selling indulgences to build St. Peter's in Rome. We sell the grace of God; we don't administer it.

STOEVER: Is a salary any different? Is it better to do as you plan, to demand a certain salary of every congregation in your church?

MUHLENBERG: Fair wages only, so that ministers be not distracted and burdened, wondering how they shall eat. And if we are to bring ministers to this country, if we are to train men for ministry, they must know that they will not starve. And we must train them, Herr Stoever.

STOEVER: As you would have them trained, at Halle?

MUHLENBERG: We must, one day, have our own seminaries. To train our pastors, in the Scripture, in the Confessions.

STOEVER: With you as their head. Pope Muhlenberg.

MUHLENBERG: If I wanted power, why am I not to be elected superintendent?

STOEVER: How do you know that?

MUHLENBERG: I know.

STOEVER: You know, because whoever is officially elected does not matter. Ultimately, this new church has you as its head, official, or unofficial. Luther denied being the head of his church, and what name do we bear?

MUHLENBERG: I am called to serve here. Can I deny the way people look to me?

STOEVER: Look to you? You are opportunistic.

MUHLENBERG: Yes, opportunistic! That I am. If there is an opportunity to build and strengthen God's church, to save souls, to bring order to this chaos and wilderness, I will do it. God is a God of order, and in his congregations everything must be done orderly.

STOEVER: And all true pastors of this God will abide by your order, ecclesiastical and liturgical.

MUHLENBERG: Yes.

STOEVER: So it's true, that you will ask — no, demand — that all churches, all pastors, of this new Ministerium abide by your liturgy.

MUHLENBERG: It is not my liturgy.

STOEVER: It has your stamp upon it. We must all worship with the same words. You go too far, Muhlenberg.

MUHLENBERG: Am I on trial here?

STOEVER: Yes. Yes, you are. And like all accused, I am after your motives.

MUHLENBERG: My motives?

STOEVER: If you can convince me, the jury of your peer, that your motive is the salvation and care of the poor souls of this land, and not the mere building up of some institution, I will not invade your precious Ministerium.

MUHLENBERG: What must I do to convince you?

STOEVER: I don't know.

MUHLENBERG: You don't know, yet you demand proof?

STOEVER: Why must there be so much order? Why must you order the lives of pastors, the structure of the church, even the words of worship? What do you fear? Why do you fear the Holy Spirit? People need to worship in spirit and in truth.

MUHLENBERG: But we too often neglect the truth. Don't you see? Many claim to worship in the spirit, and even claim to be Lutheran, claim loyalty to our Confessions. This liturgy will be the test, the plumb line that we can hold up to pastors and churches alike. If you are Lutheran, if you claim that name, stand next to this line, this liturgy, and see how you stand.

STOEVER: If that is so, then why not use the words of institution that are truer to our Confessions?

MUHLENBERG: Those complaints have reached me.

STOEVER: They are valid.

MUHLENBERG: We use the very words of Christ, as recorded in the Gospels, "Take and eat. This is my body. This is my blood."

STOEVER: Yes, but Moses, as they walk between the walls of water, these people must hear the truth loud and clear. We must ask what does Christ mean, more than what Christ said. That is what it means to be confessional.

MUHLENBERG: It shall be changed, as you and others requested. This is my TRUE body, this is my TRUE blood.

STOEVER: It is ironic. You hate me.

MUHLENBERG: You anger me because you hurt the church. We must have pastors who are both educated, and moral. In Lancaster you were so drunk you vomited publicly. We cannot have pastors behaving thus.

STOEVER: You could find no one more true to our Confessions. I would make a fine ally.

MUHLENBERG: I have one and only one ally.

STOEVER: We all need allies, Herr Muhlenberg.

MUHLENBERG: Then this new Ministerium shall provide me some.

STOEVER: All clergy.

MUHLENBERG: Yes.

STOEVER: You do not trust the laity, Herr Muhlenberg. It will be your downfall. I have been in this country longer.

MUHLENBERG: I love the people, but I need not trust them to lead. Peter was charged to feed and lead the sheep.

STOEVER: But admit it, you think that they are as ignorant as sheep.

MUHLENBERG: About farming? No. About the church, the Confessions, even the Gospel? Often. And if we want them not to remain ignorant, we must take this horse by the reins.

STOEVER: Will the people vote in this new Ministerium?

MUHLENBERG: They will attend. They will be at the dedication of St. Michael, and at the Ministerium meeting.

STOEVER: Will they vote?

MUHLENBERG: You know that they will not. They will speak. They will voice concerns. But we must battle this temptation to control the church that leaves pastors begging these laypeople for our bread. Now every peasant wants to act the part of a patron of the parish for which he has neither the intelligence nor the skills. It is not good. We must have authority.

STOEVER: Be careful, Herr Muhlenberg. I have heard rumors that there will be complaints lodged against you by these ignorant people. Maybe you meddle too much.

MUHLENBERG: Then we will listen to their complaints.

STOEVER: And then?

MUHLENBERG: Then? We shall listen.

STOEVER: There are those who may ask why I am not there.

MUHLENBERG: So I have heard. We shall listen to them, and by listening, we shall strengthen the church. Stoever, this is a strange and difficult land and people we serve. You know, possibly better than I, that we must have an American clergy, for an American church. I know it, from before I landed in Georgia on board that wretched ship. There was such a diverse group on board. Englishmen, and crude sailors, a Roman Catholic cook, a merchant, a lawyer, a customs clerk, and a Lutheran family from Salzburg, and I worried so for them. I had worship for them, giving them the true word and sacrament, so that this family of Lutherans in this land, who will fall prey to worse things than wild animals and weather . . . who will face heresies and wretched doctrine, crude and vulgar influences, like those sailors on board, drinking, cursing, singing not hymns of the faith but filthy songs. If we do not have a church, planted firmly in this land, with pastors to serve them, these travelers and pilgrims are lost. Surely lost.

STOEVER: Those were just sailors, Herr Muhlenberg.

MUHLENBERG: This country is like Israel in the time of the judges. "In those days there was no king in Israel, but every man did that which was right in his own eyes."

STOEVER: They have clergy. And they have God's word. Why must they have your ordered church?

MUHLENBERG: They need a church as a vessel and guardian of our Confessions, true to God's word. We must be bound together in this land, Herr Stoever, for a twisted cord of many threads is not easily broken. We must be bound together. By the Gospel. By our Confessions. By our liturgy. So that we can be strong in this world, as I had to be on that boat. What was most interesting, Herr Stoever, on that boat, was that as I ministered to these Lutherans, the captain brought out his Prayer Book, and another his Bible. As they witnessed our faithfulness, their souls were touched. Many discussions began. Doors were opened for salvation. And for those who would not listen to the gospel, I was not afraid to give them the law.

STOEVER: I am sure you spoke forcefully.

MUHLENBERG: As we must. As the church must. But before we are speakers, we are pastors, Herr Stoever. That is what you do not understand. I was pastor to that family. That mother had no idea of true conversion. We talked. She learned to recognize more and more that she was a great sinner, estranged from God, and his Son. She felt, however, a yearning desire to be truly reconciled and united with God through her savior.

STOEVER: I want nothing less for God's people here.

MUHLENBERG: Yes, but those people on that ship, those events were also a mirror in which I could see my own heart as it was created by nature. . . . I could see my own desires. My own sinfulness, which I must always face. You do not face yours.

STOEVER: Why should I, when I have you to do it for me?

MUHLENBERG: You jest, about something like your soul.

STOEVER: Do you care for my soul, Herr Muhlenberg?

MUHLENBERG: More than you know, Herr Stoever.

STOEVER: You know the irony in all this is that despite the fact that you despise me, I have laid the groundwork for you. I have planted many seeds of faith in this territory and beyond.

MUHLENBERG: Yes, you have. But they need support, or they will never grow. Herr Stoever, if you do love these people, as you claim, you must not disturb this gathering. You must let the dedication, the ordination, the meeting, go as planned. You must step aside and see if it takes root.

STOEVER: You seem so certain.

MUHLENBERG: I am certain. I believe that God has brought me to these shores and this moment . . . , this kairos. It is God's providence at work.

STOEVER: How can you be so certain? Maybe your sin is not ale, or women, but pride? It is the first sin, Herr Muhlenberg. It is a deadly sin. Your certainty that God is using you, that the church you desire so to be planted, is God's church for the saving of souls, and not simply your church, for the glory of Muhlenberg.

MUHLENBERG: Nothing could be further from the truth. If that were the case, God would not bring us here. God will not let it take root.

STOEVER: It hasn't. Not yet.

MUHLENBERG: So we are left like those rival prophets, Jeremiah and Hananiah. . . .

STOEVER: How is that?

MUHLENBERG: Jeremiah spoke one word of God. Hananiah claimed another. They disagreed. Hananiah told Jeremiah to remove the yoke, that God had spoken to him. Jeremiah said, I hope that you are right, but God spoke to me and said to keep it. In the end, they agreed that only time would tell. And you know what happened.

STOEVER: In a year, Hananiah was struck dead.

MUHLENBERG: Only time will tell if it is God's word I proclaim, and God's will that is done as this church is gathered.

STOEVER: On that we agree.

MUHLENBERG: Funny thing about time though. How much time do you need to tell? Ten years? One hundred? Two hundred? More?

How long do you seek to know if the church you plant is truly God's vessel?

STOEVER: I venture forever. We see in a glass dimly, but then we shall see face to face, and fully understand, even as we are fully understood.

MUHLENBERG: Will you let the Ministerium meet, without you, and without malice?

STOEVER: I should be there. But maybe it is God's providence that we meet here, this night, instead of at the Ministerium.

MUHLENBERG: Mend your life, Herr Stoever. You must.

STOEVER: Time will tell there as well. I will leave you be, tonight, and tomorrow. I must retire. The ale has made me sleepy. I will leave you in peace, Herr Muhlenberg, and go my way. Maybe, one day, you will be gracious enough to see me as one of those twisted cords.

MUHLENBERG: But you must not stand alone.

STOEVER: A good little soldier.

MUHLENBERG: Good night, Herr Stoever.

STOEVER: Cheers, Herr Muhlenberg. Girl! Miss!!

GIRL: Yes, what now? You've had enough ale.

STOEVER: I simply need to know which is my room. It is time for me to sleep off this "ale-ment."

GIRL: Top of the stairs.

STOEVER: Thank you, my dear.

GIRL: Welcome, I'm sure. *(STOEVER EXITS)* He's an interesting preacher.

MUHLENBERG: Sometimes. What I mean is, he is always interesting. I think that he is sometimes a preacher. But some people will follow him.

GIRL: Oh well, any port in a storm, I guess.

MUHLENBERG: Unless that port is dangerous.

GIRL: I wouldn't know about that, sir. Are you done with that?

MUHLENBERG: Yes.

GIRL: I didn't understand what you were arguing about.

MUHLENBERG: We were arguing about . . . , we were arguing about something very important to me.

GIRL: So it seemed. I've never understood why there's always so many arguments between preachers and in churches.

MUHLENBERG: Let me ask you, you are German, aren't you?

GIRL: Mostly.

MUHLENBERG: Lutheran?

GIRL: My family was.

MUHLENBERG: Where is your church?

GIRL: You're in it.

MUHLENBERG: I want to know.

GIRL: There is no Lutheran gathering close enough to me. Not that I know of.

MUHLENBERG: That is what I feel so strongly about.

GIRL: All I know is that two years ago, when my father died, I needed a pastor. You, that other man, someone. We called on schoolmaster Hendrick to bury him.

MUHLENBERG: I am sorry.

GIRL: Oh, my father is still in the ground. But at that time, when he died, before he died, he desired Holy Communion, but there was none for him. In Germany, he never missed worship. Here, well, it's a difficult land, isn't it?

MUHLENBERG: Indeed, it is. So have you been baptized?

GIRL: Oh, yes. In Germany, years ago.

MUHLENBERG: And have you received instruction in the church?

GIRL: No, not me.

MUHLENBERG: You need to learn your catechism, your Creed, your Lord's Prayer.

GIRL: I know them. Not the catechism by heart, but I have it.

MUHLENBERG: But do you understand them?

GIRL: As best I can, by myself.

MUHLENBERG: Let me teach you.

GIRL: Oh no, not now.

MUHLENBERG: It's important to me.

GIRL: I have dishes to wash.

MUHLENBERG: We can talk while you wash. You shall be both Mary and Martha.

GIRL: I don't understand.

MUHLENBERG: Which is why we must talk.

GIRL: If it will please you.

MUHLENBERG: It would.

GIRL: I have always wondered about this Trinity. How Christ was in the beginning.

MUHLENBERG: Let's begin with a poem I wrote, to help people under-

stand. My "Glaubenslied." You could learn it. . . .
I believe in God, the Lord of hosts,
And in his Son and Holy Ghost,
The author of the universe
which by his providence he bear'th.
GIRL: I have heard much better poetry.
MUHLENBERG: No doubt. But no better doctrine for your soul.
GIRL: Go on . . . , it will pass the time.

(AS THEY EXIT)

MUHLENBERG: The first man of the human race
was full of light of love and grace;
his willful turn from righteous path
brought him to darkness, wrath, and death.
Yet did God thus abound in love
that he gave his Son from above. . . .

(THEY EXIT TOWARDS THE KITCHEN. THE PLAY ENDS.)

"The Good Old Days":
The Social Context of Muhlenberg's Times —
Letters of Anna Maria Weiser Muhlenberg
to Christine Engelhart

Louise Proehl Shoemaker

Originally developed for a lecture series at the Philadelphia Seminary in honor of Muhlenberg, this carefully researched and imaginative presentation about Henry Melchior's wife was a feature at the banquet during the 1999 Symposium. Dr. Shoemaker was Professor and Dean of the School of Social Work at the University of Pennsylvania. Long active in church activities, she was elected Vice-President of the Southeastern Pennsylvania Synod of the ELCA in 1997. Her exploration of Muhlenberg's social world adds more than a feminist dimension to the picture that is needed to recapture the dynamics of his day.

• •

The presentation has been made very specific to southeastern Pennsylvania, where Muhlenberg served most of his years in the American church. Some of the general categories of the social context of that time and place are covered: who the people were who lived in southeastern Pennsylvania; some of their economic problems; issues of safety and security; the nature of slavery in this area, especially in Philadelphia; the status of women; and the mobility of the population. Through information on these topics and what follows, I hope to transplant you into Muhlenberg's day.

> Thousands and thousands of English and non-English flooded the shores of North America seeking the main chance . . . they hoped for land, modest amounts of wealth, freedom to act out the drama of the Protestant Reformation, or some measure of control over their own

destinies in a political sense. Above all, the colonists asked for and expected autonomy. . . . The colonists were . . . a peculiar people. They
were anything but representative of the common English or European
citizen. On the contrary, they were the disaffected and alienated segments of society. (Paul Lucas, *American Odyssey 1607-1789* [Englewood
Cliffs, NJ: Prentice-Hall, 1984], 220)

It was to serve such people that Henry Melchior Muhlenberg was
sent by the mission institution at Halle, Germany. He was to bring some
order in a rather chaotic situation: schoolteachers were serving as pastors
in some places; discredited pastors from Germany were continuing to dis-
credit themselves and the church in the new world. And those who were
faithful were faltering under the load of scattered preaching places, unsafe
living conditions, and little pay.

To give some flavor of the social context of the Muhlenberg era, consider some vignettes, facts, and figures, especially about southeastern
Pennsylvania:

In southeastern Pennsylvania, one of the most productive agricultural
regions of the eighteenth century, English, Scotch-Irish, and Germans
predominated. By 1790 the area supported 92,000 English; 57,500
Scotch-Irish, Scots, and South Irish; and 128,000 German-speaking
peoples. These non-English immigrants moved beyond subsistence-
level farming quickly. Indeed, by 1750, farmers in southeastern Pennsylvania consumed only about 60 percent of what they produced.
(Lucas 149)

In 1763, the "Paxton Boys," a group of Scotch-Irish immigrants living
on the frontier of Pennsylvania turned into vigilantes when the
Quaker-dominated Pennsylvania legislature failed to give them sufficient protection from Indian raids. . . . They marched on to Philadelphia to state their grievances to colonial officials. They complained of
underrepresentation in the legislature . . . , inadequate protection from
Indian forays, etc., etc. It was a list of grievances which might have
come from frontierspeople in any of the colonies during hard
times. . . . A delegation from Philadelphia, led by Benjamin Franklin,
met the frontierspeople, listened to their grievances, and promised
that, at the very least, the legislature would create a bounty on Indian
scalps! (Lucas 162-63)

Another group that troubled people of conscience were the slaves owned by whites in the North. Those in the North were mainly agricultural workers but with only one or two owned by one master. They were highly prized and, in contrast to the South, had much better treatment, often becoming, like their masters, semi-skilled artisans. In Philadelphia they were longshoremen, teamsters, and sailors, and worked in the iron foundries and tanneries. In Philadelphia they were the mainstay of the iron industry, Pennsylvania having the largest number of such industries in the eighteenth century.

> Two important facts emerged from the character of slavery in the North during the colonial period. First, though not accepted as members of white society, rural slaves nonetheless mastered the complexities of white culture. Second, urban slaves, because they rarely lived with their masters, possessed a degree of autonomy not enjoyed by slaves anywhere else. (Lucas 155)

While slaves may have had some advantages from being in the North instead of in the South, the status of women differed little, North or South. While the scarcity of women led to some advancement in their status in society, Old World mores won out and women "advanced" only marginally during the eighteenth century. The following notation from a young farmwoman's diary written in 1775 described the experience of most Anglo-American women throughout the colonial era:

> Fix'd Gown for Prude Just to clear my teeth — Mend Mother's Riding hood — Ague in my face — Ellen was spank'd last night — Mother spun short thread — Fix'd two Gowns for Welch's girls — Carded tow-spun linen — worked on Cheese Basket — Hatchel'd Flax with Hannah and we did 51 lb a piece — Pleated and ironed — Read a sermon of Dodridges — Spooled a piece — milked the cows — spun linen and did 50 knots — made a broom of Guinea wheat straw — Spun thread to whiten — Went to Mr. Otis's and made them a swinging visit — Israel said I might ride his jade (horse) — Set a red Dye — Prude stay'd at home and learned Eve's Dream by heart — Had two scholars from Mrs Taylor's — I carded two pounds of whole wool and felt Nationly — Spun harness Twine — Scoured the Pewter. (Lucas 199)

In contrast to the peasants in Europe, this young farmwoman could read and write, as could many of her colonial sisters. This can be attributed to the early development of schools, at first largely schools developed by various churches. But we learn that,

> As churches moved from being sharply defined means of child social-
> ization and social control, as conceived by [William] Penn, to voluntary
> means of social participation, secular schools gradually appeared. The
> earliest schools were explicitly denominational, organized by Quakers,
> Presbyterians, and others. Among Lutherans and Reformed Germans
> the first buildings often were schoolhouses and teachers became minis-
> ters through consent of the people. (James T. Lemon, *The Best Poor
> Man's Country* [Baltimore: Johns Hopkins University Press, 1972], 113)

These may be interesting facts, but what of the people who lived in that period? What was life really like for them? Were there appreciable numbers of Lutherans in those days? In southeastern Pennsylvania in 1790, German Lutherans numbered 45,000, 14 percent of the population, and made up perhaps 20 percent of the population in the city of Philadelphia (Lemon 47). But we know too that they moved around a lot.

Pennsylvanians were more mobile than people in other colonies. "Muhlenberg reported in 1747 that half of his congregation of 1742 in up-per Philadelphia County was no longer with him, suggesting a rate of attri-tion approximately the same as that during the Revolution. Even if some of the departed had died (and Muhlenberg may have overstated departures to impress upon the church fathers of Halle, Germany, the frustrations of trying to impose discipline on Lutherans), there is little doubt that these people were mobile" (Lemon 73-74). "Many 'church' Germans" were fron-tiersmen, denying "the conventional belief that the Scotch-Irish were the only true frontiersmen" (Lemon 69).

But this still tells us little that makes those times real. We have the re-markable *Journals* of Henry Melchior Muhlenberg himself, giving in won-derful detail his life and ministry; many points that follow in the letters are drawn from the *Journals,* cited in their shortened form, Muhlenberg 1959, *Notebook of a Colonial Clergyman.* Digging around in the Seminary library, near the shelf on which the *Journals* are kept, I found a box in the shape of a book, a very old box, and this is what I found in it: a series of letters, some scraps of lace from a handkerchief or garment, some separate slips of paper with remarks written on them, and this small, very old book. I have put the letters into chronological order, but begin with a letter from Peter Muhlenberg to Miss Christine Engelhart, a lifelong friend of his mother.

January 1802

Dear Aunt Christine,

The collection of letters my mother wrote you arrived safely, I am happy to say. I have been reading them and find them most interesting. Yes, my father did keep his journal quite faithfully (Muhlenberg 1959: v-vi, "mixed straw and grain," to be sifted). Each of us children has some parts of it and I think we should one day bring all the pieces together.

Because you were such a close friend of my mother for so long, you and we, her children, probably knew her best. She was sickly, as you point out, and much of her life she was plagued with bodily complaints. But she had a robust personality and despite her illnesses, she took good care of us and father and the household.

You are quite right about our heritage from my mother's side (Muhlenberg 1959: 16). My grandfather Weiser's friendliness with many of the Indian nations and his knowledge of their ways have been a source of great pride for me. I can remember Mother trying to teach us children some of the Indian words she knew. And I will never forget the stories she told us when we were small which her parents had told her. The ones about animals were especially dear to me. I told them to my children when they were young.

Again, my sincere thanks for your thoughtfulness in sending my Mother's letters. I have put them in a box with the letters I saved when Frederick and Henry and I were studying in Germany, and a few scraps of paper on which she had written down some of her thoughts. They are in safekeeping for our children.

Greetings from my wife and best wishes for your continuing good health. I remain your faithful servant, Peter Muhlenberg

1747

Dear Christine,

Please forgive me for not writing since just after the wedding almost two years ago but as you can imagine, life is very busy. Our first child, Peter, was born two months ago. Thank God, he is a healthy baby and sleeps well.

But first I should congratulate you on your new position. I am glad that the children are well behaved and that you are giving music lessons — which you love — as well as teaching penmanship and literature and beginning Latin. All that and being matron for the older girls should keep you very busy. I am happy too that the church you are attending there has many young people and that you are getting to know them through your church activities. Although you don't seem to have as many Germans there in New York as we have here, you certainly know English well enough to keep up with them! I hope there is a fine young man among them whom you like.

You sound like Henry when you ask me what I am doing with all my time. Don't you remember when you were still at home and your mother kept herself and you and your sister busy all the time? We have one older German lady from the congregation here in Providence who helps me in the house, but otherwise I do all the work. With the baby, now, Mrs. Schmidt is staying overnight for a few weeks and that is a great help. She likes gardening as much as I do, so we work together outdoors as well as indoors.

We seem to have company all the time. If it were not for our generous congregation members I don't know how we could make ends meet. They bring chickens and eggs and lard and bread when they come to announce themselves for communion on the Saturdays before communion. I asked Henry if he thought they would take their gifts back if he said they couldn't receive communion the next day, and suggested he be especially careful with Mr. Katzwinkle when he brings elderberry wine. Henry laughed and said "the last batch was so sour, it would serve old Katzwinkle right for making such bad wine."

Henry is away a good deal preaching in the congregations out in the countryside and even as far away as Delaware and New Jersey. He says he must go when he has told them he will be there. Otherwise many would have come very far in vain and the sectarian people say to our people "That's the way your parsons are; they promise much, but keep little" (Muhlenberg 1959: 29). So far Henry has a good reputation for keeping his word. He says the further west he travels in Pennsylvania the poorer our churches are. He says it's because our people are the most recent immigrants and so we have only the leftovers — "the English and German Quakers and the small denominations came to this country in the earlier, good times when land was still cheap" (18-19).

Dear Christine,

How happy your letter made me! Wasn't it good that you could hear Henry preach this summer when he served your church in New York? He tells me that your church wants him to come full-time but that the folks here in Pennsylvania won't hear of it. It would be so nice to live close enough to you to see you often!

(Anna Maria writes extensively about each of the children in their growing family, about her father's commission by the royal government of Virginia to visit the Indian nations on the border of Canada [Muhlenberg 1959: 32] since the French in Canada were reported to be winning them over from the English [36] and of domestic matters, especially of the garden she loved.)

Henry told me that the ships bringing Germans to New York are loaded with "brazen and unruly sinners" (39) and those coming into Philadelphia are just as bad. Since I don't get into the city often, I can only judge from what I hear, and that is that there is much crime everywhere. Farmers and their families are murdered and their buildings burned down. Henry says "the country people are becoming embittered because the authorities are taking no adequate measures for defense. So now we are beginning to hear that the people from the country are about to come to the city in droves and destroy everything in revenge. The city itself is swarming with unruly mobs which are ready to join with any hostile group and wreak havoc. "In short, the cup of sin is full" (94). It makes me think of the good old days when I was a little girl and most of what we worried about was wild animals since my parents knew the Indians well and they were all our friends.

My dear Christine, did you ever think that things could change so fast? Shiploads of people almost every week and new towns springing up; schools starting up all over and even for girls, like yours. Henry says people are even talking of flying machines and going up in balloons, which reminds me: one of the newer pastors from Halle was staying here last winter for a few days with Henry. He claims he must have had something to eat which made him dream that someone was taking his children away in a balloon. Can you imagine!? Anyway, he woke up only when he heard a tearing sound which was my new curtains that he had grabbed, thinking that they were balloon ropes! So, there went my new curtains! And not even an apology from the man.

1762

Dear Christine,

Yes, we are finally settled in Philadelphia. We actually moved last year but with the death of our last child just before we moved things have been very difficult. Henry still has to travel out to the congregations. When he is to go near Providence, I ask him to place flowers on the graves of the two little ones we left behind there.

Your last letter disturbed me because you feel you will never marry and that makes you very unhappy. I can understand that, but let me assure you that being married is not always a bed of roses either. Since you and I are now both 36 years old and have known each other that long, you know that I am being truthful in what I write you. You know what everyone says of women, "Kinder, Kirche and Kuche" [Children, Church and Kitchen]. That is all right by me if that includes growing flowers as well as vegetables and being able to visit friends and being taken seriously in one's opinions. Here you are a respected teacher and parents entrust their dear children to your care. Not that I would take anything in exchange for Henry and the children, but I am weary to the bone sometimes and long to be just a girl again in the home of my parents. Henry becomes very impatient with me, but then I am often impatient with myself, often about the same things. He says that if he had remained a confirmed bachelor he would be able to move about freely. Despite this, he is a good husband and father but much more stern with the children than my father was. I think he is very German in that regard. In fact, I think the mother has the better part because it is to me that the children come for comfort and reassurance.

I should not burden you in this way, but I think you will understand just as I understand your sorrow at not being married. Perhaps the right man will still appear.

1763

"My Dear Sons"

Anna Maria writes telling how their first letter from Halle, Germany, was delivered by one of the new young preachers sent from there. She goes on to write, "It is the same with all the new young preachers: they are astonished and seem disappointed when they arrive. I don't know just what they expect but someone should tell them before they come what it is like here. They all want to stay in the city and when they find they are to live in the country and stay with a family until a house and church are built some are even angry. Your father has to deal firmly with them, reminding them of their commitment to God in becoming ministers" (Muhlenberg 1959: 127).

I hope you will not forget your home and find life too comfortable there. Since you are using German every day and are learning your Greek and Hebrew and Latin in school, perhaps you should speak English and Indian with each other so that you don't forget the language you will need back here (196). And Peter, although you may admire the way pastors are respected there, remember we are all sinners in the sight of God and we are also all equal before him. Although, Henry, you are only nine, you can polish your own shoes and not order a maidservant to do it for you as was reported to your father.

Further motherly admonitions follow regarding the care of their clothing and that they shouldn't mind that they are not as modish as what the German boys wear. "They are fine homespun and the handwork is as well done as any I have seen from Germany or even from England."

She even mentions the nice furniture the boys describe that they have been given to use while they are at school. "I have seen furniture like that in some homes here. The English, especially the wealthy Quakers, have beautiful pieces which they bring from England. But do not be envious or if you are, you should learn how to make such nice things for yourself. Frederick, you are clever with your hands; the cradle you made for your sister's doll is still in one piece and being used. Or you may be able to bring one small piece back with you. It is very difficult to save enough English pounds to buy things overseas, especially since the English government will not allow us to print our own money over here (196).

1776

Dear Christine,

What a sad and dreary time this war is! Frederick's wife and children have left New York, as you probably know and are back with her parents here in Philadelphia (159). I shouldn't say "here in Philadelphia" because we are actually living in Providence again. We bought and fixed up a house with a few acres for garden, etc. I put 120 pounds into it, some of my inheritance from my father (159). Henry thought we should be in a safer place and this house gives us space for any of the children and their families if they must flee the city.

Henry was predicting war for some time before it came, saying bad things were happening but not many people were paying attention to them. He is very critical of the Quakers who are making great profit on what they are selling but, of course, will not go to war themselves (167). Some of the Quakers here are German and some are just as rich as the English but the English still look down on them. All of the Quakers may not be doing the right thing but I differ from Henry about the war. Sometimes I think that since there is a war, we should all be part of it since we live here while Henry says because he is a pastor he cannot be involved. On the other hand, the Quakers may be right about not fighting any wars since we are Christians, we ought to do what Jesus says in the Bible. I feel as you do — I am confused and glad to be out of it all here in the country.

The last time you wrote you asked why I had gone to South Carolina with Henry two years ago. You know how I feel about pulling my weight. Also, I wanted to prove to Henry and myself that I could make the journey. Do you know what happened? Henry and Sally our daughter who accompanied us were very seasick and I was not seasick at all! I did have an inflammation in my feet but otherwise I took the journey — both ways. Actually, the ship was miserable with many mosquitoes and cockroaches and rats. I did have to admit to Henry that I could see why he doesn't like to travel by sea and why he thought I shouldn't come along (146-47).

In South Carolina we stayed with a Lutheran family. Friends of theirs from out in the country visited our host. They are prosperous farmers without using black slaves (144). Henry says that is the way things should be, and I certainly agree. I hate to see anyone take advantage of another: even the indentured servants among our German Lutherans are to be pitied, as hard as they have to work and in the end receive their freedom but no wages.

The weather in South Carolina was too hot, and I really did not like to see the Negroes treated poorly and so was glad to get home. I have even heard some of the Germans say they hope the British win the war because the slaves will be set free. We don't talk about this though because in earlier days the Germans were accused of not fighting the backwoods settlers — many of whom were Germans — who were coming to seize Indians being protected by the Quakers and

Moravians. They build small fortresses, etc., and Henry said "it seemed strange that such preparations should be made against one's fellow citizens and Christians, whereas no one ever took so much trouble to protect from the Indians His Majesty's subjects and citizens on the frontier" (97).

That was the same year we got our trustee Mr. Heppele elected into the Assembly — it really upset the Quakers and Moravians, to lose that power (111).

Our house is still open to the many who travel through here or who come to see Henry on church business. I once said that every minister in the Ministerium had slept in my sheets and Henry chided me, but I pointed out how often we had to buy new bedding for all the company we have.

1783

Dear Christine,

I am having my daughter write this because the terrible accident I had almost two years ago prevents me from being able to use my right hand. All the family send greetings and we are happy to know that you are living with the Nissens in your retirement. Please do come to see us once more if you can — before the sun sets!

Henry was so upset when it appeared that the new government would be put together without any mention of our heavenly Father or of the Christian religion at all (164). The president of the English Academy [later, the University of Pennsylvania] visited Henry and the two discussed how this might be remedied. To show you how God takes care of things in His own time, this is what General Washington said in his farewell address to the Congress:

"I now make it my earnest Prayer, that God would have you and the State over which you preside, in his holy protection; that He would incline the Hearts of the Citizens to cultivate a Spirit of Subordination and Obedience to Government: to entertain a brotherly Affection and Love for one another, and their fellow-Citizens of the united States at large, and particularly for their Brethren who have served in the field; and finally, that He would most graciously be pleased to dispose us all, to do justice, to love Mercy and to demean ourselves with that Charity, Humility and pacific Temper of Mind, which were the characteristics of the Divine Author of our blessed Religion and without an humble

Imitation of whose Example in these things, we can never hope to be a happy nation." (228)

Dear Christine, I knew you would like that. Doesn't it remind you of the pastor's words or way of saying things when we were children? Those were the days! And they will never come again.

Yours faithfully,
Anna Maria

I hope that my fantasy of "Anna Maria and her letters" has helped you feel as well as understand the social context of Muhlenberg's time.

Muhlenberg's Mission

Philip Krey

This address to the changing "Mother Synod," the Southeastern Pennsylvania Synod of the ELCA, a successor to the Muhlenberg Ministerium, May 1, 1998, was one of several at ELCA synods during the anniversary year. As a church historian and resident in "Muhlenberg country," Dean Krey brought both scholarly insights and contemporary reflections as a former urban pastor in Baltimore on the incredibly diverse constituencies of East Coast metropolitan areas today. Yet many in attendance even at a Southeastern Pennsylvania Synod Assembly, from the five-county area in and around Philadelphia, are persons new to the Lutheran Church, unfamiliar with this history. The presentation thus provides a primer on the Muhlenberg anniversary, as well as comparisons and contrasts with the pluralistic situation at the close of the twentieth century.

•   •

It is a joy and honor to address you. Although I am on the roster of another synod, it has been my privilege to serve three Southeastern Pennsylvania Synod congregations as interim pastor: Trinity, Germantown; St. John's, Overbrook; and now as mentoring pastor at Emanuel, South Philadelphia. My family and I are members of historic St. Michael's in Germantown.

I dedicate this presentation to a former colleague at the Lutheran Theological Seminary at Philadelphia who did much to keep the life and mission of Henry Melchior Muhlenberg alive, Dr. Helmut Lehmann, who devoted almost all his energy in his last years to Muhlenberg. Dr. Lehmann died April 6, 1998. For me, his death seems like the passing of an era. He knew many of the German immigrant pastors who went to seminary in

Germany, with my father, in the early part of [the twentieth] century, and came, like Muhlenberg, to this country to serve German-speaking Lutherans in the United States and Canada.

On Muhlenberg's gravestone there is an inscription that reads: "Who and what he was future time will know without a monument of stone" (T. Schmauk, *Muhlenberg: The Organizer of the Lutheran Church in America*). We do have a statue of Muhlenberg at the Lutheran Theological Seminary, Philadelphia. There are living monuments, an institution named after him, in Allentown — Muhlenberg College. We have, as a result of Muhlenberg's labors, a Lutheran Church in the eastern part of this country and its daughter institutions around the country. There used to be a Muhlenberg Press. But Helmut Lehmann and others have in recent times done much to reintroduce "who and what Muhlenberg was" to our consciousness. I have borrowed from him and his 1992 series ("Missioner Extraordinary") for the 250th anniversary of Muhlenberg's arrival in Pennsylvania. I am also indebted to a wonderful summary article written by Dr. Robert Marshall, "The Church Still Being Planted" (*Currents* 1998).

Some scholars have said that what we are celebrating in 1998 is the most important date in the history of the Lutheran Church of America (Tappert 1975, *Lutherans*, p. 49). Celebrations and observances have been held now for several years under the leadership of Dr. Kenneth Senft and the Vice President of the Southeast Pennsylvania Lutheran Synod, Dr. Louise Shoemaker, and the Mission Resource Institute, with the major event scheduled at Muhlenberg College on the weekend of August 7-9, 1998.

The event being celebrated is the founding assembly of the Ministerium of Pennsylvania on August 15, 1748 at Old St. Michael's in Philadelphia. The occasion was the dedication of the building of Old St. Michael's (now also Zion). (Because of a change in the calendar, the date would now be August 26.) Henry Melchior Muhlenberg (1711-1787) was the moving force behind this historic convention. German Lutheran pastors and laypersons were called together in a meeting. "Six ministers were present, including the dean of the Swedish chapter and a minister from upper New York. There were lay representatives from the original 'united congregations' (Philadelphia, Trappe, and New Hanover), and the congregations more recently added to their number (Germantown, Upper Saucon, Zionsville, Stouchsburg [Tulpehocken], Bernville, Lancaster, and New Holland, Pa.)." A new church building was dedicated for Old St. Michael's in Philadelphia, the state of parishes and schools was reviewed, and they approved and regularized a liturgy. One young pastor from Halle in Germany was also examined and ordained (Tappert 1975: 49-50). The preparation and oversight over ministers to supply the parishes scattered over Pennsylvania and adjacent states became a key purpose of future assemblies.

A contemporary account of this first assembly noted the central role of the ordinations and recorded the purpose of the meeting: "for the closer union of the preachers and the united congregations among themselves, . . . a meeting of the preachers, elders, and deacons of all the frequently mentioned congregations was appointed to be held in Philadelphia on August 15, 1748" (Tappert 1975: 49-50).

A ministerium was a body of ministers — a collegial, not a top-down, gathering — for planning and organizing for mission of the church around common purposes. These purposes were to provide 1) regularized and creditable leaders in ministry (lay representatives were consultants without vote; later, of course, this would thankfully change); 2) a clear focus on the roots of the tradition in the Lutheran Confessions as a basis for its beliefs and practices; 3) a common form of worship (Marshall 1998: 89-91).

I shall organize my remarks around two themes: Muhlenberg's mission, and the ecumenical and pluralistic context in which both Muhlenberg and we live. There are differences and commonalities between our context for mission and his. First, a little about this man for the neophytes in "things Muhlenberg."

Henry Melchior Muhlenberg was born in Einbeck in the state of Hannover, Germany, in 1711. He died in 1787. Einbeck is better known for its beer than its famous native. (The royal family of England was also from Hannover, and this caused some ambivalence in Muhlenberg regarding the American Revolution.) On September 6, 1741 (his thirtieth birthday), Muhlenberg received a "term call" — for three years to Pennsylvania. This was a call to three Pennsylvania congregations that were frustrated by a lack of pastoral attention and wanted program support from Halle in Germany. The congregations were located in downtown Philadelphia, New Hanover, and Trappe. Pennsylvania was Muhlenberg's second, perhaps third choice for a call. He had wanted to be a missionary. He was earlier recruited by missionaries to Jews, but he really wanted to go to India. He notes in his journal (*Journals* 1:5), when other missioners were chosen for India, "the all-knowing Saviour knew my witness for such extremely important work. . . . O what a wise God, whose thoughts are not our thoughts! He had not elected me for East India. . . . I recognized the wise guidance of God." He had opportunity to become the superintendent of schools and pastors, perhaps even the court preacher, but thinking himself too square *(quadrat)* for this he declined (Lehmann, p. 1). His first call had been to the town of Grosshennersdorf in Germany, where he would also serve a school. Like many new pastors, he grabbed at the call because it was open, but the call to Pennsylvania changed this.

Muhlenberg studied, among other places, in Halle, the great Pietist center, the place of origin for many missionaries and charitable social service institutions. He was ordained and examined in Leipzig, having to prove that he was prepared in Hebrew and Greek and the Confessions of the Lutheran Church. Ordination was on August 24, 1739 in Leipzig, with the whole ministerium present. Scholars have called him an "orthodox pietist" (Roeber). He was not the usual stereotype of a pietist, in that he both smoked and drank in moderation.

Muhlenberg's journey to the new land was harsh. He traveled to Pennsylvania via Georgia, arriving in 1742. It was a rough voyage of fourteen weeks, with rowdy sailors, and he was sick to his stomach a good portion of the way. After a brief stay in Georgia, he traveled alone by ship along the coast to Philadelphia, and again he complained that he was deathly seasick and covered with lice.

He had been called as a missionary from Halle to provide pastoral care to Germans in diaspora in this country. He found them a rough-and-tumble lot — uncommitted, a flock in need of a shepherd. He found that the children were growing up like pagans, with no knowledge of Luther's Catechism.

Serving three congregations from the start, he was an itinerant, riding from congregation to congregation in all kinds of weather (later in severe pain from hemorrhoids). He often prepared his hour-long sermons in the saddle. He wore out more than one horse; his pay was next to nothing, and he found himself borrowing money to buy clothes and horses. After three years he decided to stay beyond his term and married the resourceful Anna Maria Weiser, with whom he had eleven children. They were married for forty-two years. They took out a mortgage for the large plot of land in Providence, what we now know as Trappe, not far from Philadelphia. Helmut Lehmann suspected that Anna Maria was the reason he stayed beyond three years.

Muhlenberg faithfully traveled to his congregations in southeast Pennsylvania. Our mission-minded Pastor Muhlenberg saw that the Lutheran Church needed to be expanded beyond the three churches he served. He proclaimed his famous motto, *Ecclesia Plantanda*, "The church still has to be planted." This was in distinction from the church that had already been planted in Europe, *Ecclesia Plantata*, especially the Lutheran state church in Germany and those supporting his mission work. He kept going farther and farther out into the colonies, to support and plant the church in Lancaster, York, Frederick, Maryland, New Jersey, and New York City.

He had heard and experienced the gospel and wanted to make Christ known and to teach the gospel to hungry persons whether in their homes or in the open air, baptizing, catechizing, and administering the Eucharist. He notes in his journals that, unlike Germany, sometimes the scattered Germans were so hungry for the gospel that they were willing to listen for hours. The gospel was an experience for him, but a message that came from the outside, in the preached word and Baptism and the Lord's Supper. He was an orthodox pietist.

Muhlenberg's Mission

It is important to recognize differences at the same time we consider the similarities, if, as church historian Martin Marty has said, we want to find a useable past. I will argue that Lutherans, then and now, find themselves in a missionary context, and secondly, we find ourselves in both an ecumenical and a pluralistic situation. Muhlenberg's genius was to plan and organize in the American colonial context. We have a similar agenda in a different context.

Muhlenberg came as a missionary pastor to Germans in diaspora (scattered about the land), and he focused on this assignment. His mission, as he saw it, was to gather them into a church in touch with its confessional heritage. He found himself, however, in a new context. He had moved from a state-supported, established church to a voluntaristic society. In America people could belong or not belong to the church of their choice. The existence of the church was dependent on their giving, or on support from abroad. He could not count on civil authorities in Pennsylvania for the support of his mission. He wrote in his diary: "One has not the slightest support from the secular authorities, but each one has the greatest freedom in this respect." There was no support from government, which had nothing to do with church matters in a free colony. He had no force or authority at his command to gather people into congregations other than the sword of the Spirit and faith in the living God who makes promises.

Muhlenberg's Pennsylvania had a majority of Germans but was dominated by English-speaking Quakers, who were religiously tolerant but controlled most of the economic resources. German Lutherans were on the outside, looking in. Muhlenberg's missionary genius in this context was to organize Lutherans, proclaim an embodied/sacramental gospel, and provide an organized structure whereby this could be delivered in a new context, a mixture of centralization and local creativity.

Our current situation, you will recognize, is one in which the government and culture at best compete with the church and at worst are outright hostile to the church's agenda, especially in the media. A most important difference in our contexts is that, whereas Muhlenberg did his mission in a struggling colony whose immigrants remembered the importance of the church in their lives, we struggle to do mission in an American empire that offers pacifying substitutes for the church: consumerism, sports, the entertainment media.

The Muhlenberg tradition has given us both strengths and weaknesses, in the face of a disestablished church. As a weakness, I suggest that we have transferred Muhlenberg's grief for the loss of state and societal support to a grief that our centralized church structures cannot produce more in the way of mission and support. But the highly centralized and collegial structure that is part of the Muhlenberg tradition is both a strength and a weakness. Our national church, synods, conferences, and ministeriums with their resources can, on the one hand, give us an organized way of planning and proposing mission in a chaotic context; on the other hand, our complex structures can immobilize us in the face of mission opportunities. Nevertheless, the positive side of the Muhlenberg tradition is the enterprising church-planting missioner. (Muhlenberg got on his horse and kept pressing beyond the boundaries of established congregations to plant the church; we need to do the same on foot, by bicycle, in the car, and with all the media and technologies at our disposal.) In the same way, in a voluntaristic society and in a missionary context, we need to work all the harder to develop good stewardship and evangelism expectations in our mission situations and where the church has already been planted. In a voluntaristic situation, organization, creativity, and accountability on the local level are key.

Furthermore, we also need to support and build that creative and flexible side of the Muhlenberg tradition symbolized in many of our social ministry organizations, which were often formed by individual mission-minded pastors and societies. These institutions give Lutheranism a "public service" face and a lasting organized place in society. It is time to support and reclaim them.

We know that we have an embodied word to proclaim and teach and catechize, and people to gather. (I'll return to this.) We have many people in this tradition among us; we need missioners and institution builders.

The Ecumenical and Pluralistic Situation

When Muhlenberg arrived, he found German Lutherans scattered among a host of religious groups: Quakers, Anabaptists (i.e., those who, among other things, insist on "believer's baptism"), Schwenkfelders, Moravians, Spiritualists, Mennonites, and "Sabbatarians," in addition to the Reformed and Episcopalians. To a more limited extent, he experienced African Americans, slaves and freed, and Native Americans. From the beginning, America has always been pluralistic. Muhlenberg's mission, as he saw it, was to gather Lutherans and plant individual congregations in the outparishes of the colonies, Lutherans deeply rooted in their tradition and gathered along ethnic lines.

There were other models at the time: his archrival, Count Nicholas Ludwig von Zinzendorf, founder and guiding spirit of the Herrnhuter Brüdergemeine (Moravians), attempted to organize Lutheran congregations in and around Philadelphia, but he wanted to tie them into a top-down (noncollegial) "Brotherhood of the Spirit" — a union of denominations — without recognizing the loyalty to individual roots of the other confessional families (Lehmann). Zinzendorf also saw himself as a kind of "inspector" of established congregations and was not always mission-minded about establishing Moravian congregations in Pennsylvania, apart from supervision in Germany, as some Moravian scholars now recognize.

Muhlenberg was also confronted with the revivalist model, such as that of George Whitefield, who practiced a more radical pietistic model of conversion and spirituality that led to the renewal or transformation of the individual. This model was much more intent on crossing racial and ethnic boundaries in mission, and converted African Americans and Native Americans to Christianity. It was a nonsacramental model. As we have seen, Muhlenberg stood for a confessional Lutheranism, emphasizing the importance of the external preached word; a catechetical spirituality, and a sacramental piety.

At Muhlenberg's first assembly, which we celebrate this year, there were a variety of Lutherans present: pietists of all stripes, Germans of different dialects, customs, and liturgies. There were Swedes, and some pastors from the Reformed tradition as observers. In Muhlenberg's opening address he commented, "A twisted cord of many threads will not easily break." Coming from a religiously divided Europe that exported its wonderful resources and many divisions to America, Muhlenberg saw it as his mission to organize European Lutherans into one strong cord. As one scholar has pointed out, it is a mystery why the Halle orthodox pietist, who wanted to be a missionary to India, never missionized the freed African Americans of Pennsylvania, leaving this to the revivalistic denominations.

We find ourselves in a different context today, although ecumenical and pluralistic issues are still at the forefront. Muhlenberg found himself, and to some extent was, one of the architects of American denominationalism. We find ourselves at its end as laypersons who cross denominations at will, as new ecumenical proposals and agreements augur a new day in American and universal Christianity. We insist that these threads maintain their own distinctive colors. Our cord now has a variety of racial and ethnic threads, all of which have their own authenticity and integrity. We can recognize the value of a common worship but also acknowledge the faithfulness of other liturgical traditions.

In addition, having come to agreement on many doctrinal issues that have been church-divisive, and sometimes agreeing to disagree, we have already made historic ecumenical proposals with some of the same traditions that Muhlenberg confronted: the wonderful agreement with the Reformed traditions in 1997, Moravians and Episcopalians in 1999. We can now see a variety of doctrines and peoples making a stronger cord beyond Muhlenberg's vision and yet consistent with it, because our agreements and new partners proclaim Christ, maintain the sacraments, and are faithful to the roots of the individual traditions. "These are roots. What will be the new plantings?"

When Muhlenberg addressed the first assembly of the Ministerium of Pennsylvania in 1748, organizing Lutherans for his era with a regular clergy, a confessional witness, and common worship, he described the new organization as "being only a trial and a test" (Lehmann 1992: 8). As you find yourselves assembled in a new context, what "trials and tests" will you faithfully shape, in dialogue with the tradition and context?

Today, at this Southeastern Pennsylvania Synod assembly, I see many more racial and ethnic threads that need to be in a cord that will not break, to maintain a free and democratic society and for the sake of mission. This is also part of the Muhlenberg trajectory — Muhlenberg's mission. Muhlenberg pressed on to new communities with his limited focus, but you have gathered as African Americans and others of African descent, and Hispanics, and Russians, and Asians of all types, and from the community of the deaf. In fact, Muhlenberg did not make it to India, but India has wonderfully come to our shores to share its rich traditions of mission.

I look to you, as a church having been planted, the church that also has to be planted with flexibility and planning for a rapidly changing context, with organization and a passion to proclaim the embodied gospel.

Anniversary Sermon

The Rev. Barbara Berry-Bailey

This sermon was preached at the Gideon F. Egner Memorial Chapel, Muhlenberg College, August 9, 1998. As she indicates in the sermon, Barbara Berry grew up in a Lutheran Church–Missouri Synod congregation (in Detroit). Her desire to become a pastor was impossible in the LC-MS, but she did not forget the dream after college, while working at Temple University, Philadelphia. She was graduated from the Lutheran Theological Seminary, Philadelphia. At the time of the Muhlenberg Symposium, she was pastor of Trinity Lutheran Church, 5300 Germantown Avenue, Philadelphia, with its motto, "A New Mission in an Historic Place." Subsequently she became Associate Director of Worship & Music, ELCA Division for Congregational Ministries, Chicago. The first two lessons were those appointed for the 10th Sunday after Pentecost, August 9; August 15 commemorated Mary, Mother of Our Lord.

•   •

Scripture Lessons
Genesis 15:1-6
Hebrews 11:1-3, 8-16
Luke 1:26-38

Grace to you and peace from God our Father and the Lord Jesus Christ.

I

It is of course an honor to stand before this assembly of God's people to bring the Word of the Lord, but also a humbling experience. I must say, when I was approached by Dr. Louise Shoemaker about preaching at Muhlenberg, without hesitation I said, "Yes, of course!" She has been a source of strength for my son who is still in the discernment process of answering God's call to word and sacrament ministry . . . and I love her and respect her expertise and judgment.

It was not until I saw the brochure weeks later that I realized to what I had agreed. And honestly, if I knew then what I know now, I would not have agreed so quickly.

Down in Southeastern Pennsylvania, the code name for this event is "The Big Henry Bash," and as a former Missouri Synod girl, I'm not sure who is spinning the fastest right now, Muhlenberg or C. F. W. Walther.

But that is exactly what the appointed texts for this Sunday are all about . . . knowing what you are in for when you say "yes to the Lord." I believe that is one of the issues my son faces. He wants to know the details of how everything is going to turn out. And I guess that is normal, to want to know. But the truth is, when God calls us, we really don't get specific details.

Consider in Luke 1, the messenger's words to Mary, who was to be the mother of the "Son of the Most High God." She was told that he will be great, he will reign over the house of Jacob forever; and of his kingdom there will be no end. And so she said, "Let it be to me according to your word." And the angel departed from her.

The angel departed without giving her what I believe was some vital information necessary to really agree to this whole conception-out-of-wedlock deal. She had already asked one question, "How can this be, since I have no husband?"

And the messenger was ready for that one: "Oh, um, yes. You see, the Holy Spirit will come upon you and the power of the Most High will overshadow you, *that* is why the child to be born will be called holy and the son of God." (The messenger kind of reminds me of those telemarketers that have an answer for whatever response you may give them. They're always ready.)

Mary doesn't respond.

The messenger goes on, "Look, look, your cousin Elizabeth, she's in her forties and she's six months pregnant. And you know everybody used to say she was barren. With God, nothing will be impossible."

So Mary thought and said, "Yes, you're right. Well, what do you know! I am the handmaiden of the Lord; I'm on board. Just like you said." And the angel got out of there before she could ask any more questions.

What the messenger left out was: "Oh, by the way, your son, the fruit of your womb, will be misunderstood even by his closest friends who, most of the time, will have no idea what he is talking about; the very people he will come to save will be instrumental in his death on the cross. And his followers for centuries will be persecuted, people will wage wars and enslave other people in his name."

But I guess Mary didn't want the details. The conception alone would have made me say, "No! No way! Pick somebody else, I have my own troubles. Thank you, but no."

Even though we know no one says no to the Lord, and gets away with it, I know I would not have been as trusting as Mary. I would not have had the faith that Mary had. I would have wanted some more details.

Or, maybe that is what faith is, accepting God's will, without knowing the details.

The second lesson says, "Faith is the assurance of things hoped for and the conviction of things not seen." In other words it's the opposite of "what you see is what you get." Faith says, "What you do *not* see is what you get."

That is why people who do not walk by faith think that what we do on Sunday is a stupid waste of time. (I have had people tell me that.) But in all fairness, I must say people who supposedly walk by faith seem to have as difficult a time as nonbelievers.

How many times have you heard, "Pastor, what is your vision for the congregation?" And I think about Jeremiah, and what I *want* to say is, "I see a boiling pot . . . and if you don't stop asking me what *my* vision is. . . ." When in reality the vision has been articulated time and time again, in sermons, in committee and council meetings; the vision has been written in newsletters, in bulletins, in Council minutes, announcements, in memoranda, but because they do not have all the specific details of the *outcome*, people cannot see it. And if they can't see it, they won't believe it.

According to our second lesson today, faith is being convinced of something that there is no concrete evidence to support. Faith is believing that God is good all the time, even when your world is coming apart. Faith is believing that [as we sing] "God will take care of you through every day, o'er all the way." . . . Faith is having no fear even when you walk through the valley of deep darkness, and that deep darkness can take on many different forms:

it can be a dreaded disease;
it can be a prison sentence;
it can be a messy divorce;
it can be an unbearable family situation;
it can be relocating to an unfamiliar place, or a familiar place with no clue of what is going to happen in the future.

Abraham is cited as the premier model of faith.

Our Old Testament lesson gives us a picture of one who walked by faith — Abraham. When God called Abram initially (in Genesis 12), God said, "Pack up all your things and go. Get moving. Leave the land of your family and go to a place that, well, I won't tell you about now, but when you get there I will let you know."

And unlike Mary, Abraham did not ask one question — no if's, no but's, no maybe's. The text says, "so Abram went."

In a new book titled *The Gifts of the Jews*, Thomas Cahill points to this as the pivotal event in human civilization. Prior to this event, primitive peoples were geared to cyclical movement. Days, seasons, clans, tribes, life itself was of a cyclical nature. Abram's response to the command to "Go" breaks the cycle and allows for the beginning of something new and different, something never before experienced. An unfamiliar place with unfamiliar people makes for unfamiliar events.

Now, in today's lesson in Genesis 15, God came in a vision (an authentic, concrete method of communication, just like receiving a fax, right? NOT!). God promises Abram that God is his shield and that his reward will be great.

Now since Abram set out, a lot has occurred:

1. They get to Egypt and Abram fears that they will kill him and take his wife, so he lies and says that she is his sister. Plagues afflict Pharaoh because of this lie and they are sent on their way.
2. He and Lot literally have a parting of the ways because of the strife between them.
3. There is a military skirmish between Abram and an alliance of four eastern kings. So by now Abram has seen some hardship and, well,

maybe he is having his doubts about having left his native land. So when God comes to him this time, he is curious.

This time Abram has questions. He remembers the promise God made: "I will make of you a great nation." A lot has happened, and still no offspring.

He says, "What will you give me? I don't have any children and so a slave will be my heir." But God tells him that his own biological descendants will be as countless as the stars in the sky.

And he believes the Lord.

He has no concrete evidence to believe a communication that couldn't be scientifically documented. For Abram and Sarah time keeps slipping into an uncertain future; they are getting older. But at this point in the Abraham story, **he believed the Lord.**

And both St. Paul (Rom. 4:3) and the Letter to the Hebrews cite that as an example of faith.

II

When you're under the gun, so to speak, that is when your faith is most obvious.

Faith is a gift of the Holy Spirit that works when it will and where it will, as Luther said, but I want to add that it works through all sorts of ways that we tend to discount.

The story of *Indiana Jones and the Last Crusade* is the story of two men, a father and a son. One whose life work was a pursuit of holy things, the other's the pursuit of facts, concrete evidence. One, an obvious man of religion, though I don't think he was Lutheran; the other seemingly a man who discounted religious matters. But the boy did grow up with and was influenced by his father's faith; he didn't practice it but when it came down to the test of faith — that is, the belief in things that he could not see, he did have faith. If you watched your parent spend his/her whole life working on the pursuit of religious matters, you must have a spark of faith. Maybe it takes coming face to face with the crises in life to make it obvious to us.

In the most memorable scene in the film Indiana has to step out on faith — he has to make a leap from a gorge at least forty feet wide. "No one can jump it. It is a leap of faith." And so he stands there at the edge of the gorge and with seemingly nothing to support him, he steps out. . . . He steps out and his foot lands on a support that was always there, but from the perspective of the sojourner, it was hidden. Only in believing in something that he could *not* see could he continue the quest.

Now many will say that it was not a leap. To leap you must get a running start. It is not that he did not have faith, because one can't just have faith all of a sudden. If he didn't have faith, he never would have stepped off. Faith is not something magical that just appears.

Faith is not something you earn or achieve through your own hard work.

Faith is a lifelong process. . . . You don't just get it and keep it in your wallet like a driver's license and pull it out when you need it.

A contemporary theologian defined faith as the process of constant overcoming of doubt.

And brother Henry Melchior, didn't he step out on faith? To leave his familiar place to go to an uncertain place with uncertain people, struggle with issues he would never have had to face in his homeland?

But, by faith, Henry boarded that ship to cross the Atlantic. But still, I wonder if he had known all the specific details of his mission, would he have stepped onto that ship? Consider his fourteen-week voyage, bad food, bad water, threats from pirates and enemy ships.

Consider his compensation package. I understand his pay was so little he had to borrow money to buy clothes and a horse. He had no travel allowance.

Consider the status of women and people of color. Can you imagine his reaction to the Word of the Lord saying, "And from your mission, slave and Indian women will be in the pulpit teaching men!" That's one detail the messenger certainly left out of Muhlenberg's call message.

But, as I have learned for the first time in my life, when planting, your harvest is often times greater than what you expect. (Can anybody use some tomatoes or zucchini?)

While visiting some of my members in the Germantown Home, one of the residents gave me a small tomato plant. The gift of a green thumb was not my gift, and I worried about this little plant, but not wanting to insult the woman and refuse her gift, I took it. With fear and trepidation, I planted it in a sunny spot, as she suggested. That one little plant has grown into more than seven branches. I have had to prop it up, tie it up. Some true gardeners in the congregation have given me marigold to plant to keep certain pests away from the tomato plant.

And now, I am beginning to see the signs of the fruit. All from that one little plant that I feared may never live once it was planted.

Two hundred and fifty years ago Henry went, and without knowing all the details of his vision he planted a church. Henry was a man of faith.

And while we thank God for Abraham's faith, for Henry's faith, let us pray that the Spirit may continue to move us, to ignite our faith. Because the church continues to be planted through us. We have not been given all the specific details of who will be the church, how the church is going to look. But we have been given the command to make disciples of all people; nobody, not Henry, not Bishop Anderson, not you, not me, *nobody* stands here in 1998 and determines who will be called Lutheran in 2098. God knows.

For us then, faith is assurance that, regardless of what we see in *The Lutheran* magazine, God is in control. Faith is the assurance that the fruits of our labors in the gospel will be pleasing to God. Faith sees not necessarily all Lutherans singing hymns out of a book that looks the same but rather, singing praises to the one true God, knowing without a doubt that it is by grace we are saved through faith in Christ Jesus. Faith for us, in this place, binds us in love, regardless of where we live, how much we have in the bank — and I mean that "1 Corinthians 13 love," not the polite superficial stuff that ends with "Go in peace, serve the Lord."

Because it is through that love that the planted church is nurtured,
it is through that loving in faith that the church can grow, and
it is through that loving in faith that the church will glorify not us, not Henry, but God.

May Almighty God — who created us and sustains us, who, when we died through sin bought us back and gave us life, who continues to move in us and makes us holy — surround us, guide us, keep us in steadfast faith, now and forever. Amen.

Keynote Address at the Dedication of the Muhlenberg House, Trappe, Pennsylvania, August 9, 1998

Charles H. Glatfelter

We have come today to dedicate a house standing in a place that Henry Melchior Muhlenberg called home for most of his forty-five years of pastoral service in what he often called the Pennsylvania wilderness.

In 1761 one of his German Reformed colleagues tried to explain to the Dutch Reformed authorities who had sent him to America just what being an energetic Pennsylvania pastor entailed. "It is almost impossible to convey any idea with how much difficulty all these congregations are maintained," he wrote. "Everything, so to speak, has been started anew, and without hard labor not one congregation can be built up. With faith, love, hope, zeal, patience, and readiness to serve in preaching, catechizing, and family visitation, by constant riding about (because the people are so scattered), we must carry on the work."[1] If Muhlenberg had read what George Alsentz of Germantown was writing, he most certainly would have proclaimed: You can say that again. In fact, he had already written substantially the same thing, and more than once.

When Muhlenberg came into Pennsylvania in November 1741, he experienced for the first time in his life a degree of religious freedom all but unknown elsewhere in the western world, different even from that in Virginia or Massachusetts. William Penn's 1701 Charter of Privileges, Pennsylvania's constitution, guaranteed that no one who acknowledged "one Almighty God the Creator upholder and Ruler of the world" and who was willing to live quietly under the civil government would ever be compelled to support any religious institution. Consequently, the provincial govern-

---

1. Report of the Rev. John George Alsentz, 1761, in *Minutes and Letters of the German Reformed Congregations in Pennsylvania, 1747-1792* . . . (Philadelphia, 1903), p. 202.

ment in Philadelphia would not hinder those who wanted to establish such institutions. At the same time, neither would it help them.

Every pastor who came to colonial Pennsylvania quickly learned that it took laymen little time to understand that its religious affairs were going to be conducted differently from what they were accustomed to in Europe. While it is evident that most of these people wanted to have the church in their midst here, they wanted it on substantially their own terms, terms that vested final authority in the congregation. Woe to any pastor who did not learn that lesson along with his potential parishioners.

Unlike the commission that Dutch Reformed authorities gave Michael Schlatter in 1746, which directed him to visit wherever there were German Reformed in Pennsylvania and determine what level of support they would promise if a pastor were sent to them, Muhlenberg's call was to three specific congregations, only one of which had a church building when he arrived and all three of which were being served by other men.

Because he could prove that he was a properly ordained Lutheran pastor in good standing (he had his credentials with him) and because there were soon good reports of how he was handling himself in Pennsylvania, several of the twenty or so other Lutheran congregations in the province began asking him to minister to them and help obtain regular pastors. As he began responding affirmatively, he wrote in his journal that "we have never forced ourselves upon anyone or invited ourselves, only going when we were almost compelled and the utmost necessity required it" (*Journals* 1:169).

Nowhere can we find evidence that Muhlenberg ever believed he had been called to Pennsylvania because a church must be planted there, but it is easy to find evidence that he knew full well he was part of a church that was being planted there. Always he accepted that this church was going to remain different from the church in Europe. Even as he saw much that he did not like about it, he clearly treasured its religious freedom. Since he firmly believed that all persons, including himself, were far gone in sin, he lamented the fact that most Pennsylvanians were not taking advantage of their freedom to live the true Christian life, one of awakening, conversion, repentance, and daily renewal. Always he was critical of what he took to be the shortcomings of everyone in sight, including himself.

And yet, this was a man who understood how important it was for Pennsylvania pastors to come to terms with what he and others called the customs of the country. Certainly this never meant accepting every practice he believed sinful, but it did lead him to preach in English and Dutch, when deemed necessary, as well as in German. "We should look at language as we look at a bridge over a river," he wrote in 1761. Whether it is oak or whatever is not important, only that it "hold and enables us to get across and toward our goal."[2] It sometimes led him to shorten winter worship services, once he realized how much warmer his clothing was than that of his fellow-worshipers. When he recalled how difficult it was for many of his people to pay his salary, he wished that it would be possible for him to earn his income in some other way. "I can affirm," he once write, "that many a time have I wished that I had the Apostle Paul's gifts and was able at the same time to practice his trade so that it would not be necessary to live by the bitter sweat and blood of the poor people" (*Journals* 1:365).

In less than a week we shall observe the 250th anniversary of the first meeting of what is best known as the Ministerium of Pennsylvania, but which Muhlenberg called by many different names. In the earliest days it was a far cry from what it later became. He first saw it as nothing more than a gathering of the few pastors and catechists who had followed him from the University of Halle. Significantly, it was the Ministerium that ordained Nicholas Kurtz in 1748; that took place the day before it was organized. Absent from this first meeting, because they were not invited, were those pastors who either were not ordained according to the applicable European rules or who, if ordained, had come to Pennsylvania without having a regular call from a parish. Nevertheless, they and others similarly not invited were then ministering to very many German Lutherans. Finally, Muhlenberg did not consider it necessary to convene the Ministerium every year. During the twenty-eight years between 1748 and 1776, at a time when the number of Lutheran congregations in Pennsylvania was increasing from 40 to 126, there were no Ministerium meetings in eight of those years. Meanwhile, the German Reformed coetus and the Presbyterian synod of New York and Philadelphia found it possible, even necessary, to meet during every one of those twenty-eight years.

But this is only part of the story. Especially after the Ministerium resumed in 1760, after having missed five possible annual meetings, an increasing number of other pastors and congregations were admitted to membership. Now the Ministerium began to deal with requests from many of the pastors and congregations who no longer wanted to function entirely on their own. Now the Ministerium began to perform as the syn-

---

2. Henry Melchior Muhlenberg to Charles Magnus von Wrangel, August 12, 1761, trans. Heinrich P. Suhr, *Lutheran Church Quarterly* 13 (January 1940): 82.

odical body that the growing Lutheran church in free Pennsylvania sorely needed. By 1776, be it remembered, judged by the number of congregations, the German Lutheran was the largest church in Pennsylvania.

It is a tribute to the good sense of Muhlenberg that the evolution of the Ministerium from an organization of a small group of Hallensian pastors into one that embraced a larger and larger percentage of pastors and congregations occurred without any evidence of opposition on his part and without any hint of dissatisfaction with his continuing leadership.

In 1772, after the members began discussing the need for a written constitution as a sound guide for future meetings, he agreed that such a document was necessary. "A poor father would be foolish," he wrote, "to insist that his twenty- or thirty-year-old children should continue to wear clothing which fitted them when they were three, six, or nine years old" (*Journals* 2:515).

In 1745 Muhlenberg married Anna Maria Weiser; she was eighteen and he was thirty-four. Of their eleven children, seven reached maturity. All three of the surviving sons became Lutheran pastors. Two of the daughters married Lutheran pastors from Halle.

Despite the vast bulk of Muhlenberg's writings, we know less about life in his growing family than we would like to. On occasion, however, the curtains part a little. In 1762, he wrote that he punished the fifteen-year-old Peter, "who went out without permission and did not come home until about nine o'clock" (*Journals* 1:489). And they part again just two years later to allow us to learn how father and mother took turns holding the dying five-year-old Samuel on their laps, telling him, "in accord with his little understanding, about the loving Saviour and heaven and blessedness" (*Journals* 2:31). About 10 o'clock, as his father was returning Samuel to bed, the boy kissed him goodbye and died.

There is every reason to believe that the loving care these two incidents from the journals demonstrate characterized the family and fitted the children to grow into responsible adults. When the American Revolution occurred, and their father wrestled long and hard with what his conscience required of him, all three of his sons considered leaving the ministry. Two of them did. Peter entered the military. Frederick entered politics. Clearly, this was definitely not what their father would have advised them to do, but when he learned in 1779 that Frederick had been elected to the Continental Congress, he wrote in his journal: "If I were to give my judgment concerning the matter, it would be expressed somewhat like John 9:21, 'He is of age; ask him: he shall speak for himself'" (*Journals* 3:220).

What sounder pronouncement can come from a parent who has worked diligently at the craft of parenting? He might have added something about the proper clothing for a nine-year-old and a thirty-year-old and how it differed.

For about twenty-eight of their forty-two years of married life, Henry and Anna Maria lived here in Providence. Here eight of their children were born; here one died. As the Revolution was beginning, they returned here, to stay, in 1776. For some time thereafter Henry Melchior Muhlenberg took up a role that was almost new to him in America: that of a parish pastor pure and simple. No one who respects this man can fail to feel with him as he loses much of his hearing, finds it increasingly difficult to walk, and has to be lifted onto and then off his horse whenever he travels.

On a very hot August day in 1784 he officiated at the funeral of Jacob Merkle, a long and faithful member of Augustus Church. Since Merkle was to be buried on his farm, the funeral was held in his large barn, which could not accommodate more than about half of those who came. No schoolmaster being available, Muhlenberg had to lead the singing as well as preach the sermon. As part of the extensive record of this event in his journal, the old pastor wrote that "I began my ministry in barns in this region almost forty-two years ago, and, as it appears, will also end it in barns" (*Journals* 3:610).

Thereafter, on most Sundays he and his family did not attend church, but had private devotions at home. From time to time he performed a marriage or a baptism. The very last entry in his journal, significantly enough, was to record a baptism performed eight days before he died, on Sunday, October 7, 1787.

Three weeks earlier, in Philadelphia, the Constitutional Convention finished its work, signed it, and sent it on to the states. Peter was now vice-president of the Supreme Executive Council of Pennsylvania, which meant that he might be called the lieutenant governor of the Commonwealth. Within a month Frederick would be elected to the convention to vote on Pennsylvania's ratifying the document; when it met, he would be elected its president. Henry was pastor in Lancaster and three months before his father died was elected president of the short-lived Franklin College.

During the last two centuries many descendants of Henry and Anna Maria Muhlenberg have been pastors, doctors, attorneys, and business-men. Many more have used most or all of their talents in ways that entirely escaped our notice. The first person to call us to task if we gave the Muhlenberg line credit for the quality of these lives would be Henry

Melchior Muhlenberg himself. And if we acknowledged the importance of the Weisers, Meyers, Halls, Shaffers, and others, he could correct us again. The credit, he would say, goes to God alone. But the old man would have to be silent, would he not, if we gently reminded him: We are of age! Let us speak for ourselves!

Two centuries after his death he is still a worthy model for us, not because he can tell us how to handle the issues of our own day, but because by the strength of his convictions, his skill in dealing with people individually and in groups, his wisdom in determining when to change and when to hold fast, and by his sheer physical energy, he demonstrated what a godly person can accomplish in one lifetime.

IV. Retrospective

Muhlenberg's Ministerium and the Churches of Today and Tomorrow, in the Setting of the Deism of the Founding Fathers, especially Benjamin Franklin

John Reumann

How does one conclude the decade begun in 1997-98 by celebration of the 250th anniversary of the first meeting of the Ministerium of North America? It has been rounded off in 2006 by reflection, predictable results, and some unexpected twists and turns. That's the outcome of many a conversation among Planning Committee members and others. If perspective from millennia is a fortunate opportunity (Anderson, p. 144 above), modest input from a decade is also helpful.

The millennium year has come and gone. September 11, 2001 is said to have changed everything. War on terror, weapons of mass destruction, Afghanistan, Iraq, tsunami, Hurricane Katrina and destruction along the Gulf Coast, genocide in Darfur[1] were not present in even the most apocalyptic scenarios of the late 1990s.

Many of the things essayists did worry about proved less significant than expected. Full communion with the Reformed, Episcopalians, Moravians, and, soon to be added, Methodists, became a reality, with varying results. The "trial or test" of which H. George Anderson spoke (p. 148 above) is still going on. Sex scandals in the Roman Catholic Church and divisions within Anglicanism over openly gay clergy and bishops have made closer relationships less attractive for some (but more attractive for others). Little can be said to have happened in Lutheran–Eastern Orthodox and Lutheran-Lutheran (ELCA, LC-MS) relations. Bilaterals attract more interest and energy than conciliar structures.

---

1. Louise Shoemaker was mentioned in the *New York Times* in 2006 when one of the "Lost Boys of the Sudan," whom she had sponsored, was graduated from Wagner College on Staten Island.

Limited church growth and tighter dollar budgets work against expansion in the mainline churches. Worship wars? The older divides have been somewhat superseded by the Renewing Worship Project in the ELCA, leading to a new book, *Evangelical Lutheran Worship,* in October 2006.[2]

Most who took part in the Muhlenberg anniversary convocations and Symposium ended up better informed, perhaps proud of their heritage, but puzzled. Is recalling past heritages really likely to sabotage present church emphases?

The one item in the life of the ELCA in 2004-2006 that almost no one lifted up in 1997-98 was the Sexuality Study.[3] Here a series of compromises in the Task Force Report, the recommendations from the Church Council, and the 2005 Churchwide Assembly amounted to efforts to hold the church together, yet without drastic decisions in one direction or another. The Episcopal Church U.S.A. and the Presbyterian Church U.S.A. took similar actions at their conventions in June 2006. To what extent were the whole study and the feelings it generated the influence of secular society on the church? As was said in the 1960s, the world sets the agenda, the church responds.

Muhlenberg, it has been said (Reumann, p. 92 above), lived at the intersection of Lutheran orthodoxy, pietism, and emerging rationalism. Reading through our essays shows that writer after writer has given attention to Muhlenberg's pietism. Others have sought to rescue him from it by stressing his theological orthodoxy. The formula "orthodox pietist" has been much repeated in one form or another. But all too little attention was given to how it was rationalism that was in the ascendancy (Reumann, p. 93 above; H. L. Nelson).[4]

In the decades before and after Muhlenberg, reason was increasingly

---

2. There will be ten settings for the Service of Holy Communion: two are brand new; two come from the existing *Lutheran Book of Worship* (Settings One and Two there); one stresses chant (from *LBW*); one is African American, one from *Libro de Liturgia y Cántico* (1998); three more with tested contemporary materials; the Service of the Word; and 650-700 hymns and songs. The principle from Muhlenberg's day of "one book" has been stretched to the limit in encompassing diversity. Cf. *With the Whole Church: A Study Guide for Renewing Worship* (Chicago: ELCA, 2005).

3. *Journey Together Faithfully: The Church and Homosexuality.* Study Guide. Chicago: ELCA. Part One (1996); Part Two (2003). Proposed statement, 2007.

4. Cf. Brooke Allen, *Moral Minority: Our Skeptical Founding Fathers* (Chicago: Ivan R. Dee, 2006).

assumed to be something that every human being possesses. From use of reason, there comes light ("Enlightenment," Aufklärung). Effects were at least twofold: (1) Applied to Scripture, reason led to historical-critical approaches — text criticism, questions about authorship (did Moses write all the Pentateuch?), denial of miracles, resurrection, atonement, revelation itself. Such matters were especially pressed and developed in Germany.[5] Muhlenberg encountered (and liked) this approach to the Bible especially in the work of Prof. J. D. Michaelis, an orientalist, who wrote an *Introduction to the New Testament* (1750) and an annotated translation of the Old Testament in thirteen volumes. Muhlenberg was exposed to his views particularly in 1742 in London when he was preparing to come to America (*Journals* 1:18-20 refers to Magister Michaelis, who was "the teacher," *Correspondence* 1:21, cf. 16 n. 26).

(2) Applied to religion in general, reason had for some time suggested a concept of God, a Deism (Latin *deus*) shared by all religions, prior to Christianity, to Judaism, and apart from the Bible. In 1624 Edward (Lord) Herbert of Cherbury (1583-1648), in a Latin treatise, *De Veritate* (French but not English translation), concluded that all religions posit five truths. (1) There is one supreme God, who (2) ought to be worshiped, especially through (3) pursuit of virtue and piety. (4) Repentance for sin is a duty. (5) There is another life, with rewards and punishments. These truths are divinely implanted common knowledge in the human mind. Like many others, Benjamin Franklin reiterated these points in his own credo (Shaw 265, to Ezra Stiles, President of Yale, in 1790); worship and service means "doing good" to "God's other children"; Franklin added, "the soul of man is immortal." In 1732 Franklin had listed three tenets: "a rational and omnipotent God exists," who is benevolent; "humans ought to imitate his goodness" (Walters 1992a: 53).

An explosion of writings in the late seventeenth and early eighteenth century argued for Deism in a variety of ways. John Toland (1670-1722) claimed *Christianity Not Mysterious* (1696, against all notions of the supernatural and revelation). Matthew Tindal (1655-1733) wrote on *Christianity*

---

5. Space does not permit tracing here the rise of critical biblical scholarship. Cf. Edgar Krentz, *The Historical-Critical Method*, Guides to Biblical Scholarship (Philadelphia: Fortress, 1975); see William Baird, *History of New Testament Research*, Volume One: *From Deism to Tübingen* (Minneapolis: Fortress, 1992), where developments among deists and pietists are explored, and for J. D. Michaelis's (127-38) efforts to "harmonize orthodoxy with reason" (129).

as Old as Creation (1730); the religion of nature is common to all creeds; the Bible, even Jesus, adds nothing; the creation is our word of God. Free-thinking became the order of the day (Anthony Collins, 1713; German *Freidenker*), as did vigorous attacks on clergy of all sorts.

Of course, Deism took a variety of forms, sometimes allowing some role to Scripture or Providence. But generally God was conceived of as, even if personal, apart from and distinct from our concerns. The Deity is Nature's God; the cultivation of the virtues is what humans should be concerned with. Deists sought to reflect the latest in philosophy of the day (as in John Locke) and science (Newton).

Deism was at its height in England 1689-1742, strong in France (Voltaire), later in Germany. For America, the Enlightenment is said to have gone through phases (May 1976): present in "moderate form," 1688-1778; then as "skeptical enlightenment" (1750-1789); in 1776-1808, as "revolutionary enlightenment," with Philadelphia "the capital of American deism" (p. 197) and a center for science (of which Franklin was a part, experiments with electricity, etc.); in decline, the Enlightenment became "didactic" (1800-1815). The chief American advocate for Deism was probably Elihu Palmer (1764-1806);[6] its popular partisan, Thomas Paine (1737-1809, "My Own Mind Is My Own Church"). Ethan Allen (1737-89), of "Green Mountain Boys" fame, wrote a systematic treatise, *Reason the Only Oracle of Man* (1784), perhaps plagiarized from Thomas Young. Philip Freneau (1752-1832) was its poet.[7] Jefferson,[8] like Washington and John Adams, and most of the Founding Fathers

6. Walters 1992a provides excerpts from the writings of each American Deist mentioned here, plus the Conte de Volney (1757-1820), whose *Ruins; or Meditations on the Revolutions of Empires* Jefferson began to translate; and publications like *The Temple of Reason* (1800-1803); *Prospect; or, View of the Moral World* (1803-1805, ed. Elihu Palmer); and *The Theophilanthropist* (1810-11). Only Paine seems to be mentioned in Muhlenberg's *Journals* (3:286, 504 n. 1).

7. "This human mind! How grand a theme: Faint image of the Great Supreme. . . . And Nature we, by Reason's aid, Find boundless as the power that made. . . . Virtue is gained by slow degrees; and science, which from truth she draws, Stands firm to Reason and her cause" (Walters 1992a: 282, 284-85, 286). Freneau's most widely read work was probably his epic, "The British Prison Ship" (1781), on a hulk anchored in Brooklyn where patriots were jailed under terrible conditions; cf. also the "Narrative of Ethan Allen's Captivity" (1779), a sort of Devil's Island or Gulag of its day.

8. Note Jefferson's *The Life and Morals of Jesus of Nazareth, Extracted Textually from the Gospels in Greek, Latin, French, and English*, with an Introduction by Cyrus Adler (Washington, DC: Government Printing Office, 1904). Often reprinted, including *The Jefferson Bible with the Annotated Commentaries on Religion of Thomas Jefferson*, ed. O. I. A. Roche, in-

were Deists, but Franklin particularly exemplifies popular and varied Deism (its "first noteworthy American advocate," Walters 1992a: 51).

Franklin (January 17, 1706–April 17, 1790) arrived in Philadelphia from his native Boston on October 6, 1723 and walked up Market Street[9] at age seventeen, nineteen years before Muhlenberg arrived in Philadelphia (*Journals* 1:65). Franklin's experience with boat travel (Shaw 21-23) was no happier than Muhlenberg's, transatlantic or coastal. He practiced his trade as a printer in Philadelphia, then in London (1724-26), and increasingly got himself caught up in literary, scientific, and other projects in his adopted city of Philadelphia.[10] In 1759 Franklin became agent in London for the Pennsylvania Assembly; back in Philadelphia in 1762; to London again, 1764. As agent of Georgia, New Jersey, and Massachusetts, Franklin visited France and other parts of Europe. He was back in Philadelphia in 1775, but the next year was elected a commissioner to France on behalf of the Continental Congress (1778, sole minister plenipotentiary). His work there, including the Treaty of Paris with Great Britain, has been variously assessed as monumental or frivolous (he just partied and socialized). Franklin did get back to Philadelphia 1785-90 and was a delegate to the Constitutional Convention, as well as President of the Pennsylvania Council.

Franklin's civic achievements included founding or helping to establish a university, a hospital, a library, a learned society, a militia, a firefighting company, and a fire insurance company (cf. Billy Smith in Talbott 91-123). He contributed money to the college in Lancaster named for him in 1787, later merged as Franklin and Marshall, of which Gotthilf

---

troduction by Henry Wilder Foote, foreword by Donald S. Harrington (New York: Clarkson N. Potter, Inc., 1964, 2nd ed. 1967); Jefferson's *Extracts from the Gospels*, ed. Dickinson W. Adams (Princeton: Princeton University Press, 1982).

9. His description, "Gazing about till near the market house I met a boy with bread . . . and, inquiring where he got it, I went immediately to the baker's he directed me to" (Shaw 23-24), confronts me as part of the doctor's chart every time I have an eye examination.

10. For a fuller account of Franklin's achievements, see the catalogue for the Tercentenary exhibit, *Benjamin Franklin: In Search of a Better World*, ed. Page Talbott (New Haven/London: Yale University Press, 2005) at Philadelphia's Constitutional Center, Dec. 15, 2005–April 30, 2006; St. Louis, Houston, Denver, Atlanta, and Paris. The U.S. commemorative stamp for Franklin in 2005 chose to salute him as printer, postmaster, scientist, and statesman. Franklin's contributions to science and better living, including improved fireplaces, electrical apparatus, lightning rods (touching off debate whether such protection against destruction of buildings by fire was against Providence); cf. E. Philip Krider, in Talbott 162-97.

Henry Ernst Muhlenberg was president. Franklin was able to achieve much in part because he sold his printing business and in effect "retired" in 1748, though he could always return to printing, as in France where his press at Passy served the American cause well (cf. Cohn in Talbott 234-71; the "kindly old printer" still "playing at the art he began as a boy" scarcely fits the crafty way Franklin was able to provide type that American printers were otherwise cut off from, as well as the printing of passports for American citizens, not to mention propaganda for the new American nation).

Franklin several times began to write his autobiography, in 1771 while in England, in 1773 while in France (without what he had written before, without his earlier outline). Thus there are gaps in an account never completed.[11] He lacked the oversight of authorities to whom he had to report, unlike Muhlenberg, who had to report to Halle. One problem is that many things he wrote for various newspapers that he published are unsigned, and we must guess whether he authored and meant seriously what is there. This is a particular problem with some of the (satirical, polemical) writings on religion.[12]

Like Muhlenberg, Franklin was a reluctant revolutionary. Only slowly did he come to oppose the Mother Country and support revolution and independence. As with Muhlenberg, father and son(s) did not see eye to eye. Muhlenberg's sons more readily embraced the Revolution than he did. Franklin's illegitimate son, William (1729, mother unknown) whom Ben trained for service by travels in Europe and who eventually became royal governor in New Jersey (1768), ended up a loyalist (Tory). Unlike Muhlenberg, Franklin had no beloved, supportive wife like Anna Marie Weiser. There was a common-law marriage with Deborah (Reed) Rogers in 1730 (their son Frankie died at age four; a daughter, Sarah); Deborah died in 1774. Ben's neglect of her was the one "great erratum" of his life (Shaw xii, 34, 36, 39, 46; Talbott 126, the matter was complicated by the fact that Deborah was, after being deceived by John Rogers, "neither married

---

11. Among the several editions of Franklin, Leonard W. Labaree, ed., *Papers of Benjamin Franklin* (New Haven: Yale University Press, 1959-), 37 vols. to date, is definitive. *Benjamin Franklin's Autobiography,* ed. J. A. Leo Lemay and P. M. Zall (New York: Norton, 1986) and Franklin's *Writings* in the Library of America series, ed. J. A. Leo Lemay (New York: Library of America, 1987) provide the texts conveniently. The inexpensive paperback, ed. Peter Shaw, has been cited as more accessible.

12. Franklin was capable of puns, even of sexual suggestiveness ("Women are the prime Cause of a great many Male Enormities," Lemay in Talbott, p. 20). How seriously should we take his Jonathan Swift–like satire on "Exporting Felons to the Colonies" (1751)?

nor free to marry another"). Deborah's industry did help make Franklin's fortune (Talbott 131-32), but once overseas he all too easily left her to shift for herself. Even the house for which she supervised construction, Franklin Court, was razed by 1812, and the museum replica that the National Park Service has constructed on Market Street in Philadelphia must be content with an outline of the main building.

The Franklin family's religious background was English Protestant, Church-of-England roots, in Boston Calvinist Presbyterian. His father may once have envisioned a career in the church for Benjamin; hence he got a year of schooling (1714-15, Boston Latin School). But the cost of education soon made a career in trade more likely. By sixteen, Ben had repudiated Calvinism for Deism (Shaw 7-9, 73; Walters 1992a: 51-52). Aldridge (1967; cf. 1965) argued that Franklin was a polytheist, but the notion that he believed in many gods does not hold up (Walters 1992a: 382). The notion that he was "the most dangerous man in America" (Bowen) had nothing to do with religion but with his work (in France) as a threat to British interests (Bowen 252, "a dangerous engine . . . sorry . . . some British frigate did not meet with him by the way"). Rationality, the life of virtues (what Walters 1992a: 54 calls "his no-nonsense quasi-mathematical program for cultivating them"),[13] and the hope of "perfectibility of society and individuals" (Walters 1992a: 54-55) marked his outlook. His scheme "was not wholly without religion" but "purposely avoided" the "distinguishing tenets of any particular sect" (Shaw 83). His life was to be not without prayer (adoration, petition, thanks), almost litany-like ("Help me, O Father"). Franklin at times took sides in Presbyterian squabbles[14] and once in 1738 wrote his parents to squelch rumors of his unorthodoxy.[15] If he had his

---

13. *Autobiography* (ed. Shaw), pp. 76-77, the virtues of temperance, silence, order, resolution, frugality, industry, sincerity, justice, moderation, cleanliness, tranquility, chastity, and humility were to be worked at one by one, charted day by day, as to how well he had achieved the virtue of the day in activities hour by hour.

14. In 1734 Franklin took a particular liking to the sermons of a Presbyterian preacher named Hemphill (good voice, little of a dogmatic nature, but he inculcated virtue and good works). Most Presbyterians thought him heterodox. Franklin wrote pamphlets and a piece in the *Gazette,* "Dialogue between Two Presbyterians" (Walters 1992a: 82-87), defending Hemphill, whose cause was lost when he was forced to admit that some of his sermons were lifted from the writings of others (Shaw 91-92). Franklin showed little awareness of how a presbytery or church standards work.

15. Letter to Josiah and Abiah Franklin, 13 April 1738; to his father, 13 April 1738 (?), perhaps never sent; Walters 1992a: 87-88.

own version of the Lord's Prayer,[16] that was in keeping with what others of the time were doing.

The influence of Deism was most felt perhaps in colleges, universities, and seminaries of the day (Walters 1992a: 1-3). At Yale, Lyman Beecher later recalled, the college, when he entered in 1793, "was in a most ungodly state. The college church was almost extinct. Most of the students were skeptical . . . infidelity of the Tom Paine school. . . . Most of the class before me were infidels, and called each other Voltaire," etc. At Dartmouth students were "lawless, and without the fear of God"; "but a single member of the class of 1799 was publicly known as a professing Christian." William and Mary was called "a training ground for 'infidelity and . . . the wild politics of France.'" Princeton had "only three or four [students] who made any pretensions to piety." Harvard succumbed, so Gibbon's *Decline and Fall of the Roman Empire* was banned and burned as uncomplimentary to the Christian faith; each incoming student was given a copy of Richard Watson's *Apology for the Bible.* Perhaps Lutherans were fortunate *not* to have had a college as yet! On the broader scene, "the Methodist Episcopal Church urged a national day of fasting and prayer in 1796 to stem the tide of deism," as did the Presbyterian General Assembly two years later. For many Pennsylvania Germans, lack of higher education and their use of German and lack of English were barriers to absorbing the new teachings of Deism, just as in the Fundamentalist-Modernist controversy of the 1920s. Usually men, not women, were attracted to Deism; this was so, in part, because women did not attend the colleges or the Masonic lodges, which were centers for propagating the ideas of Deism.

Occasionally there is evidence that allows comparing Muhlenberg and Franklin on persons and issues in religion. While Muhlenberg did not agree on some things with George Whitefield, the Methodist evangelist (*Journals* 2:673-75, 677, 680, 684; Marshall, p. 21 above), he nonetheless met with him and often went to hear him preach (2:137-39, 230-32, 433, 545). Franklin was also interested in hearing Whitefield preach, in part because he wanted to check reports that Whitefield spoke to as many as 30,000

16. About 1768 Franklin produced a version that dropped archaic forms and reflected rational religion, i.e., promoted virtue: "Heavenly Father, May all revere thee, And become thy dutiful Children and faithful Subjects. May thy Laws be obeyed on Earth as perfectly as they are in Heaven. Provide for us this Day as thou hast hitherto daily done. Forgive us our Trespasses and enable us likewise to forgive those that offend us. Keep us out of Temptation, and deliver us from Evil" (Walters 1992a: 89).

people in the open air. When he preached in Philadelphia in 1739 (Shaw 100, before Muhlenberg arrived in the city), Franklin circulated through the crowd as Whitefield "preached one evening from the top of the Court-house steps, which were in the middle of Market Street and on the west side of Second Street which crosses it at right angles. Both streets were filled with his hearers to a considerable distance. Being among the hind-most in Market Street, I had the curiosity to learn how far he could be heard, by retiring backward down the street toward the river; and I found his voice distinct till I came near Front Street when some noise in that street obscured it. Imagining then a semicircle, of which my distance should be the radius and that it was filled with auditors, to each of whom I allowed two square feet, I computed that he might well be heard by more than thirty thousand." Franklin also thought he could distinguish from the style of delivery "between sermons newly composed and those which he had often preached in the course of his travels"; the latter were more smoothly done.

Once in a while Franklin and Muhlenberg were thrown together on political issues with religious overtones, though Muhlenberg the pastor tried to stay out of such matters, while Franklin was active on various is-sues for the sake of the colony. He long felt the pacifist Quaker power structures did not do enough to defend Philadelphia from attack by sea, and settlers on the frontier from Indian raids. In these matters he hoped for German (Lutheran) support.

In 1764 (cf. Shoemaker, p. 189 above; *Journals* 2:18-24), frontier set-tlers had had enough of Indian assaults on outlying farms and in retalia-tion killed several (Christian) Indians in Lancaster. Other Indians who were under safekeeping in Bethlehem were marched to Philadelphia for their greater security. Rumor had it that "young male Indians" had escaped and were doing harm, while their "old men and women and children were living off the fat of the land at the expense of the province." The "Paxton Boys" or "Paxton Rangers" (from the village of Paxton), after the massacre of Indians in Conestoga and Lancaster in December 1763, then marched on Philadelphia, 700 (or 1500) strong, to present their grievances to the gov-ernment and perhaps extract more vengeance on Indians protected by Quakers and Moravians, who built ramparts and fortresses for protection; one could even see Quakers drilling with muskets for possible conflict. All this prompted Muhlenberg's remark about "preparations . . . against one's fellow citizens and Christians," though there had never been efforts to pro-tect them on the frontier.

Some of the approaching mob were doubtless Germans. Muhlenberg, Wrangel, and two other pastors agreed that Scripture called for support of the government in this crisis (on the basis of Rom. 13:1-2; Titus 3:1; 1 Peter 2:12-13; Prov. 24:1; Rev. 2:1-4). Franklin, the mayor, members of the governor's council, and Wrangel were designated to meet with representatives of the militant frontiersmen. They concluded an amnesty with them. Muhlenberg was unable to participate because of illness, but regarding the Paxton Boys he and Franklin were on the same side. The outline for Franklin's autobiography simply refers to "the Paxton murderers" (Shaw 163); see further his *A Narrative of the Late Massacres;* Middlekauff, in Talbott 203-5.

Later in 1764, in the election of October 2, Franklin hoped for German support. But the Germans generally voted for Henry Keple, a trustee of the Lutheran Church, for the Assembly and "gained the upper hand — a thing heretofore unheard of," German Lutherans and Reformed, Anglicans, Presbyterians, against Quakers, Moravians, Mennonites, and Schwenkfelders (*Journal* 2:123). Franklin lost by eighteen votes and left in defeat for London, as agent of the Pennsylvania Assembly (Lemay, in Talbott 40). Against such a background, Franklin's bitter remark about "Palatine Boors" fits (Reumann, p. 105 above; Shaw 266).

Deist influence on Muhlenberg and Pennsylvania Germans did not come through Franklin and his ilk. When it did come, it was really after Muhlenberg's active time, and especially in the New York area (fewer Germans, Lutherans more caught up in English cultural issues; Scholz, p. 58 above), and then only for a time. H. G. Anderson (in 1975, *Lutherans* 90-91, 94) describes the Lutheran fight against Deism in different synods. But even Halle had become infected. One pastor protested that, "should we send for ten candidates" to place "in our vacant congregations, it is highly probable that we would have . . . nine despisers, yea, blasphemers of Christ" (105). Some Lutherans preferred to make a frontal attack on Deism, even by means of revival meetings. John George Schmucker (1771-1854), father of Samuel S. Schmucker (who gave Deists no place in his plans for church reunion, Marshall 38 = 1998: 97), was converted at age eighteen, so reason was not the way he entered the faith (Anderson 108).

The most significant Deist among U.S. Lutherans was doubtless Frederick Henry Quitman,[17] trained at Halle (under the influence of the ratio-

---

17. Anderson, 1975 *Lutherans* 105-6, 110, 206; Marshall 31 = 1998: 94; G. E. Lenski, *The Encyclopedia of the Lutheran Church* 3:1998. On Quitman's theology, see Raymond M. Bost,

nalist biblical scholar, J. S. Semler, and G. C. Storr with his "biblical super-naturalism"). Quitman came to the U.S. via Amsterdam and Curaçao. He became the second president of the New York Ministerium, elected 1807-25. Quitman wrote a catechism (1812), liturgy, and hymnal that denied the authority of both Scripture and the Lutheran Confessions. But even these efforts did not gain much of a place for Deism among Lutherans.

Deism, which once had been a (or *the*) "dominant religious attitude among intellectual and upper-class Americans" (*The New Encyclopedia Britannica, Macropaedia*, 15th ed., 1975, 5: 563), fell into place as a minor movement in American religion, famous chiefly for its influence on the Founding Fathers, but with little liveliness in subsequent decades. It contributed to tolerance at the cost of commitment to divine revelation in the Bible.

Recently Jon Meacham 2006 has claimed the time of the Founding Fathers "is like our time," with a middle ground "between religious fundamentalists and dogmatic secularists." He sees in the colonial and formative Federal periods "public religion" and concern for "morality." "All men need the gods" (18). After this uneven, scarcely academic analysis of American beginnings, Meacham hop-scotches his way through the nation's religious history: the Civil War, Lincoln, and Darwin; Franklin Delano Roosevelt against the Depression and Axis totalitarianism; and then Martin Luther King, the fight for civil rights, the new Right, and Ronald Reagan's delicate balance. This eclectic case for an "American Gospel" going back to the Founding Fathers scarcely supports a tradition of religion and public life rooted in Deism. The claim that the Deist Founding Fathers were really Bible-believing Christians fares no better; they weren't.

We do better to say that Deism, once a force, continues to linger on in some places and some denominations (Unitarianism is usually cited), in secular society, and as part of some civic religion. It should neither be overemphasized nor unstressed. It was a part of Muhlenberg's world, exemplified in Franklin and others, that may matter more today than Protestant orthodoxy or pietism. A series of articles in the *Philadelphia Inquirer* on the state of and challenges to the Roman Catholic Church (and by implication most churches) was dominated by the banner headline, "American culture is winning" (June 4, 2006, p. A12). Part of that culture is deistic.

"The Reverend John Bachmann and the Development of Southern Lutheranism," diss. Yale 1963; Bachmann was Quitman's pupil.

Bibliography

(with the assistance of John Peterson, Curator, Lutheran Archives Center at Philadelphia, and Darren G. Poley)

Aland, Kurt, ed. *Die Korrespondenz Heinrich Melchior Muhlenbergs: Aus der Anfangszeit des Deutschen Luthertums in Nordamerika*. 5 vols. Berlin: De Gruyter, 1986-.

Albanese, Catherine. 1988. "Religion and the American Experience: A Century After," *Church History* 57, no. 3: 337-51.

Aldridge, A. Owen. 1967. *Benjamin Franklin and Nature's God*. Durham, NC: Duke University Press.

Anderson, H. George. 1969. *Lutheranism in the Southeastern States 1860-1886*. The Hague: Mouton.

————. 1975. "Early National Period 1790-1840," in E. C. Nelson, *Lutherans*, pp. 79-144.

————. 1992. "The External Scaffolding of the Spiritual Edifice." ELCA Conference of Bishops, Oct. 4-6, 1992, Trappe, PA. Conference of Bishops Minutes, Exhibit P.

Arndt, Johann. 1979. *True Christianity*. Translated by Peter Erb, introduction by Heiko A. Oberman. New York: Paulist.

Atwood, Craig D., ed. 2001. *A Collection of Sermons from Zinzendorf's Pennsylvania Journey*. Translated by Julie Tomberlin Weber. Bethlehem, PA: The Moravian Church in America.

Bachmann, E. Theodore. 1994. "With Muhlenberg in New Jersey," *Essays and Reports 1992*. St. Louis: Lutheran Historical Conference.

Bachmann, E. Theodore, with Mercia Brenne Bachmann. 1997. *The United Lutheran Church in America, 1918-1962*. Edited by Paul Rorem. Minneapolis: Fortress.

Baglyos, Paul A. 1992a. "Muhlenberg in the American Imagination," *Lutheran Quarterly* 6: 35-50.

————. 1992b. "Wind and Wafers: An Appreciation of Muhlenberg's Ministry 250 Years after His Arrival in America," *Lutheran Partners* 8, no. 5: 16-18.

————. 1997. "In This Land of Liberty: American Lutherans and the Young Republic, 1787-1837." Dissertation, University of Chicago.

Baird, William. 1992. *History of New Testament Research*. Volume One: *From Deism to Tübingen*. Minneapolis: Fortress.

Baptism, Eucharist and Ministry. 1982. Faith and Order Paper No. 111. Geneva: World Council of Churches.

Bodling, Kurt A. 1998. "A Century of Muhlenberg Biographies: An Analysis," *Concordia Historical Institute Quarterly* 71, no. 2: 86-93.

Bost, Raymond M., ed. 1994. *Lutheranism . . . with a Southern Accent: Essays and Reports,* vol. 16. St. Louis: Lutheran Historical Conference.

———. 1998. "The Muhlenberg Tradition Moves South," *Concordia Historical Institute Quarterly* 71, no. 3: 128-34.

Bowen, Catherine Drinker. 1974. *The Most Dangerous Man in America: Scenes from the Life of Benjamin Franklin.* Boston: Little, Brown & Company, *An Atlantic Monthly Press Book.*

Brands, H. W. 2000. *The First American: The Life and Times of Benjamin Franklin.* New York: Anchor Books, Random House.

Brown, John D. M. 1942. "For God and Country: The Muhlenberg Bicentennial Pageant" and "The Bicentennial Hymn" (four verses, to tune of "God of Our Fathers").

Butler, Jon. 1990. *Awash in a Sea of Faith: Christianizing the American People.* Studies in Cultural History. Cambridge, MA: Harvard University Press.

Cecil-Fronsman, Bill. 1992. *Common Whites: Class and Culture in Antebellum North Carolina.* Lexington: University of Kentucky Press.

Cobbler, Michael L. 1998. "Comment" on Jeff G. Johnson article, in Lehmann Memorial volume, pp. 26-34.

"Comment: The Pennsylvania Ministerium from 1748 to 1998," *Lutheran Quarterly* 12 (1998): 185-92 (photos).

A Common Calling: The Witness of Our Reformation Churches in North America Today: The Report of the Lutheran-Reformed Committee for Theological Conversation, ed. Keith Nickle and Timothy F. Lull. Minneapolis: Augsburg, 1993.

Documentary History = *Documentary History of the Evangelical Lutheran Ministerium of Pennsylvania and Adjacent States. Proceedings of the Annual Conventions from 1748 to 1821.* Philadelphia: Board of Publication of the General Council of the Evangelical Lutheran Church in North America, 1898.

Falckner, Justus. 1708. *Fundamental Instruction: Justus Falckner's Catechism.* Translated and edited by Martin Kessler. Introduction by Johannes P. Boendermaker. Delhi, NY: American Lutheran Publicity Bureau, 2003.

Fevold, Eugene L. 1975. "Coming of Age 1875-1900," in E. C. Nelson, *Lutherans,* pp. 255-356.

Florida-Bahamas Synod of the ELCA, "Leaders for Tomorrow." 1998. Florida-Bahamas Synod Point Paper.

Fogelman, Aaron S. 1996. *Hopeful Journeys: German Immigration, Settlement, and Political Culture in Colonial America, 1717-1775.* Philadelphia: University of Pennsylvania Press.

A Formula of Agreement Between the Evangelical Lutheran Church in America, the Presbyterian Church (USA), the Reformed Church in America, and the United Church of Christ on Entering into Full Communion on the Basis of A Common Calling: Ecumenical Proposals, Documents for Action by the 1997 Churchwide Assembly. Chicago: Office of the Bishop (Department of Ecumenical Affairs), ELCA, 1996.

Franklin, Benjamin. 1987. *Writings.* Edited by J. A. Leo Lemay. Library of America Series. New York: Viking.

Freeman, Arthur. 1998. *An Ecumenical Theology of the Heart: The Theology of Nicholas Ludwig von Zinzendorf.* Bethlehem, PA: Board of Communications, Moravian Church in America.

Frick, William K. 1902. *Henry Melchior Muhlenberg: "Patriarch of the Lutheran Church in America."* Philadelphia: Lutheran Publication Society.

Fritz, William Richard. 1971. "Beginnings — Before 1803," in *A History of the Lutheran Church in South Carolina.* Edited by Paul McCullough. Columbia, SC: R. L. Bryan Company, pp. 1-149.

Gifford, Hartland H., and Arland J. Hultgren, eds. 2002. *The Heritage of Augustana: Presentations at Rock Island and Lindsborg.* Chicago: Augustana Heritage Association (Lutheran School of Theology, 1100 E. 55th Street, Chicago 60615-5199).

Gilbert, W. Kent. 1988. *Commitment to Unity: A History of the Lutheran Church in America.* Philadelphia: Fortress.

Glatfelter, Charles H. 1980, 1981. *Pastors and People: German Lutheran and Reformed Churches in the Pennsylvania Field, 1717-1793.* 2 vols. Breinigsville, PA: The Pennsylvania German Society.

————. 1992. "Muhlenberg West of the Susquehanna," *Lutheran Theological Seminary Bulletin: Henry Melchior Muhlenberg: Forbear for Whom?* 72, no. 4.

Graebner, August L. 1892. *Geschichte der Lutherischen Kirche in America.* St. Louis: Concordia Publishing House.

Groh, John E., and Robert H. Smith, eds. *The Lutheran Church in North American Life 1776-1976, 1580-1980.* St. Louis: Clayton Publishing House and the Lutheran Academy for Scholarship, 1979.

Gummere, Richard M. 1967. "Henry Melchior Muhlenberg: A Spiritual Trouble-Shooter," in *Seven Wise Men of Colonial America* (Cambridge, MA: Harvard University Press), pp. 50-63.

Hall, David D. 1989. *Worlds of Wonder, Days of Judgment: Popular Religious Belief in Early New England.* New York: Alfred A. Knopf.

Handley, George E. 1996. "The Ministerium of Pennsylvania, from 1748," *Lutheran Quarterly* 10, no. 4: 363-83. The entire issue is on "Lutheranism in the Delaware Valley."

————. 2003. "A Look at H. M. Muhlenberg, the Pennsylvania Ministerium and the Development of Lutheranism in the Northeast," in *Eastern Lutheranism and the National Church — Influence and Foil: Essays and Reports,* 18, ed. David J. Wartluft (St. Louis: Lutheran Historical Conference).

Havens, Mary. 1990. "Zinzendorf and the 'Augsburg Confession.'" Ph.D. dissertation, Princeton Theological Seminary.

Holmes, David L. 2006. *The Faiths of the Founding Fathers.* New York: Oxford University Press.

Jacobs, Henry Eyster. 1893. *A History of the Evangelical Lutheran Church in the United States.* New York: Christian Literature Co.

Johnson, Jeff G. 1998. "Muhlenberg's Relationship to African Americans," in Lehmann Memorial volume, pp. 21-26.

Joint Declaration on the Doctrine of Justification: The Lutheran World Federation and the Roman Catholic Church. Grand Rapids: Eerdmans, 2000.

Kleiner, John W. 1990. *Henry Melchior Muhlenberg: The Roots of 250 Years of Organized Lutheranism in North America.* Studies in Religion and Society, vol. 41. Lewiston, NY: Edwin Mellen Press.

―――. 1998. "Comment" on Marianne Wokeck article in Lehmann Memorial volume, pp. 106-10.

Kolb, Robert, and Timothy Wengert. 2000. *The Book of Concord: The Confessions of the Evangelical Lutheran Church.* Minneapolis: Fortress.

Kreider, Harry J. 1954. *History of the United Lutheran Synod of New York and New England.* Philadelphia: Muhlenberg Press.

Kuenning, Paul P. 1988. *The Rise and Fall of American Lutheran Pietism: The Rejection of an Activist Heritage.* Macon, GA: Mercer University Press.

Kurtz, Stephen G., and James H. Hutson, eds. 1973. *Essays on the American Revolution.* Chapel Hill: University of North Carolina Press / New York: W. W. Norton & Company.

Labaree, Leonard W., and Whitfield J. Bell, Jr. 1959-. *The Papers of Benjamin Franklin.* New Haven: Yale University Press. 37 vols. to date.

Lehmann, Helmut T. 1978. "The American Revolution in Henry Melchior Muhlenberg's Experience," *Essays and Reports 1976.* St. Louis: Lutheran Historical Conference.

―――. 1992. "Missioner Extraordinary," in *Partners in the Spirit* (newsletter), a ten-part series. Wescosville, PA: Northeastern Pennsylvania Synod, Evangelical Lutheran Church in America; reprinted in *Concordia Historical Institute Quarterly* 71, no. 2 (Summer 1998): 56-71; 71, no. 3 (Fall 1998): 107-27.

―――, and J. Woodrow Savacool. 1992. "Muhlenberg's Ministry of Healing," *Lutheran Quarterly* 6, no. 1: 51-68.

Lehmann Memorial volume = *Henry Melchior Muhlenberg — The Roots of 250 Years of Organized Lutheranism in North America. Essays in Memory of Helmut T. Lehmann,* ed. John W. Kleiner. Lewiston, NY: Edwin Mellen Press, 1998.

Lemon, James T. 1972. *The Best Poor Man's Country: A Geographical Study of Early Southeastern Pennsylvania.* Baltimore: Johns Hopkins University Press.

Lewis, A. S. 1962. *Zinzendorf the Ecumenical Pioneer: A Study of Moravian Contributions to Christian Mission and Unity.* Philadelphia: Westminster.

Lucas, Paul. 1984. *American Odyssey 1607-1789.* Englewood Cliffs, NJ: Prentice-Hall.

Mann, William J. *Life and Times of Henry Melchior Muhlenberg.* Philadelphia: G. W. Frederick, 1887; 2nd ed. 1888.

―――. 1891. *Heinrich Melchior Muhlenberg's Leben und Wirken. Zum 150. Jahrestag von Muhlenbergs Ankunft in der Neuen Welt.* Philadelphia: Pastor A. Hellwege, Roxborough.

―――― et al., eds. *Nachrichten von den vereinigten Deutschen Evangelisch-Lutherischen*

Gemeinden in Nord-Amerika, absonderlich in Pennsylvanien. 2 vols. Allentown and Philadelphia: Brobst, Diehl & Co. & G. C. Eisenhardt, 1886, 1895.

Marshall, Robert J. 1998. "The Church Still Being Planted," *Currents in Theology and Mission* 25, no. 2: 85-100.

May, Henry F. 1976. *The Enlightenment in America.* New York: Oxford University Press.

Meacham, Jon. 2006. *American Gospel: God, the Founding Fathers, and the Making of a Nation.* New York: Random House.

Meuser, F. 1975. "Facing the Twentieth Century 1900-1930," in E. C. Nelson, *Lutherans,* pp. 359-449.

Muhlenberg, Henry Melchior. *Correspondence = The Correspondence of Heinrich Melchior Muhlenberg,* edited and translated by John W. Kleiner and Helmut T. Lehmann. Vol. 1: *1940-1747.* Camden, ME: Picton Press, 1993; vol. 2, 1997. For German, see Aland, K., ed.

———. *Journals = The Journals of Henry Melchior Muhlenberg in Three Volumes,* translated by Theodore G. Tappert and John W. Doberstein. Philadelphia: The Evangelical Lutheran Ministerium of Pennsylvania and Adjacent States and Muhlenberg Press, 1942, 1945, 1958. Reprinted, Evansville, IN: Lutheran Historical Society of Eastern Pennsylvania and Whippoorwill Publications, 1982.

———. *Notebook = The Notebook of a Colonial Clergyman; Condensed from the Journals of Henry Melchior Muhlenberg.* Minneapolis: Fortress Press, 1959, 1987, second Fortress Press paperback ed. 1998.

———. *Selbstbiographie. Heinrich Melchior Muhlenberg, Patriarch der Lutherischen Kirche Nordamerikas. Selbstbiographie, 1711-1743,* ed., with additions, W. Germann. Allentown, PA: Brobst, Diehl & Co., 1881. See *Journals* 1:xxi and xxii, 1-2 and passim (note p. 2 n. 1).

Nelson, E. Clifford, ed. *The Lutherans in North America.* In collaboration with Theodore G. Tappert, H. George Anderson, August R. Sueflow, Eugene L. Fevold, Fred W. Meuser. Philadelphia: Fortress, 1975. Rev. ed. 1990.

———. 1975. "The New Shape of Lutheranism 1930-," in E. C. Nelson, *Lutherans,* pp. 453-541.

Nelson, Harvey L. 1980. "A Critical Study of Henry Melchior Muhlenberg's Means of Maintaining His Lutheranism." Dissertation, Drew University, Madison, NJ.

Nolt, Steven M. 2002. *Foreigners in Their Own Land: Pennsylvania Germans in the Early Republic.* Pennsylvania German History and Cultural Series, 2. University Park: Pennsylvania State University Press.

Oldenburg, Mark. 1998. "The 1748 Liturgy and the 1786 Hymnal," in Lehmann Memorial volume, pp. 61-76.

Peterson, John. 1998. "Archival Resources for Muhlenberg Research," in Lehmann Memorial volume, pp. 151-62.

Pfatteicher, Helen E. 1938. *The Ministerium of Pennsylvania: Oldest Lutheran Synod in America, Founded in Colonial Days.* Philadelphia: The Ministerium Press.

Reumann, John. 2003. "The Priesthood of Baptized Believers and the Office of Ministry in Eastern Lutheranism from Muhlenberg's Day to Ours," in *Eastern*

Lutheranism and the National Church — Influence and Foil, Essays and Reports 1998, vol. 18, ed. David J. Wartluft (St. Louis: Lutheran Historical Conference).

Richards, Henry M. M. 1993. "Muhlenberg — A Man in a Dilemma," *The Periodical* (Lutheran Historical Society of Eastern Pennsylvania) 38: 1-3.

Riforgiato, Leonard Richard. 1980. *Missionary of Moderation: Henry Melchior Muhlenberg and the Lutheran Church in English America*. Lewisburg, PA: Bucknell University Press.

Roeber, A. G. 1993. *Palatines, Liberty, and Property: German Lutherans in Colonial British America*. Baltimore: Johns Hopkins University Press.

————. 1998. "Henry Melchior Muhlenberg: Orthodox Pietist," in Lehmann Memorial volume, pp. 1-15, with "Comment" by Sally Schwartz, pp. 15-20.

————. 2003. "Lutherans, Antinomians and the Pastoral Office in Early North America," in *Eastern Lutheranism and the National Church — Influence and Foil, Essays and Reports 1998*, vol. 18, ed. David J. Wartluft (St. Louis: Lutheran Historical Conference).

Rohrbough, Faith E. 1996. "The Political Maturation of Henry Melchior Muhlenberg," *Lutheran Quarterly* 10, no. 4: 385-408, reprinted with revision in Lehmann Memorial volume, pp. 35-53.

Sattler, Gary R. 1989. *Nobler Than Angels, Lower Than a Worm: The Pietist View of the Individual in the Writings of Heinrich Müller and August Hermann Francke*. Lanham, MD: University Press of America.

Schjørring, Jens Holger, Prasanna Kumari, and Norman A. Hjelm, eds. 1997. *From Federation to Communion: The History of the Lutheran World Federation*. Viggo Mortensen, Coordinator. Minneapolis: Fortress.

Schmauk, Theodore E. 1903. *A History of the Lutheran Church in Pennsylvania, 1638-1820*. Philadelphia: General Council Publication House.

————. *Muhlenberg: The Organizer of the Lutheran Church in America*.

Schmucker, Samuel Simon. 1965. *Fraternal Appeal to the American Churches with a Plan for Catholic Union on Apostolic Principles*. Edited, with Introduction by Frederick K. Wentz. Seminar Editors. Philadelphia: Fortress.

Scholz, Robert F. 1979. "Was Muhlenberg a Pietist?" *Concordia Historical Institute Quarterly* 52, no. 2: 50-65.

Scott, Edwin J. 1884. *Random Recollections of a Long Life, 1806-1876*. Columbia, SC: Charles A. Calvo, Jr., Printer.

Seebach, Margaret R. 1924. *An Eagle in the Wilderness: The Story of Henry Melchior Muhlenberg*. Philadelphia: United Lutheran Publication House.

Shaw, Peter, ed. 1982. *The Autobiography and Other Writings of Benjamin Franklin*. New York: Bantam Books.

Skardon, Alvin W. 1971. *Church Leader in the Cities: William Augustus Muhlenberg*. Philadelphia: University of Pennsylvania Press.

Spener, Philipp Jacob. 1964. *Pia Desideria*. Translated, edited, and introduction by T. G. Tappert. Seminar Editions. Philadelphia: Fortress.

Stoeffler, F. Ernst. 1973. *German Pietism During the Eighteenth Century*. Leiden: E. J. Brill.

Strohmidel, Karl-Otto. 1992. "Henry Melchior Muhlenberg's European Heritage," *Lutheran Quarterly* 6, no. 1: 5-34.

Sueflow, August R., and E. Clifford Nelson. 1975. "Following the Frontier 1840-1875," in Nelson, *Lutherans*, pp. 147-251.

Suhr, Heinrich R. 1940. "Muhlenberg's Opinion on the Introduction of English into the Churches, 1761," *Lutheran Church Quarterly* 13: 79-85.

Talbott, Page, ed. 2005. *Benjamin Franklin: In Search of a Better World*. New Haven: Yale University Press.

Tappert, Theodore G. 1942a. "The Muhlenberg Tradition in the Nineteenth Century." *Lutheran Church Quarterly* 15: 394-403.

―――. 1942b. "Henry Melchior Muhlenberg and the American Revolution." *Church History* 11: 284-304.

―――. 1948. "John Casper Stoever and the Ministerium of Pennsylvania." *Lutheran Church Quarterly* 21: 180-84.

―――. 1953. "Was Ecclesia Plantanda Muhlenberg's Motto?" *Lutheran Quarterly* 5: 308-11.

―――. 1957. "Orthodoxy, Pietism, and Rationalism 1580-1830," in Harold C. Letts, ed., *Christian Social Responsibility: A Symposium in Three Volumes*. Philadelphia: Muhlenberg Press, 2:36-88.

―――. 1975. "The Church's Infancy 1650-1790," in E. C. Nelson, *Lutherans*, pp. 1-77.

――― et al., eds., trans. 1959. *The Book of Concord: The Confessions of the Evangelical Lutheran Church*. Philadelphia: Muhlenberg Press.

Wagner, Walter H. 1998. "A Key Episode in American Lutheranism: Zinzendorf's Encounter," *Concordia Historical Institute Quarterly* 71, no. 2: 72-85.

―――. 2002. *The Zinzendorf–Muhlenberg Encounter: A Controversy in Search of Understanding*. Bethlehem, PA: Moravian Historical Society.

―――, and Arthur Freeman. 1998. *Following Our Shepherd to Full Communion: Report of the Bilateral Dialogue of the Moravian Church in America and the Evangelical Lutheran Church in America*. Minneapolis: Augsburg Fortress.

Wallace, Paul A. W. 1950. *The Muhlenbergs of Pennsylvania*. Philadelphia: University of Pennsylvania Press.

Walters, Kerry S. 1992a. *The American Deists: Voices of Reason and Dissent in the Early Republic*. Lawrence, KS: University Press of Kansas.

―――. 1992b. *Rational Infidels: The American Deists*. Wolfeboro, NH: Longwood.

Weinlich, John R. 1956. *Count Zinzendorf: The Story of His Life and Leadership in the Renewed Moravian Church*. Nashville: Abingdon; reprinted Bethlehem, PA: The Moravian Church in America, 1984.

Wentz, Abdel Ross. 1964. *A Basic History of Lutheranism in America*. Rev. ed., Philadelphia: Fortress, 1964.

Wentz, Frederick K. 2003. "Lutherans and Ecumenism: The General Synod Tradition into the Twenty-First Century," in *Eastern Lutheranism and the National Church — Influence and Foil, Essays and Reports*, vol. 18, ed. David J. Wartluft (St. Louis: Lutheran Historical Conference).

Williams, Kim-Eric. *The Journey of Justus Falckner.* Delhi, NY: American Lutheran Publicity Bureau.

Winters, R. L. 1948. "John Casper Stoever: Colonial Pastor and Founder of Churches." *Pennsylvania German Society Proceedings and Addresses,* p. 53. Norristown, PA: published by the Society. Diss. Hartford Seminary Foundation.

Wokeck, Marianne S. 1998. "Henry Melchior Muhlenberg's Views of the Immigrant Church: 'The Desert Is Vast and the Sheep Are Dispersed,'" in Lehmann Memorial volume, pp. 85-106.

Zeiser, Samuel R. 1989. "*Ecclesiolae in Ecclesia* and *Ecclesia Plantanda:* Conflicting Approaches to Mission Among the German Protestants in Colonial Pennsylvania." S.T.M. dissertation, Lutheran Theological Seminary at Philadelphia.

———. 1998. "Comment" on Faith Rohrbough article in Lehmann Memorial volume, pp. 53-59.

Zinzendorf, N. 1746. *Nine Lectures on Important Subjects in Religion.* Translated with introduction by George W. Forell. Iowa City: University of Iowa Press, 1973.